Ibsen, Strindberg and the intimate theatre

Studies in TV presentation

Film Culture in Transition

Thomas Elsaesser: General Editor

Double Trouble
Chiem van Houweninge on Writing and Filming
Thomas Elsaesser, Robert Kievit and Jan Simons (eds.)

Writing for the Medium: Television in Transition
Thomas Elsaesser, Jan Simons and Lucette Bronk (eds.)

Between Stage and Screen
Ingmar Bergman Directs
Egil Törnqvist

The Film Spectator: From Sign to Mind
Warren Buckland (ed.)

Film and the First World War
Karel Dibbets and Bert Hogenkamp (eds.)

A Second Life
German Cinema's First Decades
Thomas Elsaesser (ed.)

Fassbinder's Germany
History Identity Subject
Thomas Elsaesser

Cinema Futures: Cain, Abel or Cable?
The Screen Arts in the Digital Age
Thomas Elsaesser and Kay Hoffmann (eds.)

Audiovisions
Cinema and Television as Entr'Actes in History
Siegfried Zielinski

Ibsen, Strindberg and the intimate theatre

Studies in TV presentation

by

Egil Törnqvist

Amsterdam University Press

Cover photo: Hedda Gabler, *Bengt Wanselius*
Cover design: Korpershoek Ontwerpen, Amsterdam
Lay-out: JAPES, Amsterdam

ISBN 90 5356 371 7 (hardcover)
ISBN 90 5356 350 4 (paperback)

Table of contents

1 Preface

The present book is concerned with two types of end products: the television performance and the play text on which it is based. Although the main purpose is to illuminate the former, this obviously can not be done without a close scrutiny of its textual basis. In my examination of TV productions based on thirteen plays by Ibsen and Strindberg, I combine more general aspects with close 'readings' of individual, often transcribed passages, since such a procedure in my view gives the reader optimal insight into both the transposition problems and the directorial solutions involved.

The choice of the two dramatists was determined not only by my familiarity, as a Swede, with the languages in which they wrote but also, and more importantly, by the fact that their plays have frequently been adapted for television. The thirteen play chapters are framed by a Prologue and an Epilogue. In the former, I elucidate the specific characteristics of television drama, its position between the stage play on the one hand and the cinema film on the other. In the latter, I discuss briefly to what extent the dramaturgy of Ibsen and Strindberg suits television and summarise, under five headings, the problems involved when presenting their plays, written for the study and the stage, on the small screen.

Quotations from Ibsen's and Strindberg's source texts are in my own rendering, although I naturally owe much to existing translations. Faithfulness to the source texts prevails. This is true even of the punctuation, which at least in Strindberg's case is often surprising. Unlike English usage, three dots within quotations indicate a pause; when indicating an omission, the dots are put within brackets. Quotations from the English-speaking productions are, naturally, in the form used there.

The typography of drama texts varies somewhat. Since such variation seems both irrelevant and disturbing, I have deemed it desirable to standardise the typography as follows:

1   For stage and acting directions, I use italics throughout. The same principle is applied in my transcriptions of performance passages.
2   Cue designations are put in low-case capitals and printed in roman.

Titles of non-English works are usually given in English translation. The original titles are added in the index.

In the transcribed sections, the occasional figures indicate shots. The following abbreviations are used both there and in the quotations from the dramatists' stage directions (where left and right always mean 'as seen from the audience'):

L   =   left
R   =   right
BG   =   background
FG   =   foreground
CU   =   close-up
ECU   =   extreme close-up
MCU   =   medium close-up
MS   =   medium shot
LS   =   long shot
HA   =   high angle
LA   =   low angle

Should one use the past or present tense when describing TV drama? Both alternatives can be defended. Since a teleplay, like any other production, is time-bound and most people watch a teleplay only once, the choice of past tense, as in the case of a stage production, may seem natural. On the other hand since teleplays, unlike stage plays, are durable and, with the now common use of domestic video recorders, repeatable, I have deemed it more appropriate to apply the practice of film criticism and use the present tense.

The illustrations are often approximations rather than exact reproductions of what is seen in the TV performances.

A substantial part of this book has appeared earlier in various publications. The chapter on *A Doll's House* is based largely on the chapter "*A Doll's House* as teleplay" in my *Ibsen: A Doll's House*, Cambridge: Cambridge University Press, 1995; I gratefully acknowledge permission from the publisher to reprint passages from this work. The chapter on *Ghosts* relies in part on an article entitled "Page, Stage and Screen: The Opening of Ibsen's *Gengangere (Ghosts)*," in *Tijdschrift voor Skandinavistiek*, Vol. 17, No. 1, 1996. Part of the chapter on *Hedda Gabler* earlier appeared as "Screening *Hedda Gabler*" in Maria Deppermann et al. (eds.), *Ibsen im europäischen Spannungsfeld zwischen Naturalismus und Symbolismus*, Frankfurt am Main: Peter Lang, 1998. The chapter on *The Father* is to some extent based on an article entitled "A 'Play'-within-the-Play: The Opening of Strindberg's *The Father*" in the Supplementary Issue, entitled *Strindberg in Performance*, appearing in *Theatre Research International*, Vol. 18, 1993. The chapter on *Miss Julie* owes much to the chapter "*Miss Julie* as TV Play" in Egil Törnqvist & Barry Jacobs, *Strindberg's Miss Julie: A Play and Its Transpositions*, Norwich: Norvik Press, 1988. The chapter on *Thunder in the Air* is partly based on an article in Kela Kvam (ed.), *Strindberg's Post-Inferno Plays*, København: Munksgaard/Rosinante, 1994. The chapter on *The Ghost Sonata* has much in common with the chapter dealing with that play in my *Transposing Drama: Studies in Representation*, London: Macmillan, 1991. The chapter on *The Pelican* appeared earlier as "Strindberg och den intima teatern: *Pelikanen* som TV-drama" in *Strindbergiana*, Vol. 12, 1997. All articles/chapters have been thoroughly revised for this book.

For their invaluable assistance I wish to thank the respective staff of the BBC Written Archives Centre, Reading; the BBC Photographic Library, London; the Drama Department of the Norwegian Television, Oslo; the National Archive of Recorded Sound and Moving Images, Stockholm; and the Photographic Archive of the Swedish Television, Stockholm.

The illustrations have been made possible thanks to grants from the Norwegian Research Council and the Swedish Institute.

PROLOGUE

2 Page, Stage and Screen

What happens when a play, written for the stage, is presented on television? What occurs when a drama, intended for recipients of one language, is translated into another language? What are the problems involved when plays written a century ago are presented today? Or when plays originating in one culture are transferred to another? Where does the play text end and the performance text begin?

Despite the overwhelming number of books that are being published about the mass media, despite the fact that television plays attract an audience which far outnumbers those of the hits on the London, Paris or New York stage, and despite the fact that the bulk of plays presented on radio and television are still transposed stage plays, remarkably little attention has been paid to these questions.

Let us approach our subject slowly and begin by asking: What is the difference between the *drama text*, experienced by a reader, and the *performance text*, experienced by a spectator (or listener)?[1] The most obvious answer to this question is that since drama to the reader is textual, while performance to the spectator is audiovisual, the two kinds represent different semiotic systems.

"Reading a play," says Strindberg,

> is almost like reading a musical score: it is difficult, and I do not know many who can do it, although a lot of people say they can. The very arrangement of the text, where the eyes have to wander from the name of the speaker to his speech, demands close attention; the seemingly uninteresting exposition has to be got through and carefully recorded in one's memory, since it contains the warp, by means of which the whole weaving is set up. The action noted within the parentheses delays and distracts one, too. Even to this day when I read Shakespeare I have to pencil in notes to keep the characters and particularly the numerous minor speaking characters straight, and I have to go back constantly to the list of characters and to [...] the first act to take a look at what the characters said then.[2]

Reading a play may be difficult – even for playwrights. Yet watching a play is hardly easier, since the spectator is constantly faced with such a richness of simultaneous impressions that s/he is only able to grasp part of what s/he sees and hears.[3] In a stage performance "the [spectator's] eye will err," to paraphrase Strindberg, from the speaker to the listener(s), from faces to costumes, from scenery to properties. Although this is less true of screen productions, where the camera guides our gaze, many shots,[4] especially in cinema films, will contain more visual and aural information than we can cope with at a first viewing.[5]

The audiovisual information provided by the performance text relates to five different *codes*: (1) language, (2) culture, (3) medium, (4) directorial and (5) actorial signals.

Each of these codes can be related to a number of *sign categories*. Kowzan, concerned only with live performances, distinguishes thirteen such categories,[6] Fischer-Lichte adds one more.[7] Esslin, dealing with both stage and screen performances, discerns five "sign systems common to all dramatic media" and another three confined to cinema and television.[8] Although Esslin's wider scope coincides with the one applied here, his somewhat unsystematic classification seems problematic. Granted that any classification suffers from overlapping and borderline cases, the following combination of the three schemes seems helpful for a comparative approach to performance analysis:

Text, stage and screen categories

1   play area
2   scenery
3   properties
4   light
5   sound
6   music
7   physical constitution
8   mimicry
9   gestures, movements
10 positions, grouping
11 make-up, hair
12 costume
13 paralinguistics
14 dialogue

Screen categories

15 camera work
16 editing

Because of the constant interaction between verbal and non-verbal elements, the performance text has a much wider polysemic range than the drama text. On the other hand the polysemic range of the dialogue shrinks in performance simply by being spoken. As readers we may think of numerous ways of phrasing a speech. As spectators we experience one of these ways, chosen by the actor.

Despite the marked differences between drama text and performance text, there is a considerable overlap. This explains why we can witness two radically different productions – even within different media and/or different languages – and yet sense that we are confronted with the same underlying play text.

Even if the drama text is the only thing that provides a *tertium quid* by means of which different productions can be compared with one another, this does not mean that it is sacrosanct. When in the following chapters, one production is found to be more faithful to the source text than another, this should be seen as a factual observation, analogous to the distinction between literal and free translation, not as an evaluative statement. Obviously, both more faithful and less faithful productions may be either good or bad.

There is an old, regularly revived dispute about whether text or performance, author or director, should reign supreme. Far from being an academic question, this controversy mirrors two different attitudes to the relationship between drama text and performance text, which have far-reaching practical consequences. Defenders of the priority of the drama text tend to protest against significant changes of it in performance, arguing that such changes can only spoil what has been designed as an autonomous, coherent work. Uncompromising advocates of the play text would, in addition, dismiss any meddling with it by referring to the author's intention. Like those who claim that Bach's *Goldberg Variations* should be played on a harpsichord, for which they were written, and not on a piano, defenders of the play text would argue that plays written for the stage should only be done there. Even those who do not share this historicist view may still find that, just as we do not shorten Bach's compositions, so we should leave those of competent dramatists intact.

Defenders of the priority of the performance text, on the other hand, argue that since the drama text is merely a blueprint and since the transposition from book to stage means a transference from one semiotic system to another, the performance text must be considered a separate, autonomous work.[9] Defenders of the performance text may also point to the fact that the director has, or should have, a vision of his/her own, which will hardly in all respects coincide with that of the dramatist; and that at the same time s/he must seek to establish vital contact with his/her audience, often far removed in time and space from the audience the dramatist had in mind. In the last instance this standpoint leads to the view that, in Elsaesser's words, "every adaptation is a reading, every reading a 'performance', and every performance the creation/writing of a text."[10]

Moreover, since most plays are nowadays performed in an abridged form, particularly when presented on the screen, arguments in favour of the drama text have become undermined by stark reality. To defenders of the performance text, they appear anachronistic. Their answer would be: Had artist X (composer, playwright) been familiar with the new instrument (piano, television), s/he would either have composed for it or adjusted his/her own composition to suit the new medium.

Although the relationship between drama text and performance text was discussed as early as in the eighteenth century, especially by Diderot and Lessing,[11] it is only recently, with the launch of new research areas like semiotics, media studies, performance analysis and reception theory, that we have become aware of the fundamental difference between these two forms of presentation and of the radically different situations of reception they give rise to.[12]

The difference between the reader of a drama text and the viewer of a performance based on this text has partly, as already indicated, to do with quantity: the sparsity of audiovisual indications in the drama text as compared to the wealth of such indications in the performance text. To put it differently: while the drama text is necessarily unsystematic and fragmentary in its recordings of audiovisual signifiers, the performance text is in this respect consistent and complete. The blueprint, to use the traditional imagery, makes room for the building, the executed play. Whether the dramatist more or less refrains from stage directions (Shakespeare) or makes frequent use of them (Ibsen, Strindberg) – to register everything is, of course, impossible – the text remains a blueprint to be filled in by the performance.

In a performance, every character has by necessity a particular appearance, says his or her lines at every moment in a particular way in a particular place, moves and gesticulates in a special manner, etc. Even when stage directions are provided in the drama text, they are almost always indeterminate when compared with their audiovisual equivalents. Choose any semiotic category and you will find the same difference between indeterminateness in the textual description and precision in the audiovisual execution. The verbal information that a character walks to the left, for instance, will necessarily be less precise than the (audio)visual information about this action.

Whether readers or spectators – the latter short for the more correct spectators-cum-listeners – recipients approach plays with very different pre-knowledge. Some recipients have no pre-knowledge whatsoever. Others have a very general pre-knowledge. They have in advance been confronted with the name of the dramatist, the title and date of the play, the names of the characters, etc. They may even have read a synopsis.

This more general kind of pre-knowledge should be kept separate from a more thorough type: direct familiarity with the play one is about to read or see, as text or as performance. We may in this last respect appropriately distinguish between the *first-time recipient* – someone who reads or watches a play for the first time – and the *re-recipient*, someone who does it for the second or hundredth time – *recipient* serving as an umbrella term for both categories. Unlike the first-time recipient, the re-recipient knows how the play develops and how it ends. As a consequence, s/he is able to see correspondences between the early and late parts of the play, correspondences which the first-time recipient will at best discover when s/he has experienced the whole play. As readers and spectators we are often first-time recipients, as theatre critics and scholars we are re-recipients. This is why it is not possible for a scholar to recapture what we tend to see as the 'normal' reception, the first-time reception, of a play. The scholar inevitably knows more than the normal reader or spectator, the average recipient. The dramatist's position differs from that of the critic and the scholar in that although s/he is basically a re-recipient of his/her own play, s/he must try to remain a first-time recipient of it, share this recipient's gradual experience of the play. One of the assets of Ibsen's and Strindberg's plays is that, as all great drama, they are constructed in such a way that they can captivate both first-time recipients and re-recipients.

Transposing a play from stage to screen necessarily involves a number of adjustments originating in the difference between the media. In the theatre we have a fixed seat from which we can hopefully see the whole stage. When the curtain rises we see it, if it is a proscenium arch stage, through the absent fourth wall. Throughout the performance the characters remain at roughly the same distance from us. A screen version, on the other hand, may well open with a shot of merely a part of the visualised space or even of a small object in it. Unlike the situation in the theatre, we are then for a while at a loss as to where we find ourselves. A *locus dramaticus*, Bazin points out, is in contradiction with the concept of the screen.[13]

In the theatre we normally have several characters in view, and we have the freedom to choose on whom we wish to focus. In a screen performance the camera, functioning as 'narrator,' usually presents the characters by turns, often in the form of shot-reverse shots, forcing us to concentrate on one face and momentarily disregard another.

The differences between stage and screen are fundamental and have far-reaching consequences both at the production and the reception end. The most fundamental one, perhaps, is that the stage relies on continuous space, whereas the screen depends on discontinuous space. While in stage drama we remain visually in the same environment within each act/scene, in screen drama the visible surroundings will change with each shot. And while in the 'democratic' stage drama we have, in principle at least, the freedom to focus on whatever we like on the stage, in the more 'authoritarian' screen drama the camera will successively turn our attention to whatever the director wishes us to see. We must note that a screen director has a variety of choices between rapid cutting and a mobile camera at one extreme and long takes and a static camera at the other.[14]

Stage, film and television drama differ in many respects. Some of the more important are:

- A stage performance, being live, is unrepeatable, unique.
  A screen performance, being canned, is repeatable, copyable.

- In a stage performance the actors receive feedback from the audience.
  This is impossible in a screen performance.

- A stage/film performance takes place in a public space especially designed for the purpose.
  A TV performance (usually) takes place at home. As a result, the recipient will be more easily distracted than his counterpart in the theatre or in the cinema.

- A stage/film performance is experienced collectively, a circumstance that favours certain reactions, especially laughter.
  A TV performance is experienced in isolation or with a small group of people.

- A stage/film performance has a select audience. You have decided to go to the performance and to pay for it. As a result, you are likely to watch it to the end.
  A TV performance has a mass audience and is practically free of charge. You can switch it off whenever you like or turn to another channel.

- In a stage/film performance you are totally dependent on how the play/film is being presented.
  In a TV performance you can adjust brightness, contrast, colour, volume and pitch to suit your own taste.

- A stage/film performance has nothing or little surrounding it.

A TV performance is "embedded in a continuous flow of largely non-fictional items."[15]

- In a stage performance characters and properties are three-dimensional. In a screen performance they are two-dimensional.

- In a stage performance the spectator follows the action from one and the same optical point of view: his/her seat.
  In a screen performance the optical viewpoint – distance, angle – is constantly changed by means of the camera.

- In the theatre we can decide for ourselves what we wish to focus on: the speaking or the listening character, the scenery, a prop, etc.
  On the screen the camera does this for us. The choice and linking of shots highly determines our view of events and characters.

- The stage offers nothing but 'long shots'.
  The screen, notably the small screen, prefers medium shots, medium close-ups and close-ups.[16] This has to do with the reduced visibility of the TV screen.

- The characters on the stage are normally of human size.
  On the film screen they are often larger than this. On TV they are usually smaller than this.[17]

- A stage performance has limited possibilities with regard to changes of time and place.
  In a screen performance there are no such limitations.

- In the traditional proscenium arch stage the fourth wall, facing the auditorium, is gone.
  On the screen there is no 'fourth wall'.

- A stage and especially a film performance can show mass scenes.
  A TV performance prefers scenes between two or three people.[18]

- A stage performance has a more select audience than a film, whose audience is again more select than that of a TV performance.[19]

TV's orientation towards psychological realism is indissolubly linked to the miniaturization characteristic of the medium; in Zitner's words:

As the visual focus narrows from group to individual, body to face, face to eye, the implications of the visual field shift from the social to the psychological, and this inevitably prompts directors and actors to offer a psychologized construction of the text.[20]

It follows from all this that screening a play written for the stage necessarily means deviating in a number of ways from what the dramatist had in mind and what a stage director can and cannot do.[21] The preference for close-range distances in screen versions means that the 'intimate' codes – make-up, mimicry, paralinguistics – receive greater attention than they do in stage productions. The screen director can show

- characters at varying distances; emotional intensification can, for example, be created simply by gradually tracking or zooming in on someone's face

- human faces in close-up, thereby visualising the most minute changes in them

- objects in close-up, thereby making them more prominent

- the face of the listener rather than that of the speaker, that is, focus on the reaction of the listener

- characters and props at significant angles and change these angles significantly.

The screen director can also juxtapose faces in close-up, thereby revealing parallel or contrasting reactions. S/he can juxtapose characters and parts of the scenery or characters and props, thereby establishing suggestive connections.

As for sound, we may note that sound effects and music are used to quite another extent than in stage presentations. Thus, music is regularly used non-diegetically to heighten the mood at certain moments. It may also be used to link different shots and sequences acoustically. Especially on the small screen, acoustic signifiers may even replace visual ones, as when the crying of seagulls would indicate the proximity of the sea. Intimacy of voice is decidedly better suited to the screen than the stage. The stage whisper is a contradiction in terms which we accept as a theatre convention. Similarly, voice-over is a screen convention by means of which the thoughts and feelings of the characters are made audible.

Unlike many stage performances, a screen version usually represents only part of the dialogue. If a play runs to some two and a half hours in the theatre, a TV version of the same play is likely to last at least half an hour less. Only when a play is presented as a TV serial can the whole dialogue in principle be retained.[22] Although cinema film versions may have about the same showing time as stage versions, drastic cuts in the dialogue are called for even more here, film being a much less verbal medium than TV.

Within the screen media there is the basic distinction between film and television, between the big and the small screen, between large and low density, between a "hot" medium, containing a high amount of data and a "cool" one containing a limited amount.[23] Both media make use of close-ups. This is especially true of TV, which has been called "a close-up medium," in addition to being a more verbal medium than film. Significantly, relatively few dramas are adapted for the big screen, whereas most teleplays are adapted stage dramas.[24]

Environmental descriptions and mass scenes remain more suited to the large screen with its better visual quality than to the small one, which favours drawing room shots (medium to close-up). To get a multitude of people into the small screen simultaneously, a director would either be forced to use long shots, which would impoverish the visibility, or cut between different groups or individuals, which would confuse the viewer. "Rapid change of images rather than richness within one image" is characteristic of TV.[25]

Sound in the most general sense of the word is exceedingly important to TV because, as Ellis reminds us, television offers "a small image of low definition." His claim that sound "is crucial in holding the spectator's attention,"[26] is more debatable. It is at least unlikely that it applies to television drama which caters for a rather select audience watching more actively than the average TV viewer.

Television drama, Eaton remarks, was originally a hybrid form:

> It borrowed its dramatic construction entirely from the theatre but its syntax was that of classical continuity editing in terms of camera angles, movements and cutting, more because of lighting conditions than any limitations of technology.[27]

In many ways this description still holds true. Yet, like any other art form, television drama has not been unaffected by the technical development. Originally shot live in a studio – a situation approaching that of a stage performance – teleplays are since around 1960 taped and edited, that is, produced in a manner closer to that of film. In the late 1960s colour began to replace black-and-white. The colours made it easier to distinguish details than when the screen was limited to whites, greys and blacks. As a consequence, long shots became more meaningful and therefore more frequent. Visibility, not least of subtitles, has been improved.[28] And bilingual reception has in recent years been made accessible in some countries.

Because of these gradual changes, it is difficult to give anything other than a very broad characterisation of what a teleplay really is. Many attempts in the past have turned out to be "merely interim statements."[29] There is no doubt, however, that television drama has generally speaking moved away from its theatrical origin in the direction of cinema. Teleplays "are increasingly cinema films in all but name; they rely upon cinematic techniques."[30] This development is likely to continue when widescreen television becomes common property.

Along with the technical development, the last decades have been marked by the globalisation of TV transmission, proliferation of the number of channels, a growing commercialisation and, as a result of this, a diminishing concern for programs with low viewing figures. In the United States,

> the commercial nature of television has been detrimental to the development of drama: plays are too costly to produce relative to the size of the audience they can command.[31]

There "the single play has virtually been killed off to make way for machine-made series and serials with high gloss, canned laughter and routine violence."[32] In Europe, especially in Scandinavia, the single play or one-off produced directly for television has fared somewhat better, but even there it has become more and more scarce, nudged away by the immensely popular soap operas.[33] In this connection we may note the marked difference in reception, also of single plays, between commercial and non-commercial channels. In the former a teleplay will be surrounded and interrupted by commercials.

In view of this development, an examination such as the present one takes on an almost historical character. What is described is less characteristic of the present situation than of the situation from the early days of television until the 1990s, a period marked by greater concern for the classics, including those stemming from domestic dramatists. In countries like Norway and Sweden, it has been natural for a long time to consider television drama an alternative to stage drama for those living in densely populated areas and a substitute for those living far away from theatres. In either case television drama lacked a clear profile. Gradually, however, as this kind of drama has gained momentum, it has come to be seen not only as a practical but also as an aesthetic alternative to stage theatre and even to film. This change has naturally also affected the presentation of the classics.

Also, the way in which television is received makes it legitimate to speak of a 'historical' period. It is generally recognised that in the last few years viewers have become both more passive – paying distracted attention and talking through the programs – and more restless, having now almost un-limited possibilities to zap between programs. Although it is likely that our adapted, classical one-offs could still count on more attentive viewers than most TV programs, these viewers have presumably not been unaffected by the general development. If this is true, it may be argued that the reception of television drama has increasingly estranged itself from the concentrated attention typical of theatre and film reception.

What we loosely refer to as television drama falls into three distinct cate-gories:

- drama texts written directly for television

- drama texts adapted from plays written for another medium, usually the stage

- drama texts adapted from other fictional modes (short stories, novels).

Only the second category concerns us here.

Turning to the way in which this type of television drama is produced, we must distinguish between:

- registrations of stage performances in the theatres where the plays are staged, with or without an audience

- adaptations of stage performances produced in a TV studio

- adaptations of play texts made directly for TV production.[34]

While the first category is the normal one in Germany, the second is com-mon in the United Kingdom, and the third is dominant in Scandinavia. Al-though it can sometimes be difficult to make out whether we deal with an adaptation via a stage production or one made directly for TV, the distinc-tion is important, since it may explain differences in scenery, acting, etc.

It is obvious that the first, financially attractive category is an undesirable hybrid of two media. A presentation intended for the stage – that is, for dis-tant reception – is forced onto the small screen, watched from nearby. As a result, the characters' gestures and mimicry seem exaggerated and their voices unduly loud. Poorly suited for the TV medium, this category will hardly concern us.[35]

When a production is rendered in a target language, the translation forms an important 'intertext' between the source text and the performance. Specific for the translation for the stage is that it "reaches the audience by way of the actors' bodies" and that "heterogeneous cultures and situations of enunciation that are separated in space and time" are involved.[36]

Concerned with stage-oriented translations, Pavis prefers translations that predetermine the *mise en scène* to those that do "not encroach on the work of the director."[37] I do not share this view. Few would deny a director a great amount of freedom with regard to the text on which s/he is basing his/her production. But a translator, especially one who translates from minor, little-known languages like Norwegian and Swedish, must certainly adhere faithfully to the source text and render all of it. This is especially important if the translation is published, that is, intended also for the general reader and not for a particular production. The whole point is that the director must understand what is in the source text when dealing with the target text. This does not mean, of course, that the translation cannot *at a later stage* be turned into a more playable, target-oriented, even updated version, either by the translator alone or by him/her in collaboration with the director. The problem is that a drama translation serves many purposes. Distinguishing no less than six "consumer constituencies" for each drama text, Hanes Harvey argues for as many renderings.[38]

When the source text is a classic, "the translation will be more readable for a target audience than the source text" is for a source audience. Shakespeare is the obvious example.[39] It is doubtful whether Ibsen and Strindberg can in this sense be called classical dramatists.

In the first paperback volume of his Ibsen translations, Michael Meyer, whose renderings of these two playwrights have been standard fare with the BBC for a long time, has a "Note on the Translations" which begins:

> I have translated Ibsen's text faithfully, but have allowed myself a certain amount of liberty as regards cutting. I do not think Ibsen can be played without cuts today [...] and judicious cutting seems to me to be almost as essential as accurate translation.
>
> Ibsen, though marvellously taut in his construction, was not always taut in his phrasing and, especially in the opening and expository scenes of a play, underlines his points to a degree which today would sound tiresomely repetitive. I have trimmed these repetitions and have thinned out the language elsewhere, retaining some additional cuts which were found necessary in rehearsal and production.
>
> Above all, I have not hesitated to strip the dialogue of many of its stage directions.[40]

Whether or not we agree with Meyer's opinion about Ibsen's text – this is, not the issue here – his view of the role of translator is dubious. Meyer confuses his role as translator with that of the director when he is handing the latter a text that has already been unduly 'adapted.' Unless the director is familiar with the source language, s/he will be at a loss, unable to discover the deviations from it. As the end of the quotation makes clear, Meyer's translation is, in fact, a hybrid between a 'general' version intended for the reader and a presumably commissioned acting version, made for a particular production.[41]

A very different approach is taken by another translator of Ibsen's and Strindberg's plays, Inga-Stina Ewbank. In the introduction to a recent volume of three of Strindberg's chamber plays, she writes:

> The aim has been to be as faithful as possible to Strindberg, that is to preserve a sense of his style and use of language: not to explain or clarify his sometimes apparently irrational associations and incoherent sentence structures and dialogue patterns. (Where explanations seemed necessary, they have been placed in the notes, which were primarily aimed at the directors but may also help readers.)[42]

This description, which I fully subscribe to, is a good illustration of the drama translator's boundaries and possibilities. With its many helpful notes, Ewbank's volume is a rare example of what one would like to see as standard fare in future published drama translations.

Some ten years ago Martin Esslin observed that "there is as yet hardly any serious criticism of drama on television."[43] This statement is on the whole still valid. When we turn to the field of *comparative* performance analysis, we may almost speak of a *terra incognita*. Such analyses could concern stage performances based on the same drama text, a difficult undertaking since the considerable problems related to the analysis of a single live performance would multiply here. An easier project, from a practical point of view, is what is attempted here: the comparison of screen productions based on the same drama text. Moreover, although Pavis is of course right when stating that to notate a performance "inevitably means to interpret, to make a more or less conscious choice among the multitude of signs of the performance deemed *noteworthy*,"[44] screen productions have the advantage over stage performances that they, being fixed on tape, are controllable to quite another extent.[45] In this respect drama texts and screen performances have something in common.

What is then the aim of this type of research? Esslin has argued that

> only by starting from an overview of all the aspects of dramatic performance can we arrive at a clear differentiation of those features that each of the separate media –

stage, film and television – can claim as specifically their own, as against the much larger number of aspects they have in common.[46]

This applies *mutatis mutandis* to the area mapped out here: printed version, intended stage version and screen presentation. By examining various productions based on the same text, we obtain a good perspective on the relationship between constants and variables in the play text itself, its potential range. At the same time we can more clearly see what individual directors are doing with it, his or her obligatory and voluntary choices.

By limiting the examination to TV presentations of plays written for the stage, comparability is increased – especially since all the plays were composed in the same relatively short period by merely two dramatists, who could both be seen as ancestors of the intimate realism characteristic of television drama.[47] The realism, or better illusionism, that in Ibsen's and Strindberg's time dominated the stage has, with the arrival of the screen media, come to be associated with these media – whereas the stage has come to be seen as a place where stylisation, non-illusionism, should reign supreme. Paradoxically, the more or less mimetic kind of presentation intended by the two Scandinavians is nowadays largely taken care of in media that existed hardly (film) or not at all (television) in their time.

PART ONE – IBSEN

3   A Doll's House (1879)

Ibsen's second realistic play in prose, *A Doll's House*,[1] has been extremely popular also on the small screen. Of the four TV productions dealt with here, all of them in colour, those of Arild Brinchmann (Norway, 1973) and David Thacker (UK, 1992) adhere rather faithfully to the play text, whereas those of Per Sjöstrand (Sweden, 1970) and Rainer Werner Fassbinder (West Germany, 1974) adapt the play in very different ways.

The play opens with the protagonist, Nora Helmer, returning home on Christmas Eve, loaded with Christmas gifts for her three children and for her husband who has just been appointed manager of the Credit Bank. Nora reveals a secret to her old friend Mrs Linde. Years ago she falsified her dying father's signature to secure the money needed to save her husband's life. When Krogstad, one of Helmers' employees who had committed a similar crime, risks being dismissed from his job, he threatens to reveal the forgery to Helmer. Confronted with two letters from Krogstad, the first threatening, the second conciliatory, Helmer reveals his egoistic nature. Realising that *she* is not fit to educate their children and that *he* is not fit to educate her, Nora decides to educate herself. She leaves her family.

As a realistic drama with few characters and one setting, *A Doll's House* is, arguably, even more suited today for the screen than for the stage. For a long time the Helmer living room was presented in a minutely realistic way on the stage. With the arrival of film and, later, television, which could present environments in a much more authentic way, meticulous stage realism was gradually replaced by selective realism and even by highly stylised presentations. Not surprisingly, three of the TV versions we are considering are in a realistic mode, while one, going against the grain, is highly stylised.

This development means that the play's few unrealistic ingredients are now easier to accept on the stage than they were at the time when illusionism held sway in the theatre. While these ingredients no longer present a problem to the stage director, they do to the director of the realistically oriented screen media. Nora's thirteen soliloquies form a case in point. Let us see how they are handled in the four teleplays.

It is a commonplace to state that especially in the screen media the physical distance between spectator and character implies a mental distance. A Nora who delivers her soliloquies in long shot is not a Nora we easily identify with. Understandably, none of the directors have chosen this solution. They all have Nora soliloquise in close-up, usually turned to the camera. Thacker at times even resorts to extreme close-ups.

While he retains most of the soliloquies, the other directors omit many of them. Brinchmann, being the most consistent realist of the four, frequently replaces the soliloquies with pantomime, making us guess from facial expressions what is on Nora's mind. When he retains a soliloquy, he makes it realistically more acceptable by reducing it to a few words. In these pantomimic passages, we see

> another Nora, a Nora Helmer has never known. In this way the great scene of transformation – when Nora discards her masquerade costume – was prepared from the first moment.[2]

All the directors, except Fassbinder, keep the soliloquy that provides a strong curtain for Act II, opening with "Five o'clock" and concluding with "Thirty-one hours to live." In the play text this soliloquy is somewhat loosely motivated by Nora looking "*at her watch*." Sjöstrand's Nora, standing next to the clock on the mantlepiece, starts to soliloquise about the time left to her as the clock strikes five. The outer stimulus motivates her thinking aloud. Similarly, Nora's "Corrupt my little children!," which is in Ibsen's version not directly related to anything around her, is in Sjöstrand's performance motivated by her looking into the nursery. The director even has us share her optical point of view when she is peeping at her children, asleep in their beds – a sentimental touch akin to that of Ibsen's alternative German ending.[3]

Thacker adds soft mood music to a couple of the early soliloquies, flute or strings. The non-diegetic music here serves to underline Nora's development from relative harmony to an increasingly disturbed state of mind. However, this concretisation of the idea that the 'music' gradually disappears out of Nora's life seems both sentimental and trite. Fassbinder, too, adds non-diegetic music to the few soliloquies he retains, but in his case it functions rather as an ironic comment on Nora's statements.

A major question when producing *A Doll's House* concerns the relations between the sexes. Since these have changed considerably since 1879, modern productions must take this into account. Ibsen, Sprinchorn points out,

> was writing at a time when the sympathies of the audience would lie mainly with the husband [...], whatever sort of man he was. To give Nora a fighting chance in the struggle for the sympathies of the audience Ibsen had to darken the character of Torvald.[4]

Today the situation is different. The more dislikeable Helmer appears, the more we ask ourselves why Nora did not leave him long ago. Modern productions therefore tend to play down his authoritarian self-complacency. Creating a bullying nineteenth-century Helmer for a late twentieth-century audience, as Thacker does, is hardly recommendable. Sjöstrand and Brinchmann settle for considerably milder Helmers, who function as father substitutes for Nora. Fassbinder's Helmer is about the same age as his Nora, a logical choice since in his version society itself is the tyrant, victimising *both* of them by forcing them into their imprisoning gender roles.

Ibsen's description of the setting is, as usual, fairly detailed:

> *A pleasantly and tastefully, but not expensively furnished living room. A door to the R in the BG leads to the hall; another door to the L in the BG leads to* HELMER's *study. Between these two doors a piano. In the middle of the L wall a door, further downstage a window. Near the window, a round table with armchairs and a small sofa. In the R wall, somewhat at the farther end, a door, and against the same wall, closer to the FG, a porcelain stove, with a couple of arm-chairs and a rocking-chair in front of it. Between the stove and the side door a small table. En-gravings on the walls. A what-not with china and other bric-à-brac; a small bookcase with richly bound books. Carpet on the floor; fire in the stove. A winter day.*[5]

The very first sentence of the stage-directions reveals the authorial narra-tor's double message. He makes the *reader* visualise a pleasant and tasteful room. At the same time he suggests to the director and the scenographer that they recreate a pleasant and tasteful room on the stage for the *spectator*. While the reader can easily accept the idea, since the narrator's description allows him or her to imagine what *s/he* finds pleasant and tasteful, the spec-tator who is confronted with a visual concretisation of the room may experi-ence it as unpleasant and tasteless. Judging by the way people furnish their living rooms, taste varies considerably.

When first confronted with this living room, we find it hard to see much significance in it. It is said to be attractive – as a room in a doll's house is likely to be. The piano (music), the engravings (art) and the books (litera-ture) suggest that at least one of the inhabitants has cultural interests. That is about all. Again there is a discrepancy between the reader and the spectator. The latter will not be immediately aware of what is behind the doors in the background nor of the fact that it is *"a winter day."*

However, when we reread the play, the setting becomes more signifi-cant. Nora's remark that Torvald has the talent "of making a home bright and beautiful" causes us to see the room as an expression of his rather than her taste.[6] *He* is the ruler in this household, and *he* is the one who explicitly voices his aesthetic interests. Therefore, as Helmer is gradually revealed as a man hiding behind a socially impeccable façade, the living room takes on other qualities. The properties we took to be signs of genuine cultural inter-est now appear to be merely status objects, social icons. Like the play title, the setting is, in other words, vested by Ibsen with a concealed pejorative meaning.

We may also regard the fact that the whole action takes place in one and the same room as a sign that Nora is imprisoned in a doll's house existence – although the room has "no fewer than four doors, one of which leads to a fifth and a sixth."[7] This raises the question of whether this is an open or a closed environment. As appears from the acting directions at the beginning of Act III, the Helmers live on one of the upper floors of an apartment house. Ibsen

> could have given the Helmers a house, or even an apartment on the ground floor, without changing the play's surface at all. [...] The elaborate separation between the inner and the outer world increases the gaps between them; we feel that Nora's "doll house" is a refuge from the cold, hard world outside, a safe haven – or a prison.[8]

A comparison of Ibsen's opening with the way in which the various TV versions open is revealing.[9] Ibsen's play opens on a harmonious note:

> *A bell rings out in the hall; after a moment we hear a door being opened.* NORA *enters the living room, humming contentedly to herself; she is wearing outdoor clothes and carrying a lot of parcels, which she puts down on the table R. She leaves the door to the hall open behind her and out there we can see a* PORTER *carrying a Christmas tree and a basket. He gives these to the* MAID, *who has opened up for them.*
>
> NORA. Hide the Christmas tree well, Helene. The children mustn't see it until tonight, when it's decorated. *To the* PORTER, *taking out her purse.* How much – ?
>
> PORTER. Fifty øre.
>
> NORA. Here's a crown. No, keep it all.
>
> *The* PORTER *thanks and leaves.* NORA *closes the door.*

This opening immediately suggests that it is Christmas Eve. It also tells us that Nora tips the Porter exorbitantly but as first-time recipients we cannot make out why this is so. Is Nora a spendthrift? Is she unusually generous because it is Christmas? (A third possibility – that Nora is open-handed because her husband's financial position has recently improved – is still unknown to us at this point.) A stage performance will hardly settle the matter.[10]

But the opening means more than this. This is the first monetary allusion in the play, and as Bentley notes, "the references to money all lead into the play [...] and culminate in Nora's "Torvald, this is a settling of accounts.""[11]

Important, too, is that already here one of the central symbols, the Christmas tree, is literally brought into the play, thereby receiving the needed attention from the recipient. The Christmas tree may be seen primarily as a "symbol of family happiness and security";[12] or as "a natural product of the forests" that "has been prevented from full growth, cut or transplanted, then prettified and decorated in a domestic environment, like Nora herself."[13] Quigley draws the parallel to the protagonist even closer when noting that the Christmas tree "is dressed and then stripped – which links it with the later fancy-dress ball and the costume Nora first dons and later discards."[14]

Brinchmann follows the source text quite faithfully in his opening:

1 NORA *in red coat and a* PORTER *with a Christmas tree outside a door.* NORA *rings the bell.*

2 *CU of* NORA *through the glass of the door, from inside. Ringing of bell.*

3 HELMER *at the desk in his green-walled study, a book in L hand, a pen in R. When he hears the bell he smiles, gets up, goes to the door of his room, opens it, looks out.*

4 *The hall and behind it a long corridor. The door in BG is opened and the* MAID *approaches.*

5 HELMER *in door opening waves to the* MAID *with his book, indicating that she open the door.*

6 *The* MAID *opens the front door.* NORA *enters with a basket full of parcels in one hand and a big parcel in the other. Behind her the* PORTER *with the Christmas tree and another basket full of parcels.*

NORA. Hide the Christmas tree away, Helene.

7 *Pan with* NORA *as she moves into the living room, where she puts down the parcels; turning to the* MAID, *who is still by the front door.*

NORA. The children mustn't see it before it is decorated this evening.

8 *The* MAID *and the* PORTER *with the Christmas tree by the front door. The* MAID *takes the tree and the basket from the* PORTER *and disappears right.*

9 NORA *up to the* PORTER, *takes out her purse.*

NORA. How much – ?

PORTER. Fifty øre.

NORA. Here's a crown. No, keep it.

PORTER *thanks and leaves.* NORA *closes the door.*

Within nine shots Ibsen's visualised two-room set (hall and living room) has been extended with three more areas (exterior, study, corridor). In retrospect the first shot is remarkable in that it is the only exterior shot in the whole teleplay. It clearly relates to the ending, where Nora leaves her doll's house for the world outside.

Already in this brief opening sequence, husband and wife are contrasted visually. *He* is keeping check of the money at his desk. *She* has just been spending a lot of it. Helmer also immediately establishes his role as *paterfamilias*. He can guess that it is Nora who has rung the bell – is the implication here that she has no key to her own apartment? – but it is below his dignity to go to the door himself. He orders the Maid to go.

Nora's generosity towards the Porter is a brief incident that passes by rather unnoticed, partly because Brinchmann does not particularly emphasise it and partly because the brevity of the (long) shot and the fairly rapid cutting surrounding it makes it harder for us to sense Nora's exceeding generosity. To put it differently: given the cutting around it, we would need a more emphatic Porter sequence to grasp the significance of what is happening, for example in the form of close-ups showing Nora's and the Porter's facial expressions when she gives him the crown. However, as earlier indicated, there are good reasons why Brinchmann has not opted for this solution.

Adjusting the play to the dynamic TV medium, Sjöstrand divides his script into no fewer than sixty-five different scenes, each scene shift representing a change of place; in the production this number is somewhat reduced. There, in the opening, we move with Nora from the Credit Bank, where Helmer[15] has just officially accepted his new post as manager, to a tea room, then back to the bank again. Not until some twenty minutes later do we find ourselves in the Helmer interior, where Ibsen's play begins. This means that much of the conversation between Nora and Helmer and between Nora and Mrs Linde that with Ibsen takes place in the living room, with Sjöstrand occurs in the tea room. Once inside the house we see, in turn, the various rooms of the apartment: besides the living room and the hall, prescribed by Ibsen, Helmer's study, the dining room, the children's room and the kitchen.

Sjöstrand opens his performance by crosscutting between Helmer's masculine world and Nora's feminine one – a contrast that, as Steene has observed, is indicated spatially already in the play text where Rank and Krogstad but not Nora enter Helmer's study.[16] Nora's doll mentality is demonstrated from the very beginning as she listens *"with childish affection"* to her husband's speech, added by Sjöstrand, about "trustful collaboration" – a speech which seems utterly hypocritical to Krogstad, who has just learnt that he has been dismissed.

An advantage of Sjöstrand's rearrangement is that the meeting between Nora, Mrs Linde and Rank is made more plausible. The two women simply come across each other in the tea room, where Rank, by chance or not, after a while joins them. Momentarily, we even glimpse Krogstad, the lonely outsider, outside the windows. Nora's secret eating of macaroons is replaced by her revelling in pastries – against her explicit promise to Helmer. Having finished their tea, Nora brings Mrs Linde to the bank, in the hope that she can persuade Helmer to find a post for her there. From the bank the director cuts to Nora surrounded by her three little children on the sofa in the Helmer living room, the lonely Mrs Linde sitting opposite the happy family. Ibsen's opening is rearranged in this version – though much of the dialogue is retained – in favour of three lengthy sequences depicting the social environment to which the Helmer household belongs.

In Fassbinder's *Nora Helmer*,[17] which stresses the dehumanising reïfication of bourgeois society, Nora recklessly makes use of radical feminist slogans to create a comfortable position for herself within a society she claims to fight. The director

> cut all the lines which seemed to her [Margit Carstensen as Nora] most significant and which she most wanted to discuss. He had decided, unilaterally, to show Nora "as a woman who understands the means she has to get her own way, to suppress a man."[18]

The power struggle between husband and wife is indicated already in the opening shot, showing Helmer's ringed hand resting upon the back of Nora's naked shoulder and her ringed hand with its red-painted nails resting upon his, an emblematic metaphor. Fassbinder's Nora has, so to speak, the upper hand from the very beginning.

Through a lattice – part of an interior balustrade? – in the shape of two combined "hearts," we see Nora entering the apartment from far back with the Christmas presents. The colouring is pale, cool, enfeebled. The note of distance and imprisonment has been struck. In the rest of the performance we frequently watch the characters either through the ornamented glass walls – where Helmer's comparison of Nora to a lark and a squirrel seem inscribed – or via the many mirrors in the living room. The room is filled with properties, indicating the materialism of the *nouveau riche* couple, representative of the situation in an affluent society. Elegantly dressed in early twentieth century dresses, Helmer and Nora are narcissistically isolated from each other in their labyrinthine world of mirrors. Restless, they move around in the limited space at their disposal as though in a cage. The conversation between them often takes place with one of them in the foreground looking at us rather than at the addressee appearing in the background. The dialogue is rendered in a monotonous way with a minimum of mimicry, as though the characters are drained of all emotions and are mere puppets in a social machinery, victims of a deadening (bourgeois) society. As in

Brechtian theatre, empathy concerns their recognisable situation rather than themselves.

Thacker opens with a high angle shot of Nora and the Porter climbing the staircase as we receive the information about play title and author – to the accompaniment of non-diegetic string music which, synchronised with the climbing, moves from low to high. We understand that the Helmers are living high up in an apartment house. The camera shifts to the inside of the apartment as we see the Maid open the front door. Thacker's Porter, unlike Brinchmann's, indicates by the gesture of his hand and by his facial expression that Nora has tipped him surprisingly generously.

The tarantella at the end of Act II is the most spectacular part of the play. On the most obvious level, Nora dances the tarantella to distract Helmer's attention from the fateful letterbox. Her wild dancing expresses her fear that he will discover her crime. Helmer is significantly unable to guide Nora but Rank, who is doomed to die shortly, is more successful. Rank and Nora, both of them in the shadow of death at this point, understand each other intuitively. Helmer understands nothing. The many references to failed attempts at guidance help to pinpoint the fact that Nora, although she has asked Helmer for instruction, no longer follows it. Still trying to admire him, she is instinctively breaking away from him. In this sense the tarantella prepares for her discovery at the end that she and her husband have in fact never understood one another.

The reason why Nora practises of all dances a tarantella is not so much that this rapid, whirling south Italian dance reminds Helmer and herself of their happy days in and around Naples. The tarantella, as used by Ibsen, is a sophisticated motif which demands of the recipient a certain factual knowledge both of the dance and of the spider that has given the dance its name:

> The tarantula spider is reputedly poisonous, and anyone bitten by it is likely to contract the disease of tarantism. This is "a hysterical malady, characterized by an extreme impulse to dance." And the cure for this malady was held to be – dancing the tarantella. [...] The symptom of the disease and the cure for the disease are one and the same.[19]

The wildness with which Nora dances the tarantella is indeed similar to what we would expect from someone bitten by the tarantula. Squeezed between Krogstad's demands and Helmer's stern moralising, she has got the poison inside her. Suicide is on her mind. And at the same time, a vague hope that a miracle might save her. The tarantella is a fitting, theatrically powerful expression of her schizophrenic situation.

The tarantella is difficult to do on the small screen. Nora needs some space for her dancing. Moreover, at the end of it we have three other characters spread out in the room: Rank *"at the piano,"* Helmer *"by the stove"* and Mrs Linde *"in the doorway."* While on the stage Nora's state of mind at this point will be illuminated by her wild dancing, in a TV version such kinesics may, in part, be replaced by mimicry. To what extent does the director want to show the dancing itself and to what extent does s/he want to show Nora's facial expressions while dancing? To what extent, in other words, does s/he opt for long shots, medium shots, close-ups? What does s/he focus on? Nora's anguish? The master-slave relationship between Helmer and Nora? The bond, by love and death, between Nora and Rank? Or all of these things?

Fassbinder, more interested in Nora's will to power than in her anguish, omits the tarantella. Sjöstrand aborts a climactic development of the sequence by opting for crosscutting. From the tarantella he cuts to a shot showing how Mrs Linde in vain visits Krogstad. Cutting back to the tarantella he then shows how Helmer rather emphatically instructs Nora. The passage ends with Nora throwing the tambourine to Mrs Linde.

Brinchmann begins the tarantella with a long shot of Nora, tambourine in hand, then cuts to a shot showing Helmer at the piano in the foreground and Nora dancing in the background. In a series of shots, in which the camera gradually approaches Nora without actually reaching close-up distance, the director focuses on Nora's increasingly wild dance and the mimicry that goes with it.

Thacker switches back and forth between long shots, taking in a great deal of the room, two-shots of Helmer instructing Nora, and shots showing Nora's face in the foreground, Helmer and Rank in the background. Somewhat surprisingly, Mrs Linde enters in the foreground left. Carefully designed, there is nevertheless a lack of focus in Thacker's rather theatrical handling of the tarantella.

Rank's leave-taking of the Helmers – he has just learned that his days are counted – is full of double-entendres. Rank asks for a cigar. Helmer gives it to him. Ibsen continues:

NORA *strikes a match.* Let me give you a light.

RANK. Thank you. *She holds out the match for him; he lights his cigar.* And now – goodbye.

HELMER. Goodbye, goodbye, my dear chap.

NORA. Sleep well, Dr Rank.

RANK. Thank you for that wish.

NORA. Wish me the same.

RANK. You? Very well, since you ask. Sleep well. And thanks for the light. *He nods to them both and leaves.*

Nora and Rank both realise that her lighting his cigar has a deep erotic significance. Facing death, Rank has just revealed to her that he is in love with her. She can now symbolically return his love. This is clearer in the source text, where they both speak of "ild" (fire). When Nora wishes Rank a good night's sleep, they both, unlike Helmer, know that sleep stands for death. When she wants him to return the friendly wish, neither Helmer nor Rank realise that this connotation applies also to her, that suicide is on her mind.

Rank's leave-taking is omitted altogether by Fassbinder. The cigar-lighting loses all significance in Sjöstrand's version. The director has Helmer rather than Nora light Rank's cigar, and he omits Nora's and Rank's metaphoric references to fire. With Brinchmann it is a rather slow, intimate passage. We see, in close-up, the flame of Nora's match lighting Rank's long cigar. The medium here helps to clarify the sexual connotations. Rank's leave-taking is done as follows:

CU of NORA. Sleep well, Dr Rank.

MS of RANK *who turns round to face her*. Thanks...

CU of NORA. Wish me the same!

CU of RANK. Sleep well. And thanks for the fire.

In Thacker's version Rank asks Helmer for a cigar, seemingly to get him out of the room, so that he can be alone with Nora. After a close-up of Nora and Rank, which shows her lighting his cigar to the accompaniment of non-diegetic theme music, Helmer appears in the background between the two – an obstacle and an outsider.

Returning from the Stenborg party at the beginning of Act III, Ibsen's Helmer, intoxicated by the champagne, demands his matrimonial 'rights':

HELMER. [...] When I saw you chasing and alluring in the Tarantella, – my blood grew hot, I couldn't bear it any longer; – that was why I brought you down here with me so early –

NORA. Go away, Torvald! You must go away from me. I don't want all this.

HELMER. What's this? Now, Nora, you're surely playing the wag with me. Want; want? Aren't I your husband – ?
There is a knock on the front door.

The dialogue implies that Helmer considers Nora his "spøkefugl" (wag) – as he has earlier called her his "lærkefugl" (lark) – a correspondence inevitably lost in the translations. And that he is close to Nora at this point. But is he behaving gentlemanly or vulgarly? Is he softly pleading or brutally demanding? The director has a range of options here.

While Ibsen's Helmer does not even kiss his wife at this moment – he has just kissed her *"on the forehead"* – Sjöstrand's Helmer unbuttons her around the neck and kisses her with increasing intensity. Even so, he is a rather quiet seducer. What is more, Sjöstrand's Nora, still accepting her conjugal "obligations," gives way and returns her husband's kisses.

Brinchmann's Helmer is much more violent. Taking off Nora's bodice, pressing her breasts, putting his hand under her skirt and forcing himself between her legs, this Helmer is actually 'raping' his wife when Rank's knock interrupts him.

Thacker's Helmer is even more demanding. Performing much the same actions as Brinchmann's, he does it in a sadistic rather than voluptuous manner. When the knock is heard, he points an authoritarian finger at Nora, telling her to arrange her clothes and make herself presentable. The gap between appearances and reality is strongly emphasised.

Fassbinder's Helmer, on the other hand, is remarkably virtuous. Neither drunk nor lecherous, he just momentarily puts his hands on Nora's shoulders.

Brinchmann and Thacker both demonstrate the ugliness behind the proper matrimonial façade. Rather than titillate the spectator or update the play, their presentations of the seduction have an emblematic function, the rape being an extreme sign of male dominance. While such an approach seems fitting for the stage, it is doubtful whether it fits the realistic presentations adhered to by Brinchmann and Thacker.

Nothing in the play has attracted so much attention as the ending which is, arguably, the most famous – or infamous – ending in world drama. Having exchanged her fanciful tarantella costume for her *"everyday dress,"* Nora now appears in the living room in the middle of the night with *"her outdoor things"* and *"a small travelling bag."* She hands back her wedding ring to Helmer and asks him to do the same. Her wish to divorce him is made explicit. Then:

HELMER. Nora, – can I never be anything more than a stranger to you?

NORA *picks up her bag.* Oh, Torvald, then the most wonderful thing would have to happen. –

HELMER. Name it, this most wonderful thing!

NORA. Then you and I would both have to change so much that – . Oh, Torvald, I don't believe in wonders any more.

HELMER. But I'll believe in them. Tell me! Change so much that – ?

NORA. That our life together could become a marriage. Goodbye. *She leaves through the hall.*

HELMER *sinks down on a chair by the door and covers his face with his hands.* Nora! Nora! *Looks around and gets up.* Empty. She is no longer here. *With a glimmer of hope.* The most wonderful thing – ?!
The sound of a street door being slammed shut is heard from below.

Nora's slamming of the door "seems to summarize in a single action Nora's rejection of her husband, her children, her home and her social position, along with the society that taught her to need such things."[20] Her exit through the front door of the apartment significantly contrasts with her entrance through it in the opening of the play, when we see her happily returning home with the Christmas tree. "The unadorned Christmas tree, framed in the doorway at the beginning of the play" is linked "with the figure of Nora, no longer in fancy dress, passing through the same doorway at the end of the play."[21] It is also noteworthy that Nora leaves "wearing the same type of clothing Mrs. Linde had worn when she entered, having almost literally transformed herself from doll into traveller."[22]

As for Helmer, we may note that his desire to believe in miracles, followed by the (added) acting direction concerning the hope he suddenly clings to, seems to be born more out of desperation than conviction.

In Sjöstrand's version the ending is done as follows:

NORA, *wearing a white shawl, and* TORVALD *in the hall by the front door. Slight HA MCU of* TORVALD's *neck L and* NORA's *neck R. (She is facing the door.) She turns around, looks at him, smiles vaguely.*

NORA *almost pertly.* That our life together could become a marriage. *Turns toward the door, opens it and leaves.*

TORVALD *remains by the door for a while, then walks slowly back into the living room, while fingering the ring he has just got back from her. Quietly desperate he says to himself.* Nora. *Then goes to the window, opens it and shouts.* Nora! Nora! *Her name reverberates along the street. Fade-out.*

Nora here wears the same costume she wore in the beginning of the play. Only the shawl, an ironical veil or shroud, is added. Since there is no travelling bag to be seen, Nora's departure seems rather rash. Seen in relation to other directorial choices – notably the positive way in which her husband is depicted – it contributes to our impression that this Nora may well return.

As in the play text, the final focus is on Helmer. His walking through the large living room accentuates his feeling of loneliness, the emptiness of his present existence. His desperation is expressed by his calling for his wife in the middle of the night. We are a long way from the man who is afraid of making a scandal.

Brinchmann's Nora at the end puts on a brown coat with black-fur trimmings – instead of the black shawl called for in the text. She does not pick up the travelling bag until immediately before leaving. Standing by the front door of the apartment, she utters her exit line:

Straight-on CU of NORA, *looking down.*

NORA *hesitantly.* That ... our life together could become ... a marriage. *Pause. Turns towards the door.* Goodbye.

Helmer runs after her when she leaves through the cross-shaped glass-and-wood apartment door. Her steps can be heard as she walks down the stairs. Helmer turns, closes the door, looks at the ring she has returned to him, walks back into the living room and, rather superfluously, says, "Empty."[23] He sits down in the middle of the sofa, a position emphasising his loneliness, and mumbles puzzled, "The most wonderful thing." Faint door slam. Fade-out.

In Fassbinder's ending, the room has been cleared of all the properties that crammed it in the beginning. But the distance between the couple remains. The masks dropped, the gap between them has merely become more obvious. Nora's final line has, significantly, been cut. Moreover, rather than leave she stops by the front door.[24] Like Ibsen, Fassbinder ends his play with a question mark. But the question we ask ourselves is not whether Nora will return or not. It is rather whether she will leave at all.[25]

For the key line Thacker places Nora and Helmer in the living room, between the table and the piano. She has put on her black coat, he is in the same dark-green smoking-jacket he wore in the beginning. We then get:

Straight-on CU of NORA *L and* HELMER *R, both in profile, looking at one another. While the light of daybreak is faintly seen on her face, his face is slightly turned away so that we cannot see his eyes.*

NORA *softly but insistently gesticulating.* Change so much that our life together ... could become a marriage. *Soft, melancholy string music starts and continues until the end.*

NORA *still looking at* HELMER, *very softly.* Goodbye. *Looks down, turns away.*

She then moves toward the door and the camera so that we, unlike Helmer, can see her face at the moment of her departure. After a close-up of Helmer, pathetically crying, Thacker has him shout "Nora!" while rushing after her out onto the staircase. Looking down the stairs, he whispers "Empty," then returns slowly to the apartment. We see his face in close-up, on the verge of tears but with a trembling smile on his lips, as he says: "The most wonderful thing of all?" The final shot of the empty staircase as the door slam is heard reveals that Thacker was more interested in presenting an ironical circle composition – the opening and closing shot of the staircase are identical – than in showing Helmer's reaction to the door slam.

Thacker's ending is problematic. While Ibsen's Helmer meaningfully experiences the matrimonial apartment as empty, Thacker's rather pointlessly experiences the public staircase as such. Moreover, the melancholy music following directly upon the key line sentimentalises both Nora's statement and the concluding frame of the lonely, pathetic Helmer.

4 Ghosts (1881)

Ibsen's *Gengangere* has always, for want of a better word, been entitled *Ghosts* in English. The play also has a subtitle: *A Family Drama in Three Acts*.[1] Since the Alving family has never been a family in any true sense, the subtitle is obviously ironic, indicating that Ibsen is continuing the attack on the family as an institution he had begun with *A Doll's House*.

The play – once infamous, now famous and frequently performed – consists of a network of gradual revelations. Returning from Paris to his home in Norway doomed to a premature death through syphilis, Mrs Alving's son Osvald learns that he has inherited his illness from his promiscuous, long deceased father and that Mrs Alving's maid, Regine, with whom he wants to start a relationship is actually his half-sister. The asylum for poor children that Mrs Alving has erected in memory of her deceased husband burns down. Carpenter Engstrand, once paid off to play the role of Regine's father, persuades the naive pastor Manders to help him start "a seamen's home," Engstrand's euphemism for a brothel. Regine, having discovered who her real father is and that therefore a relationship with Osvald has become impossible, leaves, presumably to take up a job as a prostitute in Engstrand's brothel. Left alone, Osvald hands his mother the mortal dose of morphine and asks her to give it to him when the illness reduces him to a helpless child – which occurs shortly thereafter. Leaning over her imbecile son, Mrs Alving hesitates to give him "the last service." There the play ends. It is an ending even more provocatively open than that of *A Doll's House*.

While there is a general indication of the *place* of action – "Mrs Alving's *country estate by a large fjord in western Norway*" – the *time* of action is not explicitly mentioned by Ibsen. Yet the date of publication combined with the cultural signifiers appearing in the text suggest that the period is the contemporary one, that is, around 1880. Similarly, although there is no explicit mention of the season, we may conclude from the continuous rain and the fact that it is getting dark early, that it is autumn – implied information that would be less self-evident the further removed the recipient is from western Norway.

The visible setting represents

A spacious garden room, with a door in the L wall and two doors in the R wall. In the C of the room a round table with chairs around it; on the table are books, magazines and newspapers. In the FG L is a window and next to it a small sofa with a sewing table in front of it. In the BG the room is continued into an open, slightly narrower conservatory, closed off from the exterior by walls of large panes of glass. In the R wall of the conservatory is a door leading down to the garden. Through the glass wall a gloomy fjord landscape can be discerned, veiled by steady rain.

The play opens with two characters present in the conservatory:

ENGSTRAND, *a carpenter, is standing by the garden door. His L leg is slightly deformed; under the sole of his boot is a block of wood.* REGINE, *with an empty garden syringe in her hand, prevents him from coming closer.*

REGINE *in a low voice.* What do you want? Stay where you are. You're dripping wet.

ENGSTRAND. It is the rain of Our Lord, my child.

REGINE. The devil's rain, it is.

ENGSTRAND. Gosh, Regine, the way you talk. *Limps a few steps into the room.* What I wanted to say is -

REGINE. Don't clump about with that foot, man. The young master's asleep upstairs.

As often with Ibsen, the stage is divided into three marked areas: the two rooms, contrasting with one another, and the exterior beyond them. This tripartition has a symbolic significance. The conservatory, which is "a protected, artificial haven from the awful weather,"[2] resembles

a greenhouse, that is, a sheltered room built to grow plants by artificial means (Regine's garden syringe), where the glass walls allow forces furthering growth, like sun and warmth, to slip through, whereas destructive forces like wind, cold weather and uncontrolled quantities of rain are shut out.[3]

In her attempt to prevent Engstrand from entering the garden room, Regine invents a legitimate reason: "You're dripping wet." In the manuscript, this sentence originally read: "Det driver jo af dig." (It pours from you all right.) Interestingly, Ibsen then substituted "drypper" (drips) for "driver."[4] Why? Undoubtedly because "drypper" is very close to the noun "dryppert," meaning gonorrhea. The note of sexuality is struck in a play dealing with adultery, prostitution, inherited syphilis and incest, and in which the opening, moreover, is set in the very conservatory where the late Alving once seduced Regine's mother.[5] Now Engstrand has entered it to persuade Alving's daughter – reputedly his own – to become a prostitute in the brothel he wants to open, euphemistically referred to as a "seamen's home." The phallic garden syringe handled by Regine seems quite appropriate in the context.

Yet all this does not explain why the garden syringe is empty. Since it must be exceedingly difficult to demonstrate this in a performance without creating a farcical situation, this seems to be information primarily for the reader. But what does the emptiness signify? It is, of course, an indication that Regine has finished watering the flowers. But such a trivial explanation cannot have been Ibsen's reason for including it in the play. Downer offers another explanation when he relates the emptiness to Regine's attitude to Pastor Manders:

> Just before the entrance of Pastor Manders, "Regina glances at herself, hastily, in the mirror, fans herself with a handkerchief, adjusts the collar of her uniform. Then she resumes watering of the flowers". Since the audience already knows that the watering pot is empty and that Regina is merely a serving maid in Mrs. Alving's house, the action indicates clearly her pretension and her ambition: she assumes the pose of a lady.[6]

The problem with this interpretation is that it is based on a defective translation of Ibsen's acting directions. Rather than resume *"watering of the flowers,"*[7] Regine, in McFarlane's more adequate rendering, generally *"busies herself with the flowers"* (*gir [...] sig ifærd med blomsterne*). Even if we accept the idea that the actress doing the part of Regine does indeed at this point water the flowers, the spectators cannot grasp that she is merely feigning, since they cannot know, as Downer claims, that the pot – syringe, actually – is empty.

In fact, it seems much more natural to assume that Regine, knowing that the syringe is empty, does not *water* the flowers but *fashions* them, removes withered leaves, etc. Her reason for doing so is obviously that she wants to disguise to Manders that she has just been visited by her socially low-standing 'father'; we have just seen how she has been primping herself to make a good impression on the Pastor. But Ibsen's preference for a general rather than a specific description at this point has above all to do with the 'human' quality of the flowers, their symbolic relationship to Osvald, "a particularly frail greenhouse plant, a sensitive rose at Rosenvold."[8]

Rather than relate the empty syringe to the Regine-Manders confrontation, we should link it with the Osvald-Mrs Alving-Regine sequence toward the end of Act II. At Mrs Alving's request, Regine has just fetched a bottle of champagne from the cellar:

> OSVALD. And fetch another glass.
>
> REGINE *looks at him in surprise*. Mrs Alving's glass is there, Mr Alving.
>
> OSVALD. Yes, but fetch one for yourself, Regine.

Regine exits and quickly returns *"with an empty glass, which she keeps in her hand."* Osvald and Mrs Alving tell her to sit down:

REGINE *sits down on a chair by the dining room door, still holding the empty glass in her hand.*

We are at this point aware that Osvald wants to start an intimate relationship with Regine. And although we do not know yet that he is doomed, we understand that he needs her "joy of life" as an antidote to the somberness that surrounds him. Eventually, we learn that he has been thinking of Regine as the person who is strong enough to give him the "last service" (euthanasia), when he is ready for it. When Regine is invited to drink champagne – this joyous, life-affirming beverage – together with Osvald and Mrs Alving, it is a ritual indicating a new relationship on an equal footing between her and them.

But Regine's glass remains empty. No joy of life is poured into it. Instead, the representative of somber puritanism, Pastor Manders, enters:

MANDERS. Engstrand must be given help with his seamen's home. Regine must move to him and help him –

REGINE. No, thank you, Pastor.

MANDERS *notices her only now.* What – ? You here – and with a glass in your hand!

REGINE *quickly puts the glass down.* Pardon – !

Ironically, Manders has taken over Engstrand's initial role – again to no effect.

Let me recapitulate. At the opening of Act I, we see Regine with an empty garden syringe in her hand. Toward the end of Act II, we see her with an empty glass in her hand. Is there any connection? I believe there is.

The flowers of the garden room need water in order to survive. Watering flowers is a life-giving act. Like Osvald, the flowers need a "helping hand." We have earlier seen Regine busying herself with them. And just as the flowers long for the life-giving water, so Osvald longs for the joy of life Regine incarnates. Yet, just as Regine does not have any water for the flowers – the syringe is "*empty*" – so she ultimately, when she discovers that she is his half-sister, proves neither able nor willing to help Osvald.

The point I wish to make is that while a reader of the play text may well come up with an interpretation along these lines, a spectator witnessing a performance of *Ghosts* would find it much harder to do so. First, because the sparsity of the stage directions in the text as compared to the wealth of audiovisual signs in a production makes it easier for the reader to discover how the playwright is pointing in a particular direction. Second, because the verbal nature of the stage directions helps the reader to discover correspondences. While for him/her the garden syringe is connected with the glass through the word *"empty,"* for the spectator there is no visual equivalent of this verbal identity.

Let us now see how the play opening has been recreated in three TV productions. This is Magne Bleness' Norwegian 1978 version:

> *LS of the blue-tinted conservatory. Sound of rain. White walls, big, decorated glass windows and a glass door in BG, two white wicker chairs and a small round white wicker table, green plants in pots.* REGINE, *in BG, is watering the plants.*
>
> *Superimposed text:* Ghosts
> by Henrik Ibsen
>
> REGINE, *in grey-checkered dress and white apron, up in FG. She is watering the plants R with a green can. Out in FG L. Slight track-in on the conservatory.*
> ENGSTRAND *appearing behind the glass door, approaches it, opens it and enters. He wears a black peaked cap, grey jacket above a brown waistcoat and a striped brown shirt, black trousers. Takes off the cap, dries his nose with the back of his hand, limps forward.*
>
> REGINE *in from FG L. Hearing* ENGSTRAND'S *clumping, turns around towards him. Unfriendly.* What do you want?
>
> ENGSTRAND, *smiling, takes a few steps towards her.*
>
> REGINE. Stay where you are. You're dripping wet. *Up the steps towards the conservatory.*
>
> ENGSTRAND *smiling, waving his cap.* It is the rain of Our Lord, my child.
>
> REGINE. The devil's rain, it is. *Places herself next to* ENGSTRAND.
>
> ENGSTRAND, *cap to mouth.* Gosh, the way you talk. *Down the steps.* What I wanted to say is –
>
> REGINE. Don't clump about with that foot, man! The young master's asleep upstairs.

Unlike the reader of the play, who has both the list of dramatis personae and the cue designations at his disposal, the viewer of a screen version is not aware of the names of the characters unless they have been mentioned in the credits preceding the performance or are mentioned in the dialogue. In none of the TV versions considered here do the names of the characters precede the performance. And not until the penultimate speech of the quoted passage does the viewer learn the name of the young woman, while the name of the old man is still kept secret.[9]

From the list of dramatis personae, the reader will logically – but falsely – conclude that Regine is Engstrand's daughter, an assumption supported by their intimate form of addressing each other with "du" – a nuance necessarily lost in English translation – and Engstrand's referring to Regine as "my child."[10] Lacking pre-information about the dramatis personae, the spectator can hardly arrive at the same conclusion. S/he would be less certain that the expression "my child" should be understood literally; characteristically, Pastor Manders addresses Regine in a similar, endearing way.

Bleness' version of the opening, contained within a single shot, is quite theatrical. Variation is ensured, as in the theatre, by the characters moving around both horizontally and, assisted by the added stairs, vertically. In this way the verbal power struggle between Regine and Engstrand is under-lined proxemically.

Unlike Ibsen, Bleness opens the play by showing only the conservatory, the furniture of which – Ibsen is not specific here – is white and light and, along with the green plants (signs of summer and youth), swept in a blue light closer to romantic stage lighting than to a realistic reflection of the mis-erable weather outside. The fjord landscape, hard to reproduce on the small screen with this kind of weather, is not visible.

Beginning a little earlier than Ibsen, Bleness has Regine finishing water-ing the plants – with a green watering can rather than a syringe. Engstrand is not standing by the garden door but – no doubt to clarify the situation – enters from outside when Regine has stopped watering the plants.

Ibsen, as we have seen, says nothing about Regine's and little about Engstrand's appearance. Bleness provides them both with a servile grey and makes Engstrand darkly bicolored, thereby indicating his compound nature. The peaked cap, turning him into a would-be sailor, ties in with his plans of creating "a seamen's home."

Elijah Moshinsky's British 1987 version represents a very different ap-proach:

1 *As Schönberg's* Verklärte Nacht *is intoned, a picture of* Oswald *appears against a pur-ple-blue BG. He wears a blue costume and is sitting in a blue armchair, a blue table next to him, a newspaper in his hands. His face, in profile and strongly lit, is turned R. Slow track-in on him synchronised with increasingly louder music during the following superimposed cred-its:* Judi Dench Michael Gambon Kenneth Branagh Freddie Jones Natasha Richard-son

GHOSTS

As Oswald *turns his face towards us, half of it is covered by darkness.*

by Henrik Ibsen

translated by Michael Meyer.

Sound of tramping. Fade-out Oswald.

2 *Part of a grey-purplish door. The door is opened. Behind it CU of* Engstrand *with grey beard and moustache, black bowler hat and black raincoat.*

REGINA *offscreen, unfriendly.* What do *you* want?

3 *Deep-focus of three rooms in a row. A mirror R in the first room. Filled bookcases in the second room, everything blue-tinted.* ENGSTRAND *with a cane L,* REGINA *with long, ash-colored hair and long blue dress R, a folded white sheet in her hands.*

REGINA. Stay where you are! You're dripping wet!

Music stops.

ENGSTRAND *raising L arm.* It is God's blessed rain, my child.

REGINA *unfriendly.* The Devil's bloody rain, more like. *Walks into the rooms in BG.*

ENGSTRAND *following her.* Why, Regina, the way you talk!

REGINA *turns around abruptly, points to* ENGSTRAND's *club-foot, whispering.* Don't make such a noise with that foot. The young master's asleep upstairs.

The pre-credits here inform the spectators, not of the names of the characters but, as is nowadays common practice, of the names of the actors and actresses incarnating them. The reason is, of course, that names like Mrs Alving and Oswald[11] are less telling to a British audience than those of Judi Dench and Kenneth Branagh. The signal to the spectators is: Don't switch off! Don't zap! Stay with us! You are going to see some superb acting! Surprisingly, the name of the translator is already mentioned here. Usually this is done only in the post-credits.

The opening shot is interesting. Schönberg's *Transfigured Night*, from 1899, carries a title that excellently fits the theme and mood of the play, indicated also in the director's choice of a symbolist *l'heure bleu* colouring. What we experience along with the protagonist, Mrs Alving, in those hours before the final sunrise is, indeed, a transfigured night.

Since the young man is sitting dead still, the immediate impression is that we are watching a painting.[11] But suddenly the 'painting' comes alive. When the title, *Ghosts*, is superimposed, we realise that what we have seen is a visual counterpart of it. It is, however, not until later in the performance that we understand the full implication of this device. When the real Oswald appears, it becomes clear that it was a 'portrait' or 'self-portrait' of him (Oswald, we recall, is a painter) that we saw in the initial shot. But since Oswald is said to look exactly like his father, we may also regard this emblematic shot as a youthful 'portrait' of Captain Alving. It is not only the close relationship between father and son, the dead and the living, that is suggested here. The idea that a dead person may come alive, fundamental in the play, is also suggestively visualised. The face of the 'portrait' is double also in the sense that it shows a split face, half of it sunlit, the other half in darkness – a visualisation, it seems, of Oswald's, and Alving's, dilemma, both finding themselves torn between southern *joie de vivre* and northern puritanism.

Moshinsky settles for a monochrome blue-purplish, somewhat hazy environment, thereby creating a visually melancholic and dreamy quality harmonising with Schönberg's music. This is clearly a house haunted by memories, by ghosts. Omitting Ibsen's conservatory, with its suggestion of light and youth contrasting with the garden room, Moshinsky shows three more or less identical rooms – a narcissistic, closed-in world of culture and dreams.

Moshinsky's Engstrand looks neither like a carpenter nor like a would-be sailor; and there is nothing diabolic about his appearance. His Regina wears a blue dress, matching Oswald's blue costume. Both of them are visually very much a part of the bluish interior – as though they are products of the environment surrounding them. Having omitted the conservatory, the director also leaves out Regine's business with the flowers. Instead, he provides her with another task which establishes her servile position: the folding of white sheets. As for the dialogue, we may note that the intimate, or depreciative, quality of Regine's way of addressing Engstrand, which can be retained in, for example, German, is necessarily lost in English with its single pronoun of address.

Margareta Garpe's Swedish 1989 version of the opening is radically adapted to suit the TV medium:

1 *Black-and-white photo of a* WOMAN *with a* CHILD *on her lap. Next to them stands a* MAN . *A match is lit and a hand moves it close to the photo which is lit up, then concealed by the flames in front of it. Roar of flames.*

2 *White text on black BG:* Ghosts by Henrik Ibsen.
Piano music (Chopin's op. 28/15, The Raindrop Prelude) begins.

3 *Text:* TV adaption Margareta Garpe and Gunilla Jensen.

4 *Text:* Direction Margareta Garpe. *Dissolve to*

5 *Large light stone building in blue-tinted twilight rain.*

6 *MCU of* MRS ALVING, *in underwear, watching her face in a mirror. Track-in on mirrored face. She moves her hand with a tired gesture toward her forehead and strokes back her hair from it.*

7 *Slow track-in on* REGINE *in conservatory fixing her hair, then holding her hands as if praying.*

8 *Painting in ceiling of cherubs, a hole close to the eyes of one of them. Water is dripping from the hole.*

9 *HA CU of a bucket full of water. Drops are falling into it.*

10 *MS of* OSVALD *asleep on a sofa. A cup of tea is put down next to him. He opens his eyes.*

11 *MS of* MRS ALVING *leaving* OSVALD'S *rooms, looking at him.*

12 *MS of* OSVALD *on the sofa.*

13 *MS of* MRS ALVING *closing the door.*

14 *Pan on her as she crosses the landing and enters the door on the opposite side.*

15 *Exterior of the house in pouring rain.* ENGSTRAND *in dark clothes walks towards the house. A big white dog approaches him, barking.*

16 ENGSTRAND *and the dog, seen by* REGINE, *approach the house.*

17 ENGSTRAND *seen from behind opens the back door to the house and enters.*

18 *LS of the white conservatory.* REGINE *is sitting at the piano clumsily playing* The Raindrop Prelude.

19 *CU of* REGINE.

20 REGINE *at the piano in FG,* ENGSTRAND *outside the door in BG, knocking.*

ENGSTRAND. Open.

21 REGINE *runs to the door.*

22 REGINE'S *back by the door,* ENGSTRAND'S *face visible through the door window.*

REGINE. What do you want? Stay where you are. You're dripping wet.

ENGSTRAND. Regine, I came to tell... REGINE *opens the door.*

REGINE *whispering.* Hush! He is asleep upstairs.

The first, pre-credit, shot – a risky prolepsis since it can be grasped only in retrospect – shows the Alving family before Osvald was sent away from home. When the family on the photo is annihilated by a hand putting fire to it, it is an act figuratively indicating how the photo's semblance of family unity (the pretty façade) will be destroyed – unmasked – in the course of the play. The burning of the photo, by an anonymous hand (Fate?), anticipates both the burning of the asylum, symbol of the façade mentality, and the 'burning' inside Osvald.

The non-diegetic sound of Chopin's *Raindrop Prelude* provides a mood conforming to the weather outside; note the raindrops falling into the bucket (shot 9). Professionally played, this non-diegetic version of the prelude is contrasted in shot 18 with Regine's clumsy playing of the same piece. Like so many nineteenth-century girls, Garpe's Regine is in vain trying to elevate herself socially by playing the piano (a directorial addition) – presumably in imitation of Mrs Alving and in a modest attempt to match Osvald's artistry.

After an exterior shot of the estate, Garpe cuts to its owner. Shown in her underwear, unmasked, before the mirror, Mrs Alving is not so much scrutinising the wrinkles in her face, the sign of ageing, as her own self, thinking: Who am I? Her face next to its mirrored counterpart suggests a split ego. The middle-aged woman in shot 6 and the young woman in shot 7 – two crucial phases in life – are linked by their concern with their hair. But while the former seems to wipe cobwebs from her mind, the latter makes herself attractive. Clearly, one is concerned with the past, the other with the future. In the fashion of Edvard Munch, Garpe suggests what the two women have in common and what separates them.

Another striking difference is that Garpe pays much attention, as a film-maker would, to the environment surrounding the characters. We see the mansion first, from Engstrand's point of view, in pouring rain, as he is approaching it from the back. This is the side of the servants' entrance and the side where you can slink in unheeded. Once inside the house, we discover that its painted rococo ceiling, pointing to a more joyous period, is leaking and that one of its cherubs is 'crying.' The house and its inhabitants are clearly in a deplorable state.

The camera takes us up above, where Osvald is asleep, or pretending to sleep, and where we see Mrs Alving caring for him. Garpe then cuts back to the exterior, where Engstrand, a bit closer to the house, is now attacked by a white dog – as though the animal wanted to guard the house from the dark figure approaching it. Not until Engstrand enters the house do we 'enter' Ibsen's play.

Although Garpe's opening is the longest of the three, her dialogue is the briefest – a logical consequence of her filmic approach.

If the opening of *Ghosts* demonstrates a false father-daughter relationship, the ending dramatises a problematic mother-son relationship.[12] At Osvald's request his mother has promised to give him the mortal dose of morphine if it proves necessary, that is, when he turns mentally feeble. The play concludes as follows:

> *Sunrise. The glacier and the mountain peaks in the BG gleam in the morning light.*

OSVALD *sits motionless in the armchair, with his back to the BG; suddenly he says.* Mother, give me the sun.

MRS ALVING *by the table, looks at him startled.* What do you say?

OSVALD *repeats dully and tonelessly.* The sun. The sun.

MRS ALVING *across to him.* Osvald, what's the matter with you?

OSVALD *seems to shrink in his chair; all his muscles go slack; his face is expressionless; his eyes stare vacantly.*

MRS ALVING *trembling with fear.* What's this! *Screams loudly.* Osvald! What's the matter! *Throws herself on her knees down beside him and shakes him.* Osvald! Osvald! Look at me! Don't you know me?

OSVALD *tonelessly as before.* The sun. – The sun.

MRS ALVING *jumps to her feet in despair, tears at her hair with both hands and screams.* I can't bear this! *Whispers as though numbed.* I can't bear it! Never! *Suddenly.* Where does he keep them? *Fumbles quickly across his breast.* Here! *Shrinks back a few steps and screams.* No; no; no! – Yes! – no; no! *She stands a few steps away from him with her hands twisted in her hair and stares at him in speechless horror.*

OSVALD *sits motionless as before and says.* The sun. – The sun.

Osvald's motionlessness strikingly contrasts with Mrs Alving's mobility, just as his monotonous, obsessed repetition of those two words – the sun – markedly differs from her changing tone of voice. Beginning on a normal pitch it soon turns into a scream, then into a whisper, and again a scream. She then becomes as immobile as Osvald. Speechless, she twists her hands in her hair, a gesture indicating despair, bewilderment and identification with the brainstorm haunting her son.

Osvald's repeated reference to the sun informs her, and us, that the crucial moment has come. Like a babbling baby, he expresses his longing for something unreachable.

> But the words "Mother, give me [...]" also make us think of the promise Mrs Alving has made to give him the "helping hand." And we inevitably substitute the morphine for the sun.[13]

There is a stark irony in the fact that Osvald, who has spent a lifetime longing for the values visualised in the final sunrise – the warmth of love, the clarity of truth, the joy of living, the fresh air of freedom, the soaring white mountain tops of lofty idealism and purity – can no longer experience them. Sitting with his back to the windows of the conservatory, he can merely go on longing for them. For Mrs Alving the sunrise is ironic, too. Just before the sun rises, she tells her son:

> And, Osvald, do you see what a beautiful day we're going to have? Bright sunshine. Now you can really see your home.

But coming too late for Osvald, the bright sunshine instead forces Mrs Alving to see her home the way it "really" is. For her, the sunlight, far from signalling "a beautiful day," means a cruel illumination of all that has brought about the present catastrophe, not least her own part in it.

Will Mrs Alving kill Osvald?[14] Although Ibsen has her deny it five times and only affirm it once, this is no sure indication. When Ibsen wrote his play euthanasia was considered a crime – as it still is in most countries. No wonder he had to balance his one yes with five no's. Even today painless killing in a case like Osvald's will not be generally sanctioned. Many recipients will claim that genuine love prevents us from killing a child of our own. Others will claim that genuine love under certain circumstances forces us to kill – even a child of our own. Still others will, like Mrs Alving, vacillate between these standpoints. Ibsen's ending means that the answer to the question of how Mrs Alving should act is handed over to the audience. As a 'jury' we are invited to complete the play.

Some of Ibsen's acting directions, which may be suggestive for the reader, seem less functional as prescriptions for a performance. *"Screams loudly"* is certainly a tautology, and indications like *"with fear," "in despair,"* and *"in [...] horror"* indicate mental states that somehow must be expressed physically in performance.

Bleness stays rather close to Ibsen's ending:

1 *CU of* OSVALD, *the rising sun shining on his face.* Mother, give me the sun.

2 *LS of the blue-tinted garden room. Rosy light of rising sun streams through the window in BG.* MRS ALVING *in a black dress, stands in BG, looking at the window.* OSVALD, *in white shirt and black waistcoat, sits motionless in an armchair in FG, his back to the window, his expressionless face turned upward.*

OSVALD. Mother, give me the sun.

MRS ALVING *turns around.* What did you say?

OSVALD *dully.* The sun. The sun.

MRS ALVING *up to him.* Osvald, what's the matter with you? *Slow zoom-in to MCU. She looks at his face, whispers.* Osvald! What's the matter with you? *Touches his chin.* Look at me! Don't you know me?

OSVALD *dully.* The sun. The sun.

Mrs Alving *looks worried R for a moment, breathing hard.* I can't bear this! I can't bear it! *Screams.* Never! *Puts her face to his, whispers.* I can't bear this! *Fumbles across his breast.* Where does he keep them? *Puts her hands to her breast.* No! No! Yes! *Whispers.* No.

Osvald *motionless, dully.* The sun. The sun. *Fade-out.*

Even more emphatically than in a stage performance, Bleness informs us, via a close-up, of Osvald's imbecility before Mrs Alving grasps it. Since Bleness, like the other directors, chooses to show the final moments in medium close-up two-shot, he tones down Mrs Alving's screaming and replaces Ibsen's proxemics with gestures. As a result, his Mrs Alving becomes less mobile than Ibsen's. Instead of shrinking back *"a few steps"* – indicating that she shrinks back from what she has earlier promised Osvald – Bleness' Mrs Alving merely withdraws her hands from him and puts them to her own breast. Meant, perhaps, to provide a link between his head and her maternal breast, the arrangement is too indistinct to be suggestive. Like the other directors, Bleness avoids having Mrs Alving twist her hair, presumably finding this gesture too melodramatic for the small screen.

Although Bleness' Osvald, like Ibsen's, cannot see the sun, since he is turned away from it, the sun is nevertheless reflected in his face. Hereby the director heightens the irony. While he cannot reach the sun, the sun can reach him. To some viewers, there may be a sign of grace and resurrection in this arrangement. But most of them will probably see these values blasphemed in it.

Garpe's version of the end is more removed from the text:

1 *MCU of* Osvald *who, wrapped in a black blanket, sits motionless in an armchair, his back to the window in BG. His face, looking down, is expressionless.* Mother, give me the sun.

2 *LS of the garden room, bathing in monochrome, misty grey dawn.*

Mrs Alving, *in black dress, stands by the white-curtained window in BG, looking out.* What do you say?

Osvald *dully.* The sun. The sun.

Mrs Alving *turns around.* Osvald, what's the matter with you? What is it? *Up to him. Slow zoom-in to MCU.* What's the matter with you? *Goes down on her knees beside him and shakes him.* Look at me! Look at me! Don't you know me? Osvald!

Osvald *dully.* The sun. *Soft roar begins and grows.*

Mrs Alving. Osvald! *Her head against his breast, her words drowning in her weeping.* Where does he keep them? *Fumbles quickly inside the blanket across his white shirt. Anguished.* No! Yes! No! *Both are covered by roaring flames in FG. Fade-out.*

Although Garpe retains Mrs Alving's idea that the day that is dawning will be a beautiful one with "bright sunshine," this idea is denied visually. Instead of a sunrise, Garpe shows us a dismally grey interior. Mrs Alving's remark seems but a frail hope, an illusion without foundation in reality. Rather than receiving clarity, this Mrs Alving remains groping for a meaning in the mist of life.[15] Moreover, she ironically 'contradicts' herself by wrapping her son in a black blanket, like the white-curtained window signalling death.[16] The devouring flames tie in with this symbolism. At the same time they point back to Garpe's opening, completing in reality, as it were, the annihilation that then took place *in effigie*. The light and warmth that face Osvald in the end are not those of the sun, of life, but of its opposite.

Moshinsky's version of the end, more medium-oriented than Bleness' and Garpe's, deviates considerably from Ibsen's:

1 *MS of* Mrs Alving, *dressed in black, sitting on a black leather sofa R. The light of the rising sun, from offscreen window R, is reflected in her face.* Oswald, *he too dressed in black, is lying crouched up L with his head in her bosom, looking down. She strokes his head with one hand and holds his shoulder with the other. Behind them a purplish-blue wall, above them the black lower frame of a large mirror.*

Oswald *whispers dully.* Mother – give me the sun.

2 *CU of* Mrs Alving *looking down at him.* What did you say? *Lowers her head.*

Oswald *dully.* The sun.

3 *MS of* Oswald. The sun. *Slow zoom-in to MCU.* Oswald's *face is expressionless, his eyes closed, his mouth agape.*

Mrs Alving. Oswald, how are you feeling? What's this, Oswald? What's this? *She takes his head with both hands, raises it up, so that both heads are seen in profile, the sunlight now shining on his face. Loudly.* Look at me, Oswald! Don't you know me?

Oswald *dully.* The sun. The sun.

Mrs Alving *pressing her mouth against his forehead.* I can't bear this! I can't bear it! No! Where did you put them? *Fumbles for the morphine pills.* Oh, here! *Presses him to her breast. Screams.* Oh, nooo! No! No! *Moves to frontal position. Zoom-in to CU as Schönberg's* Verklärte Nacht *is intoned. Whispers.* Yes! *Plaintively.* No! No! *Moves her L ringed hand from his head and covers her own face with it. Slow zoom-in on her face.*

Oswald *mumbles almost inaudibly.* The sun. The sun. *His head falls down, out of screen.*

Dissolve of Mrs Alving's *face into the wall.*

By placing the characters close to the window, Moshinsky avoids 'staged' movements and groups them together even before Oswald gets his fatal attack. The highly symbolic fetal/oedipal and *pietà* grouping visualises Oswald's life span from birth to death. Death is prominent in the blackness of the sofa, the black frame threateningly hanging above the couple, in their black dresses and in the bluish-purple wall.

The sun momentarily is reflected on Oswald's face. Since it is placed behind Mrs Alving, her admonishing him to look at her also means: Look at the sun. But his eyes remain closed.

In his ending, Moshinsky focuses strongly on Mrs Alving, the protagonist. It is her reaction to Oswald's fate that is important. Moreover, his face being expressionless is much less interesting than hers. This focusing is especially obvious at the very end when his head falls out of the screen and she covers her face with the hand displaying her wedding ring – in recognition of the fact that what we have witnessed are the consequences of, to quote the subtitle, "a family drama." Moshinsky's final move is extremely suggestive. Mrs Alving's face disappears, as it were, into the wall of the house in which she has been 'imprisoned' for a lifetime. Symbolising sorrow and penitence,[17] the wall becomes the visual counterpart of the transfiguration heard once more in Schönberg's music. We are close to the miracle of St. Veronica's veil. Clearly, Moshinsky has provided his conclusion with a Christian framework that gives it dignity and universality. It is not only a son but, obliquely, the Son of Man that is sacrificed.

Interestingly, Mrs Alving's last speech differs in the four versions. Indicating no paralinguistic variation, Ibsen has her scream her five no's and one yes. Bleness reduces the number of no's to three, the last of which is whispered. Garpe rests content with two no's. Moshinsky on the other hand retains Ibsen's number and has Mrs Alving whisper her yes. There is, it seems, an indication here that the British Mrs Alving is less likely to perform the promised euthanasia than her Scandinavian counterparts.

5 *The Wild Duck* (1884)

"This new play," Ibsen told his publisher while writing *The Wild Duck*, "occupies in some ways, a unique position among my dramatic works. Its method differs in certain respects from that which I have previously employed."[1] He did not clarify in which way the play represented a new development, but it has generally been assumed that he referred to the more elusive way in which he now treated the play's complex, central symbol, the wild duck, as well as his insertion of comic elements in what is basically a tragedy.

The play is about a man who, instigated by his old friend, discovers that his wife was pregnant by another man when he married her fifteen years ago. Influenced by the friend's orthodox morals, he rejects his wife and her child. The friend tells the child that she may regain the love of 'her' father if she kills the wild duck whom she loves and whom he dislikes. Unable to do so, the child kills herself. The death of the child reunites husband and wife.

With its five acts and more than twenty roles, *The Wild Duck* is one of Ibsen's most comprehensive plays. This presents a problem in a medium where short plays with few characters are favoured, simply because the audience has neither the patience to sit through a play lasting the better part of an evening nor the energy to keep a great many characters apart. Not surprisingly, the three productions we shall examine have all been shortened.

Henri Safran's heavily adapted Australian TV film, from 1983, is not much longer than an hour and a half. Since the play is relocated to Australia in the early part of the twentieth century, the names of the characters have been modified to fit the English-speaking environment. We move between interior and exterior scenes. Shorn of Ibsen's subtle nuances, the dialogue is trivial and deprived of the humourous touches found in the text. Except for the added epilogue, the whole film is brown-tinted – as though we are watching photos in an old album. Borrowing the plot from Ibsen's play, it has little to do with its theme.

Safran's unusually lengthy initial sequence, visualising part of the background story,[2] opens with a picture of flying wild ducks. As one of them is shot, the image is frozen. Then follows the title. We see the face of the marksman, Haakon Werle, here called George Wardle. Then a shot of a swimming dog. The dog dives, picks up the duck under water and swims back with it in its mouth. The duck is not dead, only wounded. Wardle asks his servant Peters, Ibsen's Pettersen, to wring its neck but Peters wants to spare the life of the duck, saying that he knows someone who might like to get it. We then see Old Ackland (Ekdal) go hunting in his attic. Peters arrives with his gift for Henrietta (Hedvig), who emphatically states that it is now *her* wild duck.

The director has here visualised information that is related in the play; added some scenes to establish time, place and (idyllic) mood; and arranged his material thematically. Wardle's real outdoor hunting, for example, is contrasted with the imaginary indoor one of his former companion Ackland. What Ibsen serves us piecemeal via his characters – can we trust their versions? – is turned into a coherent, reliable story. As a result, there are fewer questions for the spectators to ponder. Their activity is decreased.

Unlike the other productions discussed in this book, Bo Widerberg's Swedish 1989 version is not a television one-off but a television serial of sorts.[3] Like serials, it has the same characters and storyline in the different parts, but whereas these are usually transmitted once a week, Widerberg's *Wild Duck* was broadcast on three consecutive evenings. Consequently, the time from first to last transmission did not greatly exceed the time of action in the play. As a result, the viewers could easily remember what had happened in the former part. Moreover, they could to some extent remain within the world of the play during the 'intervals.'

Of comparable duration to a stage version, Widerberg's three-part production does not follow Ibsen's dialogue to the letter. On the contrary, the director has not only shortened it in some places, he has also added brief passages of his own making. By modifying the language and by inserting bits of small talk, the director brings the play closer to modern everyday reality.[4] His 'serial' is a pronounced example of intimate realism, the primary characteristic of television drama.

Widerberg's *Wild Duck* is firmly structured. Part One ends with Hjalmar, Gina and Hedvig, close to each other on the sofa, humming "O Tannenbaum" – an idyllic picture of communion, as though taken from a family album. The director significantly freezes this frame. When Gregers enters in Part Two, the harmony is disturbed. This part ends with the arrival of Werle's letter of donation to Hedvig. In Part Three, finally, the consequences of this letter unfold. Serious complications arise and are tragically resolved.

Gregers, Ibsen himself recognised, is the most difficult character to recreate in performance.[5] Is he another innocent 'child,' believing in absolute ethics and not to blame for the calamitous consequences of his idealism? Or is he the one character in the play who is especially lacking in self-knowledge, unconscious of the oedipal basis for his need to meddle with other people's lives? A case can certainly be made for the idea that while the Ekdals somehow are aware of their life-lie, Gregers is not.

The production history of the play shows that directors tend to side either with Gregers or Hjalmar, usually with the latter, in support of Relling's proverbial statement about the universal need for illusion.[6] In all the productions considered here, Hjalmar gains more sympathy than Gregers.[7]

Ibsen is sparse with regard to the appearance of the characters. Implicitly, we can deduce that Hjalmar is somewhat fat and that he has curly hair. At Werle's dinner party he appears in the tails he has borrowed from Molvik. When he enters his home in Act II, he wears *"an overcoat and a grey felt hat."* He soon changes the tails for a more comfortable *"jacket."*

About Gregers' appearance we learn even less. The following lines look like an implicit acting direction:

GINA. Is he [Gregers] still as ugly as ever?

HJALMAR. Well, he's not very much to look at.[8]

However, rather than "ugly," Gina here means "awful,"[9] in a moral sense. Hjalmar misunderstands her. But even *his* statement, egocentric and vain as he is, cannot be regarded as objective evidence.[10] Gregers wears *"a simple grey suit of a rustic cut."*

In Arild Brinchmann's Norwegian 1973 version, Gregers is a suspicious, cold, ironic fanatic with constantly – tiresomely – staring eyes. His Hjalmar is a big spoilt child, charming despite his enormous egocentricity and false pathos.

Widerberg's Gregers is strikingly pale, his face that of a man drained of life. His oedipal hang-ups are clearly demonstrated in his explosive hostility towards his father. Widerberg's Hjalmar, on the other hand, is full of life, an egoistic but charmingly impulsive child. The rhetorical-pathetic lines Ibsen provides him with seem an expression of his theatrical nature rather than contraband from others. An embarrassed outsider at Werle's dinner party, he is the central figure at home, an actor entertaining his family with a far from truthful, self-flattering version of what he has experienced at Werle's dinner party. Since his love for Hedvig seems genuine, it is easy to accept her attachment to him.

In Widerberg's version, Gregers' meddling with the Ekdal household seems to stem from an unconscious need to destroy a communion he himself has never experienced. Or, to put it differently, it is a "dead" man's vampiric need to draw life from others in order to feel that he, too, is alive.

Act I is set in the opulent *"home of* HAAKON WERLE, *a wholesale merchant,"* where a dinner party is taking place. As often with Ibsen, the stage is divided into two rooms: downstage the study, upstage the living room. There is a striking contrast in the lighting. While there is soft green light in the study, the living room is *"brightly lit."* The soft light in what is apparently Werle's private room is motivated by his impending blindness; the light is soothing for his eyes.

But why green? The colour is the colour of forest and sea, which in the following we connect with the Ekdal loft. The forest of Höidal – the past shared by Old Ekdal and Werle – looms large both in the loft and in the study. In a wider sense, the contrast between brilliant white and soft, green light stands for the contrast between civilisation and wilderness, the wilderness that has been reduced in the Ekdal loft and repressed in the Werle study. Most clearly, this development is demonstrated in the central symbol of the play, the duck, which, once wild, has been tamed.

Bright and green light can also be linked with the opposition between truth and illusion. No-one, Relling claims, can live without illusions. As a doctor he knows that we all need the soft, green light. Gregers claims the opposite, that we all need the bright light, the moments of truth. Who is right? Both and neither of them. For is human life not a constant vacillation between the one and the other?

The green light in Werle's study, that could obviously not be retained in Brinchmann's black-and-white production, is absent also in Widerberg's colour production, where there is only a soft light in the study. (In Safran's version, the Werle interior is omitted altogether.)

In Act I, the central dialogues between Hjalmar-Gregers and Gregers-Werle take place in the soft, green light, in

> a kind of half-darkness which blurs the truth. We are viewing the truth through [...] two men who do not see clearly, as we do not see them clearly in the green light.[11]

The green light, in other words, helps to involve us in the action. The difficulty of seeing, a key motif in the play, is extended to the audience.

In the stage directions for Act I we read: *"In the study, downstage right, a small wall-papered door leads to the offices."* This is a door – a *"tapetdør"* in the original – covered with the same wallpaper as the wall that surrounds it and so, in fact, invisible. Ibsen's wall-papered door is no bizarre phenomenon. Such doors were quite common in Scandinavian homes in the last century.[12] But of course the playwright had special reasons for including it in his setting. The door, Madsen observes,

> separates the representative part of the habitation from the business part. The door at once demonstrates this boundary and the desire to liquidate it, the desire to let the private habitation of family and social life appear as the whole thing.[13]

The door receives significance when Old Ekdal, inopportunely appearing in the sitting room, enters the study:

EKDAL. [...] Be a good chap, Pettersen, and let me nip in *this* way. *Points to the wall-papered door.* I've been this way before.

PETTERSEN. Oh, all right then. *Opens the door.* But make sure you leave the proper way; we've got guests.

The translators have problems with the wall-papered door. Ellis-Fermor and Fjelde call it a *"private door."*[14] MacFarlane, closer to the source text, calls it *"a baize-covered door."* Meyer omits the whole sentence referring to the door but later mentions it as *"the concealed door."*

Ekdal's first appearance leads to expository gossip between the two servants who are *"putting the study in order."*[15] We are informed about the dubious relationship between Werle and Ekdal. Ekdal has declined socially and is now on and off receiving work from his former business partner. At this moment he wants to get to the offices to fetch a load of correction work. The "proper way" for Ekdal is the back door. But, just as he has come the wrong way, he leaves the wrong way:

GRAABERG, *the book-keeper, looks in through the wall-papered door.*

GRAABERG. Pardon, sir, but I can't get out.

WERLE. What, have you got locked in again?

GRAABERG. Yes, and Flakstad's gone off with the keys.

WERLE. Oh well, just come through here, then.

GRAABERG. But there's one more -

WERLE. Well, come along both of you; just come along.

GRAABERG *and* OLD EKDAL *come out of the office.*

WERLE *involuntarily.* Ugh!

By this time Pettersen has already informed us that when they were running the works at Höidal together, Ekdal "played Werle a low-down trick," for which he was punished with "hard labour" or "imprisonment" – we are given contradictory information. The situation around the wall-papered door clearly serves to recall this past. At this point in the play, we are asked to believe that Ekdal committed a crime for which he was punished. Later we sense that it is either Werle who is the criminal or it is a question of shared guilt. Yet while Werle was acquitted, Ekdal was imprisoned. Now Ekdal is "locked in again" – Werle's phrasing is significant – and eventually let out. Werle's sudden confrontation with Ekdal in his, Werle's, present upper-class surroundings is an unpleasant confrontation with his own past and with his bad conscience for having let Ekdal act as a scapegoat for himself. Ekdal's sudden and unexpected appearance out of the wall, so to speak, releases Werle's involuntary interjection: "Ugh!" – rather than Meyer's "Oh God!" When Werle later appears at the Ekdal front door, Gina uses exactly the same interjection: "Ugh!" Werle and Ekdal are hereby linked. Meyer ignores the connection by having Gina exclaim "Oh! Oh, no!"

In his *"wall-papered door"* sequence, Widerberg has not only Hjalmar but also Werle, in a shot showing both of them, turn away from Ekdal as soon as he appears. In an added line Werle mutters: "That damned Graaberg." When the question "Did you know that man?" is posed very loudly to Hjalmar, Widerberg's Werle quickly moves away from him to join his distinguished guests. Hjalmar answers the question evasively: "I don't know – I didn't notice – ." The allusion to Peter's denial of Christ is retained. But Widerberg's arrangement, in addition, suggests that just as Old Ekdal has served as Werle's scapegoat in the past, so young Ekdal now fulfills the same function. Once more Werle 'escapes.'

The most dramatic moment in the play occurs when Hedvig, brutally rejected by Hjalmar, in the final act

> *stands motionless for a moment, anguished and bewildered, biting her lips to keep from crying. Then she clenches her hands convulsively and says quietly.* The wild duck!
> *She steals over and takes the pistol from the shelf, sets the loft door ajar, slips in and pulls the door shut behind her.*

Hjalmar has earlier told her that he would like to kill the wild duck. Once he learns that Hedvig is not his child, he rejects her. Gregers then suggests that if she shoots the bird, she will regain Hjalmar's love. Ibsen at this point allows Hedvig a one-word soliloquy, the only one in the play, to make it clear to the recipient that Hedvig, pistol in hand, now intends to kill the wild duck.

Hjalmar's doubt about Hedvig's love for him culminates in his conversation with Gregers:

> HJALMAR. If I were to ask her: "Hedvig, are you willing to give up life for me?" *Laughs scornfully.* Oh, yes, – you'd hear what answer I'd get!
>
> *A pistol shot is heard from the loft.*

Unlike Gregers, who believes that Hedvig has made Ekdal shoot the wild duck, the recipient is at this moment supposed to believe that she has shot the duck herself. In retrospect, when we know that she has shot herself, we realise that Hedvig must have overheard Hjalmar's speech and that her suicide signifies a rejection of his scepticism. Her self-sacrifice, in the image of Christ, is meant as a proof of her love for Hjalmar.

In a stage version, Hedvig would normally remain invisible to the audience from the moment she has picked up the pistol and disappeared into the loft.[16]

Brinchmann shows Hedvig's troubled face in close-up just before she picks up the pistol, indicating that this is the moment when she decides to kill the wild duck. The camera pans with her as she moves into the loft. Arrived there, we see the upper part of her face, the glistening eyes, in frontal close-up. Omitting her soliloquy, Brinchmann tones down Ibsen's plot-oriented striving to mislead the recipient. The director is deliberately vague about whether she will kill the duck or herself.[17]

In Safran's suicide sequence we see how Hedvig, dressed in white and holding the wild duck to her breast, puts the pistol to its breast. As the director cuts to a close-up of Gina, we hear the shot. When Gregory exclaims "There's your proof!" – thinking that Ekdal has shot the wild duck – we know better. The frame arrangement of Henrietta just referred to indicates that she has not only killed the duck but also herself. In the next long shot we see, in slow motion, how the girl – just like the duck of the opening – falls down. At the same time a white dove – representing, no doubt, her pure soul – flies up.

Widerberg's suicide sequence is very different. The director softens Hjalmar's question, and obscures the Christian parallel, by changing "sacrifice your life for me" into "abstain from everything for me." As Hjalmar runs into the loft, we see Hedvig lying lifeless on the floor, while the duck, hale and sound, is splashing in its basin next to her. When Relling examines her, a close-up reveals a spot of blood by her heart. With such objective proof (difficult to furnish in a stage version), confirming Relling's diagnosis – "The bullet entered her heart. Internal haemorrhage." – Widerberg puts to shame Hjalmar's and Gregers' hope that Hedvig may have died accidentally.

As Gina and Hjalmar carry the dead girl to her room, Gina makes the significance of what they are doing explicit: "*Now* she's as much yours as mine." Ibsen does not indicate how they carry her. But in a letter he states: "When she is carried out through the kitchen door, I had imagined that Hjalmar would be holding her under the arms and Gina by her feet."[18] Brinchmann adjusts to the grouping suggested in Ibsen's letter, in which Gina, the biological parent and the one who has truly loved Hedvig, remains in her subservient role. Widerberg, who stresses the close relationship between Gina and Hedvig throughout his production, reverses Ibsen's idea of how the dead Hedvig should be carried out.

Hedvig does what none of the others dare to do. Her suicide glaringly contrasts with Old Ekdal's and Hjalmar's pseudo-suicides in the past.

HJALMAR. [...] That pistol over there, Gregers – the one we use for shooting rabbits – has played its part in the tragedy of the Ekdal family. [...] When the verdict had been pronounced and he [Old Ekdal] was about to be imprisoned – he had the pistol in his hand – [...] but he didn't dare. He was a coward. [...] Can you understand that, Gregers?

GREGERS. Yes, I quite understand.

Once Old Ekdal had gone to prison, Hjalmar pompously continues, "Hjalmar Ekdal held the pistol pointed to his own breast." But "at the decisive moment," he says, "I won a victory over myself. I remained alive." Hedvig, too, points the pistol to her own breast – but has the courage to shoot.

While it seems obvious that Hedvig's suicide will not lead to one on Hjalmar's part, Gregers is a different case. In the passage just quoted he seems to indicate that he, too, has attempted, or at least contemplated, suicide. In view of this; of the fact that his mission in the Ekdal home has failed completely; and of his final statement that his destiny is to be, "the thirteenth at table" (his earlier demonstrated self-hatred suggests that he alludes to Judas rather than Jesus) – all these matters point in the direction of suicide. Yet, since in the play's final line Relling rejects this idea, we are left with an open ending as far as Gregers is concerned.

Apart from Gregers' prospects at the end, a director has to consider those of Old Ekdal. Dressed *"in full uniform"* and carrying a *"sword"* in celebration of Hedvig's birthday, he combines Hedvig's death with what has happened to himself. In either case – this is his pipe dream – Fate has a hand in it:

EKDAL. The forest takes revenge. But I'm not scared all the same.

He goes into the loft and closes the door behind him.

This is the last we see of him. Høst sees the uniform and the sword as indications that Ekdal now musters the courage to resist the Fate he has earlier succumbed to.[19] Watts, on the other hand, argues that

[i]f Ibsen had not envisaged his off-stage suicide, the direction that Ekdal bears a sabre with him would be redundant; Ekdal's last words would remain a mere enigma; his conspicuous absence when all the other people of the household are on stage would be hardly explicable [...].[20]

But can we really believe that the man who earlier did not dare to shoot himself is now prepared to commit hara-kiri or hang himself? (The pistol is now with the dead Hedvig.) Is he perhaps going to kill the wild duck with his sabre? Or is he just imagining these things? Since Ibsen does not tell us, director and actor are free to imagine different alternatives – and eventually settle for one of them.

Widerberg reverses Ibsen's situation. Ekdal, in black uniform, remains in the studio. Sitting absolutely still, with his head hanging down, he looks dead. This is certainly not the man who is challenging Fate. Relling leaves through the door, while Gregers, fetus-like, remains sitting in the cramped space of the closet – as though in a coffin. The last we see is the door closing behind Relling, leaving two 'corpses,' separated from each other, in the studio.

None of the directors considered here indicate that Gregers' final exit is tantamount to an exit from life.[21] Brinchmann's Gregers leaves through the apartment door, followed by Relling's sceptical final remark.

Unlike the other directors, Safran provides an epilogue to Ibsen's ending. Hedvig's funeral is just over. Gregory (Gregers) and Doctor Roland (Relling) argue about whether the girl shot herself by accident or not. There is a cut to Harold (Hjalmar) alone by a tree, pensive, sad. Gina comes and sits down next to him. The romantic musical leitmotif that has permeated, and sentimentalised, the production is heard once more. This is clearly a palliative ending in the Hollywood tradition, adjusted to the taste of a mass audience. It could hardly be more averse to the 'message' of Ibsen's ending. For in Safran's version, Gregory proves to be right. Henrietta has not died in vain. Harold takes what has happened to his heart, and so the reconciliation between him and Gina holds a promise of a 'true' marriage.

6   *Hedda Gabler* (1890)

In his four-act drama *Hedda Gabler*, Ibsen is more detailed in his stage and acting directions than in any of his other plays, whether out of concern for the reader or out of distrust of the theatre makers. This presents specific problems for those directing the play for the small screen. When Ibsen, for example, prescribes *"steel-grey"* eyes for Hedda and *"light blue, large, and somewhat prominent"* eyes for Mrs Elvsted, he is obviously providing information about the contrasting natures of the two women *for the reader*. While Ibsen's prescription could hardly be communicated to a theatre audience, it could easily be communicated to a screen audience. However, eye colour would not be an important criterion when selecting actresses for the two roles. And even if the screened Hedda *has* grey eyes, few viewers are likely to link the colour with coldness, much less with steel, that is, with Hedda's pistols.

The action of *Hedda Gabler* takes place around 1890 in, as Ellis-Fermor translates, *"the Tesmans' villa on the west side of the town."*[1] This literal rendering of the source text ignores the fact that few readers would know that Ibsen is here referring to the well-to-do part of Christiania, now Oslo. Meyer is more informative when he translates the passage freely with *"the fashionable quarter of town"*[2] – although 'city' would be a better rendering for the country's capital. Yet the Norwegian setting is hardly important. *Hedda Gabler* is arguably the least place-bound of all Ibsen's plays. All the productions we are concerned with are set in the same time, and none of them contradict Ibsen's choice of place.[3]

Just returned from their wedding-cum-study trip, Tesman and Hedda have taken possession of their new home, formerly belonging to the widow of a Cabinet Minister and furnished especially to please Hedda, we may assume, by Miss Tesman and/or Brack. Ibsen's description of the unified setting reads:

> *A large drawing room, handsomely and tastefully furnished; decorated in dark colours. In the rear wall is a broad open doorway, with curtains drawn back to either side. It leads to a smaller room, decorated in the same style as the drawing room. In the R wall of the drawing room a folding door leads out to the hall. In the opposite wall, on the L, a glass door, also with curtains drawn back. Through the panes we can see part of the veranda, and trees in autumn colours. [...] Against the rear door of the inner room can be seen a sofa, a table and a couple of chairs. Above this sofa hangs the portrait of a handsome elderly man in a general's uniform.*

What we see of the Tesman villa are three parts: the veranda left, the centrally located drawing room and a smaller room behind it. Since the smaller room is apparently windowless, the distribution of light is uneven. The symbolic significance of this soon becomes clear. The drawing room, being the social area, is the room belonging to both Tesman and Hedda as well as the room where they receive their guests: Thea Elvsted, Brack, Ejlert Løvborg. The smaller room is Hedda's private sanctum, as the portrait of her father indicates. Both the exterior world and Hedda's private world, related to her past, are shut off when the curtains are drawn. In this way Ibsen can indicate Hedda's gradual withdrawal from the present into the past, a withdrawal that can be related both to her psychology – her oedipal attachment to her father – and to her ideology. The play is about Hedda's desire to escape the bourgeois Tesman world, represented by the drawing room, her fear to step outside into the exterior world and her withdrawal into her own world of the past, the paternal portrait marking the end of this withdrawal.

If, with Høst, we see the larger outer room as corresponding to the nave of a church and the inner room to the sanctuary,[4] then Hedda's suicide below the portrait of the general, placed where the crucifix is found in a church, may be called the death of a martyr, sacrificing herself less as a woman repressed by male society than as a human being in protest against the pseudo-Christian values of bourgeois society.

While this kind of architectural symbolism can be suggested in a stage performance, where we have the two rooms in full view, it is very difficult to suggest it in a TV version, which would usually show the rooms separately and display only a part of each room.

Unlike Ibsen's drawing room, Waris Hussein's, in his British 1972 production, is neither dark nor polychrome, but kept in a monochrome blue. When Thea Elvsted enters we discover that, ironically, it is *her* blue costume rather than Hedda's golden one that matches the colour of the room. Hedda is even visually out of place here. Contrasting with the cool blue of the drawing room is the passionate red of Hedda's private room. In his Norwegian version three years later, Arild Brinchmann shows a dark green drawing room that contrasts with the red of the inner room. In Deborah Warner's British 1993 performance, the drawing room is grand, high-ceilinged, sparsely furnished – it includes a huge mirror, indicating Hedda's narcissism – and it is kept in a monochrome, grey colour. The wall-papered inner room has a contrasting warm, brown-yellow colour. Turning the drawing room into a stately, aristocratic space and the inner room into a bourgeois one, Warner puzzlingly reverses the traditional pattern. Margareta Garpe, finally, in her Swedish production of the same year, settles for a light, large, attractive, aristocratically furnished drawing room with wall frescoes depicting a pastoral landscape with classical temples, a visual substitute, it seems, of Hedda's Dionysian references to Løvborg's having "vineleaves in his hair," a phrase omitted by Garpe.[5] This drawing room, being more Hedda's than Tesman's, does not markedly differ from the inner room.

The portrait presents a problem today. Many directors would feel that it is too obviously symbolic. Hussein shows a portrait of an elderly man, dressed – like Løvborg! – in black, civilian clothes, a choice indicating that Hedda's interest in Løvborg is a manifestation of her Electra complex. In Brinchmann's production the portrait of the general seems rather unimportant. It is glimpsed only very briefly in the beginning, from the side. Warner and Garpe omit the portrait altogether.

When she first appears, Ibsen's Hedda is dressed *"in an elegant, somewhat loose-fitting morning dress"* – indicating her aristocratic taste and, as we are soon to discover, her pregnancy. In Act II we merely learn that she is *"dressed to receive callers."* When Act III opens she is *"lying asleep on the sofa, fully dressed"* – from which we may conclude that she is dressed in the same way as in Act II. In Act IV, finally, she is *"dressed in black,"* realistically as a sign of mourning – Tesman's Aunt Rina has just died; symbolically in anticipation of her own death. Mourning becomes Hedda.

Hussein's Hedda, in her golden morning gown, looks both aristocratic and pregnant. His Thea wears a contrasting dark green. Brinchmann's Hedda appears first in a mauve dress, then in a grey-brownish one recalling the colour of the autumnal leaves outside, finally in a black mourning dress. Extremely thin, she shows no signs of being pregnant.

Warner's Hedda appears first in a rather fancy all-white dress, as though she is still wearing her wedding dress. In Act III, already before Rina's death, she has exchanged it for a simple all-black dress. There is a marked symbolic pattern here, especially since Thea, who in Act I wears a grey dress, in Act II appears in an all-white dress very similar to the one Hedda wore in Act I. Unlike Ibsen's, the two ladies, both dark-haired, look strikingly alike and share the same nervous, hysterical temperament. As a result, Løvborg's interest in Thea seems here determined largely by her similarity to Hedda. Hedda's pregnancy is indicated not by a loose-fitting costume but by her touching her stomach so often that her gesture, indicating how concerned she is about what is inside, becomes over-explicit.

Garpe's Hedda demonstrates a more individual symbolic pattern. She first appears in a light blue, virginal, high-collared dress, then in a red, low-necked, passionate one, finally in a black, high-collared mourning dress. Her costumes clearly serve to indicate the repression of her true, passionate nature, which is glimpsed momentarily when Garpe has her violently embrace first Thea, then Løvborg.

Ibsen pays considerable attention to the shape and colour of the characters' hair. Only for the more marginal figures, Juliane Tesman and Berte, does he refrain from any comment. Since Miss Tesman is sixty-five, we may assume that she is grey-haired – as is the case in all the productions we are considering. Tesman has *"fair hair and beard,"* Hedda's hair is of *"a beautiful medium brown, but not especially abundant,"* Thea's *"remarkably light, almost flaxen, and exceptionally rich and wavy."* Brack's hair is *"cut short, still almost black and carefully barbed."* He has *"thick eyebrows and a thick moustache, its ends trimmed."* Løvborg's *"hair and beard are of a blackish-brown."* To this list we must add the offstage Diana, referred to as a "red-haired singer," a euphemism for a prostitute.

Commenting on the hair of the characters, Northam states:

> We [...] have on one side the light-haired, warm-hearted figures; in the centre, Hedda with her ambiguous hair, at once agreeable and sparse, and her conflicting emotions; and on the other side, Brack, the dark epitome of vigour.[6]

With his trimmed hair and moustache, Brack also reveals his concern with appearances, his façade mentality – not least with regard to sexuality. Diana's red hair signals unrestrained sexuality, Hedda's attractive but scant hair suppressed sexuality and Thea's light, profuse and wavy hair sexuality coupled with generosity, love.

But the hair of the characters also has a mythological significance, as indicated in the names Diana – "a mighty huntress," as Brack calls her, relating her to her Greek paragon Artemis – and Thea, meaning 'goddess.' Viewed in this light, Diana's red hair, more generally, relates to 'pagan' life affirmation, while Thea's hair, resembling an aureole, visualises a contrasting mentality: Christian altruism. Unlike these two, Hedda's libido, as her hair testifies, is sparse, repressed. More hair-covered than the others, yet outwardly prim and proper, Brack is, mythologically, the Devil in disguise.

Ibsen draws attention to Hedda's hair at an early point when, in Act I, he has Miss Tesman kiss it. Soon after this Hedda, talking to Tesman, refers to Thea Elvsted, her old schoolmate, as "the one with that irritating hair she was always showing off. Your old flame, I've heard." Interestingly, the double meaning both of Norwegian 'flamma' and English 'flame' provide a complex pattern of hair-sexuality-fire. This is further elaborated when Thea tells Hedda that when they were both at school, Hedda once told her that she would burn Thea's hair off, and when Hedda, *"throwing her arms passionately round"* Thea, says: "I think I shall burn your hair off, after all." Before that Hedda, *"stroking her [Thea's] hair lightly,"* counters Løvborg's question whether Thea is not lovely to look at with the risqué question "Only to look at?" When burning Løvborg's manuscript, Hedda indicates that she is, in a way, burning Thea's "curly hair" as well. After Løvborg's death, her jealousy toward Thea can subside, if not disappear. Seeing Thea and Tesman trying to piece together the scraps of Løvborg's manuscript and standing behind Thea's chair – a position of power compensating for her present powerlessness – she *"ruffles her [Thea's] hair gently."* And shortly before she dies, she lets *"her hands stray gently through Mrs Elvsted's hair,"* while ironically imitating Tesman's manner of speaking.

Obsessed with Thea's hair, Hedda is obsessed also with Løvborg's, or rather, with the Dionysian "vine leaves" she wants him to wear in his hair. Just as Thea's hair represents a 'divine' libido, so Hedda's repetitive phrase "vine leaves in the hair" stands for – Dionysian and Nietzschean – life affirmation. Tesman and Løvborg have both received their doctorates in the Faculty of Humanities, Tesman abroad, Løvborg at home. Becoming a doctor in this faculty in Scandinavia still means that you receive a laurel wreath – connected with Apollo, protector of the arts – in your hair at the Commencement ceremony. Hedda's wanting to see "vine leaves" in Løvborg's hair – the name means 'leaf-borg' – shows, in other words, a concern with the Dionysian principle at the expense of the Apollonian one. The "vine leaves in the hair" are also linked with the proud "feather," a medieval panache, Hedda herself used to wear in her hat when riding out with her father, the general.

What all this amounts to is, clearly, that Ibsen, constrained by the realist demands for verisimilitude, symbolically tries to broaden the scope of the play. *Hedda Gabler* is not only a play about individuals in interaction. It is also a play that, like so many other Ibsen dramas, ideologically indicates the Nietzschean clash between Dionysian life affirmation and Christian life denial,[7] between – to reverse the pattern and indicate Ibsen's dilemma – pagan will to power and Christian humility.

Given the fact that it would be nearly impossible to find six actors whose outward appearance would fit Ibsen's prescriptions; given, too, the fact that the use of wigs is a delicate matter in a medium making frequent use of close-ups, it is not surprising that the four directors, in various ways, deviate from Ibsen's hair prescriptions. None of them suggest, for example, the sparseness of Hedda's hair.

Yet Hussein and Brinchmann stick rather closely to Ibsen's ideas. Hussein's Hedda has her brown hair up; his Thea has similarly shaped fair hair; his Tesman has abundant fair and very curly hair; his Brack has black, sleekly combed hair and whiskers; and his Løvborg black, long hair as well as black moustache and beard.

Brinchmann's Hedda has her reddish brown, hair, vaguely linking her with Diana, up suggesting her repressed sexuality; his Thea has a coiffure which corresponds to Ibsen's description; his Tesman has fair hair with whiskers but no beard; his Brack is dark but has no beard; and his Løvborg has grey hair and a grey moustache.

Much more than Ibsen, the directors, in this respect conforming to a theatrical tradition, make use of the contrast between natural and fashioned hair, an imagery suggesting the fundamental contrast between nature and culture. Thus, both Hussein and Brinchmann indicate Hedda's passionate nature by showing her alone, in a pre-title sequence, with long, loose-hanging hair. When the actual play begins her hair is fashioned. This is an effective, if conventional, way of demonstrating the difference between natural face and social persona, between unrestrained and repressed libido.

In Warner's version all the characters are black-haired. As a result there is no visible grouping of them in this respect. Warner, in fact, reverses the situation in the text by showing a Hedda with quite abundant hair, bundled in a loose plait, contrasting with Thea whose hair is short.

Garpe, finally, retains Ibsen's differentiation but changes it to a great extent. Her Hedda has fair hair, fashioned like a 'crown'; her Thea has red, pinned-up hair; Tesman's round baby face is topped by short, conventionally fashioned, black hair; her virile Brack has grey hair and a grey moustache; her rather bald Løvborg has dark hair and a scanty beard and moustache, hardly indicating vigour.

At the end of the play, shortly before she kills herself, Hedda *"begins to play a wild dance tune on the piano"* of the inner room. Except for this, Hussein's and Brinchmann's productions lack music. Warner here and there makes use of disharmonic electronic music, specially composed for her production. Garpe provides a musical leitmotif throughout her performance. No less than ten times a fragment from the slow movement of Beethoven's piano sonata no. 23 op. 57, *Appassionata*, is inserted at key moments. Better than anything else, music can express the passion that Hedda keeps repressing. Seen in this way, it is significant that the sonata we have heard so many times non-diegetically, that is, outside the space of the narrative, at the end is used for Hedda's diegetic, visualised piano playing after Rina's death, now with a more organ-like, harpsichord quality. What has been dormant in Hedda all the time finally comes to the fore. Her violent playing of the sonata before she shoots herself ties in with the passionate outbursts she has earlier shown towards Thea and Løvborg. As we have noted, Ibsen at this point prescribes *"a wild dance tune,"* arguably the kind of "popular music that would be played at Diana's."[8] This kind of music, adhered to by Brinchmann, is impossible for Garpe's Hedda who remains her father's aristocratic daughter to the bitter end.

Ibsen opens the play with the entrance of Miss Tesman, Jørgen Tesman's aunt, and Berte, a maid formerly serving Miss Tesman and now serving

Tesman and his wife Hedda. From their conversation we learn about the newly wedded couple, their wedding trip and Tesman's hopes for an academic career.

Hussein opens his production quite differently with a shot of Hedda, in her dressing gown, staring out of the bedroom window, framed by the morning sunlight. Inside we divine a dark, vaguely outlined room. The camera pans with her as she moves into a red hallway. She looks one way but moves in the opposite direction. A little later we see her in her private room sitting beneath the portrait of her father. Another long shot shows her moving into the drawing room. Hussein then cuts to a close-up of Tesman, asleep in his bed. Hedda gets into her bed, takes a look at her husband, then turns her back at him. There is a close-up of Hedda, her head on the pillow, followed by a shot of a corner of the ceiling. Then the play proper begins with the arrival of Miss Tesman.

What is here brought into picture is Hedda's state of mind. Her position by the window, later repeated several times, is emblematic for her feeling of being imprisoned in a bourgeois way of life which she detests and of her longing to escape from it. Her basically passionate nature seems indicated in the red of the hallway. There is a subtle implication that she wants to move away from her father, yet cannot do so. Her aversion against Tesman, especially as a sexual partner, is clearly demonstrated, while the close-up of the ceiling is a very marked low angle point-of-view shot, indicative of the discrepancy between Hedda's 'horizontal' existence and 'vertical' desires.

Brinchmann opens his performance in a similar way.[9] It begins with Hedda in medium close-up, apparently inspecting her own inner room. She turns around and faces the camera. We notice her red, loose-hanging hair and the sad expression on her pale, sensitive face. The camera pans around the room, taking it in with Hedda's eyes. It is an establishing point-of-view shot. So far the room is kept in a monochrome red-brown colour matching Hedda's hair. As she moves from darkness into daylight the camera picks up the red, 'passionate' furniture of the room. In a long shot we see her standing before the portrait of her general father, still on the floor as a sign that the couple has just moved into the house. Since we are never to see the portrait again, we must assume that it remains there. Through a black hanging Hedda then peeps into the more spatious Tesman living room, kept in green and brown to separate it from Hedda's private room. When she hears the offscreen voices of Miss Tesman and Berte, she does not come forward to welcome them but withdraws. Brinchmann's opening, we can see, serves primarily to show Hedda alone, without a social persona, to clarify her true attitude to her surroundings.

Warner opens with a pre-title sequence showing Hedda feeling with her hand between her legs, an indication of her pregnancy.[10] In Garpe's production, even the title frame indicates what the director is aiming at. In big white letters we read the name of the play which is identical with the woman who dominates it. The letters are seen against a black-and-red background, the black below mingling with the red above – just as passion for life and longing for death lurk behind Hedda's purity.

The performance opens with a close-up of two black riding-boots standing on a black gravel ground. An upward tilt reveals a woman from behind, dressed in white, aiming with a pistol at something. Then a cut to a branch with two apples. The woman aims at one of them. It is shot through. A cut back to the woman from behind. The *Appassionata* is intoned. The woman looks down, then straightens up. Fade-out to a black screen. Then fade-in to a shot of the Tesman villa, a huge tree in front of it. The play proper opens with a close-up of the riding-boots, the property that in Garpe's version replaces the portrait of general Gabler. The indication is that Hedda has inherited the boots from him.

Garpe's opening, emphasising Hedda's central role in her production, anticipates the ending, where again the apple and the riding-boots figure prominently. Framing the play this way makes the intervening time shrink. It is as though this Hedda has almost made up her mind to kill herself when the play begins.

Without abstaining from close-ups, Garpe, like Warner, uses them sparsely. Both directors could argue that medium and long shots, apart from allowing for more interaction between the characters and their environment, here have a special relevance. They help to characterise Hedda. It is as though she is telling the camera, that is, the spectator: Don't come too close.

Just before his aunt is about to leave, Tesman asks her if she has not noticed how much Hedda has "filled out" since Miss Tesman last saw her, adding that it is hard to see it when she has her loose-fitting gown on. Miss Tesman immediately stops and turns around. Without realising it – he appears here unduly naive – Tesman has opened his aunt's eyes to the fact that Hedda, despite her own protests, *is* pregnant:

> MISS TESMAN *has folded her hands and is gazing at her.* Lovely – lovely – lovely is Hedda. *Goes over to her, bends her head down with both hands and kisses her hair.* God bless and keep Hedda Tesman. For Jørgen's sake.

A little later Tesman wonders why his aunt suddenly became so "solemn." Miss Tesman, who is extremely attached to her nephew, is a believing Christian. She frequently refers to God. Now we see her folding her hands.

It is hardly a coincidence that her threefold praising of Hedda comes very close to the Bible's "Holy, holy, holy is the Lord of hosts" (Isaiah 6.3), especially in the Norwegian original, and that her blessing of Hedda is in the nature of the Benediction.[11] She significantly kisses Hedda's hair, hair being an ancient symbol of vitality and potency.

In a stage performance this Christian symbolism is supported by the churchlike arrangement of the two rooms, an arrangement which is likely to be lost in a screen adaptation. In none of the four productions do we see Miss Tesman fold her hands. Nor do we see her kiss Hedda's hair. The directors apparently found this latter gesture too awkward. Brinchmann's Miss Tesman kisses her on the cheek, Garpe's more solemnly on the forehead.

In Brinchmann's version, which on the whole most clearly retains the Ibsenite solemnity, there is a rather long take of Miss Tesman's gazing – to emphasise her discovery that Hedda is pregnant. Warner makes the discovery very explicit. Instead of folding her hands, her Miss Tesman keeps patting Tesman's arm while weeping with joy. And instead of kissing Hedda's hair, she presumptuously touches her stomach informing the viewer – but not Tesman! – about Hedda's pregnancy. Hussein obscures the biblical overtones by using Meyer's more everyday rendering: "She's beautiful – beautiful. Hedda is beautiful."

At the end of Act III, Hedda hands Løvborg one of her two pistols and admonishes him to kill himself "beautifully" with it. She then burns his manuscript. The end of Act IV leads up to her suicide. There are strong links between these two sequences. The two pistols, lying next to each other in Hedda's case, are used for the two violent deaths in the play, one for Løvborg's, the other for Hedda's. And the burning of Løvborg's and Thea's "child" (Løvborg's manuscript) prepares for the killing of Tesman's and Hedda's child, the fetus inside Hedda.

When Hedda hands Løvborg the pistol she had once aimed at him, he says: "You should have used it then." She replies: "There it is. Use it yourself now." Hedda here persuades Løvborg to commit the suicide which she does not (yet) dare to commit herself.

In Garpe's version the sequence leading up to this opens with a long shot of Hedda, left, in her low-necked red dress, her blond hair characteristically up, pruned. Behind her is the pastoral wall landscape – the Arcadia of antiquity – reminding us of the paradise lost Hedda is desperately seeking to regain. She takes a pistol out of the case and approaches Løvborg with it.

Unlike the other directors Garpe, simply by having Hedda turn the pistol against herself, gives a meaning radically different from Ibsen's to this passage. Lacking the courage to take her own life, Garpe's Hedda asks Løvborg to kill her. He takes the pistol, looks at it, cocks it, puts it against her throat. She looks at him, closes her eyes and trembles. He lowers the pistol, turns away. She opens her eyes. He says, offscreen: "Farewell, Hedda Gabler." The door is heard closing. The *Appassionata* bars are intoned as disgust is reflected in Hedda's face. Her death wish has been thwarted. Irrespective of whether we see her act as one of heroism or of role-playing – the production certainly points in the former direction – it relieves her of the 'murder' of her former lover she is traditionally burdened with. Garpe's Hedda is nobler than Ibsen's.

Act III ends with the climactic burning of Løvborg's manuscript. Left alone in the drawing room,

> HEDDA *throws some sheets into the fire and whispers to herself.* Now I'm burning your child, Thea! – You, with your curly hair! *Throws a few more sheets into the stove.* Your child and Ejlert Løvborg's. *Throws in the rest.* Now I'm burning – I'm burning the child.

Several translators – Arup,[12] Meyer, Ellis-Fermor – replace the last definite article with a personal pronoun: "your," thereby missing the connection between Løvborg's and Thea's "child" (the manuscript) and Tesman's and Hedda's child (the fetus). Hedda's action is not only jealously destructive. The final definite article[13] indicates that it is also self-destructive, a kind of ritual abortion.

Hussein's Hedda, Janet Suzman, has related how she would vary her acting of this passage on the stage:

> Sometimes I would squat down, cradling and rocking the manuscript to me like a baby, gazing at the awful red coals. Sometimes I would just stand there, holding it lightly, not wanting to think of its important weight.[14]

In the TV version, produced much earlier, she laughs witchfully while burning the manuscript.

In Brinchmann's rendering there is a zoom-in to a close-up of Hedda in profile as she burns the manuscript. The director has chosen very much the angle at which a stage audience would see her. In traditional manner he begins the sequence with medium shots, then moves to medium close-ups and ends with close-ups, a climactic build that, of course, could never be recreated in a stage performance.

Warner's Hedda, like Suzman's stage Hedda, carries the parcelled manuscript like a baby in her arms, hums a lullaby, then throws it into the fire and rushes to the other end of the room as if she wished to escape from it all.

Garpe's more elaborate version deserves special attention. Having sent Løvborg off with one of her, formerly her father's, pistols, Hedda moves to the Gabler chest – another substitute for Ibsen's portrait of the general – containing her riding-boots and pistols, opens it and nearly vomits, disgusted as she is with life. For a moment she seems to contemplate suicide. Changing her mind, she puts the remaining pistol in one of the riding-boots – a sexually pregnant but enigmatic act – closes the chest and caressingly touches its name-plate. She then brusquely takes the manuscript out of the drawer, where she has hidden it, walks to the stove and burns it while sobbing: "Now I burn your child, Thea." Tears are visible on her face, in which the fire is reflected. "Now I burn the child," she repeats, the change from pronoun to definite article indicating that she is figuratively burning also her own child. (The important sentence is omitted by Brinchmann.) When the flames rise, Hedda shies away from them as if they threatened to punish her for what she is doing. Her suicide, seen as retribution, is visually anticipated in this shot.

It is evident that Garpe is here expressing more than would be possible in a stage production, where the fire would hardly seem threatening; where Hedda would usually be seen in profile downstage right; and where her facial expression, because of the distance between actress and spectator, would normally be less visible.[15]

Toward the end of the play, Brack reveals that Løvborg has either accidentally shot himself or been shot – the question is left open:

BRACK. [...] The shot had wounded him mortally.

HEDDA. Yes. In the breast.

BRACK. No, it hit him in the bowels.

HEDDA *looks at him with an expression of revulsion*. That, too! Oh, why does everything I touch become mean and ludicrous? It's like a curse!

Hussein and Warner are here faced with a problem that does not affect Garpe. I refer to the word "bowels" as a translation of Ibsen's "underliv," a word which is identical in Norwegian and Swedish. Arup translates it with "abdomen," Ellis-Fermor with "stomach" and Fjelde with "stomach – more or less." This, Meyer finds, is to miss the point, since Brack

must make it clear to her [Hedda] that the bullet destroyed his [Løvborg's] sexual organs; otherwise Hedda's reactions make no sense. [...] yet Brack must not use the phrase "sexual organs" directly; he is far too subtle a campaigner to speak so bluntly to a lady. What he says is: "In the – stomach. The – lower part."[16]

However, if it is true that "underliv" was "an almost taboo word in the 1890s for a part of the anatomy somewhat closer to the sexual organs than the stomach,"[17] even Meyer's alternative seems too circumlocutory. What

Meyer in any case overlooks is that the Norwegian word relates especially to the *female* internal sexual organs. Ibsen's Brack uses a word indicating that Løvborg was killed in the place roughly corresponding to that where Hedda's fetus was conceived and which it now inhabits, the fetus she would like to abort. This, I take it, is the dominant reason for Hedda's revulsion. Viewed in this light, 'belly' may seem preferable to Meyer's four-word solution. Nevertheless, both Hussein and Warner employ Meyer's rendering.

At the end of the play, Ibsen's Hedda withdraws into her own inner room where, offstage, she shoots herself in the temple before the portrait of her father, General Gabler – to the astonishment of the onstage characters and, perhaps, of the recipient as well.

Hussein shows a Hedda whose suicide comes as a surprise – as it would in a stage performance. Unlike Ibsen's, his Hedda is seen for a brief moment inside her room before she kills herself. But since this frame is a close-up, not showing any pistol, we are not visually warned about what is to happen. Before disappearing into her room, Hedda has in fact been misleading both us and the other characters. In Suzman's own words:

> A dread lightness comes upon her. Jokes come easily. She arranges her scenario with such a sure touch that I fear, had she lived, another profession might have opened up to her [...].[18]

The last, frozen frame, which forms a background for the credits, shows Hedda lying dead on the sofa, pistol in hand and streaks of blood on her forehead. By shooting herself in the temple, she has died "beautifully."

Like Hussein's, Brinchmann's version of the end does not differ markedly from what we would expect from a stage version. As Tesman goes to the curtain separating Hedda's room from the drawing room and tells her to stop playing, we glimpse the red interior of her room. Shortly after this Hedda is seen there with a pistol in her hand, warning us of the imminent suicide. When the shot is heard, Tesman rushes to the curtain, grabs it for support and mumbles: "Shot herself." This is followed by a close-up of Brack who, shocked, gets up from his chair to deliver the curtain line: "One doesn't do that kind of thing." In the final frame the camera again enters the inner room, revealing Hedda's face on the sofa, without any trace of blood – surely a death in beauty.

Warner's Hedda, peeping through the door, pistol in hand, aims at Brack, as she had done at the beginning of Act II. Revealing to her husband that Brack now hopes to be "the only cock in the yard," she imitates a hen with her "cluck, cluck, cluck." After she has closed the door, the shot is heard. Not only Tesman but also Brack enters the inner room. Brack coolly looks at his watch as if checking the time of Hedda's death. Omitting both Brack's curtain line and the portrait of the general, Warner shows Hedda prostrate on the floor, streaks of blood on her face, confirming Tesman's "Shot herself in the temple!" The frame is frozen, and we hear disharmonic electronic music resembling noise, undermining the idea of a death in beauty.

A very different and much more cinematic approach is found in Garpe's version of the end, lasting no less than close to four minutes:

1 *Drawing room.* TESMAN *and* MRS ELVSTED, *at the desk, are arranging Løvborg's ms.* BRACK *is sitting in BG.* HEDDA's *piano playing – opening of Beethoven's piano sonata no. 23 op. 57* (Appassionata) *– is heard.*

TESMAN. But, Hedda, my dearest...

2 *CU of* HEDDA's *hands playing, a ring with a black stone on her L hand.*

TESMAN *offscreen.* ... no music this evening. Think of Aunt Rina! And of Ejlert!

3 *MS of* HEDDA *at the piano, playing.*

4 *CU of* HEDDA's *hands playing.*

5 *MS of* HEDDA, *at the piano, ending her playing by hammering a few aggressively disharmonic chords.*

HEDDA *to herself, wringing her hands.* And of Aunt Julle. And of all the rest of them. *Puts one hand against her belly.* I will be quiet in future. *Turns her head R, up from piano-stool.*

TESMAN, *offscreen.* I tell you what, Mrs Elvsted.

6 TESMAN *and* MRS ELVSTED *at desk.*

TESMAN. You shall move into Aunt Julle's and I'll come over in the evenings. And then we can ...

7 HEDDA *moves R, sits down on the piano-stool again. Next to it a table with the red apple she has recently put down on it.*

TESMAN, *offscreen.* ... sit and work there.

HEDDA, *shouting.* I can hear perfectly well what you are saying, Tesman. *Puts the riding-boots on her knee.* But how am I going to get through the evenings out here?

TESMAN, *offscreen.* Oh, I'm sure Judge Brack will be kind enough to come out and see you.

BRACK, *offscreen.* Willingly!

8 BRACK, *by the fireplace, his back to the camera, raising his R hand in which he holds a cigar.* Every single evening, Mrs Tesman.

9 HEDDA *puts on the riding-boots, stands up, straightens herself, picks up the apple, walks R to the metal chest on the floor, kneels, opens it. Non-diegetic music – from the slow movement of Beethoven's* Appassionata *– is heard from here until end. She takes the pistol out of the riding-boot, collects some (invisible) cartridges, closes the chest and tenderly strokes the golden Gabler name-plate on top of it.*

10 CU *of* HEDDA, *from behind, her hair-knot a 'crown'. She gets up. Pan as she moves L and stops in front of an outer glass door. It is dark outside. She turns around, part of her face is now brightly lit from L. Her face is calm, determined.*

11 LS *of drawing room.* TESMAN *and* MRS ELVSTED *L at desk, an 'altar' with two lit candles R,* BRACK *in BG by the fireplace.* BERTE *enters in BG from R.*

12 MS *of* HEDDA *in front of the glass door. Still brightly lit from L, she holds the pistol in her L hand. With her R hand she makes a quick brushing-away movement across her belly, turns around to face the door, opens it, and enters the darkness outside.*

13 LS *of the drawing room. A shot is heard.* BERTE, *in BG, gets up.* MRS ELVSTED, *anguished, puts a hand to her throat and looks around.*

TESMAN, *engrossed in scraps of paper, mumbles matter-of-factly.* Now she's playing with the pistols again.

14 CU *of a hanging apple being crushed as a second shot is heard.*

15 MS *of* HEDDA *slowly moving the pistol, now in her R hand, under her chin, its muzzle pointing to her throat.*

16 LS *of the drawing room. A third shot is heard.* BRACK, *still sitting by the fireplace, turns around. They all look up. Faint barking of a dog.*

17 *Vertical view of* HEDDA *lying on the ground, her riding-boots on, her hair a 'crown,' a crushed apple at her feet. Slow track-out. Fade-out.*

Far from hiding Hedda in the inner room, or showing merely glimpses of her, Garpe has the camera alternate between the two rooms while concentrating on Hedda. Tesman's and Brack's concluding lines are omitted. Two pistol shots are added to Ibsen's single shot, and there is a climactic build in the arrangement of the three shots. Two of them concern the apples on the tree outside.

This ties in with the visual apple symbolism Garpe has added to the play – at the expense of Ibsen's verbal vine leaves. At one point five half-eaten apples are seen next to Hedda. Moreover, we see her, as the only one, eating an apple. Miss Tesman keeps polishing red apples, and these are later seen on the table between Hedda and Thea. Clearly, the apples are fatefully related to the women of the play and to their archetype: Eve. The apple tree outside represents the Tree of Knowledge, the Christian Tesman values which contrast so markedly with the Greek values, Hedda's and Løvborg's values, displayed inside the walls of the villa. No wonder Hedda makes a game of demolishing apples.

But the apples also have another significance. The very first, pre-title frame shows two apples hanging close to each other. Hedda aims with her pistol at one of them. It is crushed by her bullet. This is an abortive gesture anticipating her brushing away of her fetus (cf. shot 12 above). In the final frame, we see a crushed apple at her feet. By killing herself she has also killed the child inside her. The two apples of the opening have been shot down.

More than the other Heddas we have considered, Garpe's dies a heroic death, the death of an amazone. In the final frame the riding-boots are prominent. She has remained her father's daughter. Her position recalls the longing of Strindberg's Miss Julie, her predecessor and kindred spirit, to fall not only down to the earth but also into the earth. The desolate barking of a dog in the distance – as though from another world – is the last sound to be heard until the *Appassionata* rises to a triumphant, concluding crescendo.

7 *The Master Builder* (1892)

In *The Master Builder*,[1] Ibsen develops a technique that he had touched upon in *Hedda Gabler*. Although both plays have seven characters, only two of them share a world from which the other five are excluded. In *Hedda Gabler* it concerns "vine leaves in the hair," in *The Master Builder* "castles in the air." Oscillating between an outer and an inner reality, the play essentially deals with the latter. Halvard Solness and Hilde Wangel are attracted to each other. To Hilde, Solness represents the man who dares to climb as high as he can build. To Solness, Hilde represents youth, the youth he has lost. What they have in common is an urge for life. Each sees an ideal in the other, each figures primarily in the imagination of the other. A crucial question when presenting the play is then how to deal with figures who are imagined rather than real. Since Solness, as the title indicates, is the protagonist, his situation, feelings and point of view are predominant. How does he experience Hilde? Granted that there is both a sexual and an ideological component in their relationship, how are they balanced? Can a screen presentation here offer something that a stage performance cannot?

The opening of Ibsen's play quickly demonstrates a conflict between old Knut Brovik, *"former architect,"* and his son Ragnar Brovik, a talented *"draughtsman,"* on one hand and their employer Halvard Solness on the other. Three generations are involved here. Just as Solness once deposed Knut Brovik, so Knut's son Ragnar desires to depose Solness, both to revenge his father and, as Solness did when he was young, to promote himself.

The conflict becomes acute when one of Solness' customers takes a liking to Ragnar's design for a new villa. To Solness this is a sign that his position is threatened, that his creative potency is dwindling.

Kaja Fosli, also employed by Solness, provides an antidote. Engaged to Ragnar, she is in love with Solness and can consequently give him the comforting feeling that he is more vigorous, both artistically and erotically, than the young draughtsman.

As always, Ibsen carefully describes his characters. Knut Brovik is old and sickly. His black coat, which "forewarns us of his approaching death,"[2] although *"well preserved"* is *"worn"* and his stock is *"slightly yellow."* This is apparently a man who is trying, in vain, to look respectable. Ragnar *"is in his thirties, well dressed, fair haired, with a slight stoop."* Kaja *"is a slender girl in her early twenties, neatly dressed but of sickly appearance."* Although all three obviously try to keep up appearances, their poor health reveals that they suffer from being suppressed by the master builder.

This is true also of Solness' wife Aline, who *"looks thin and haggard, but retains traces of former beauty. Fair hair hanging in ringlets. She is elegantly dressed, all in black."* Aline reveals "the same combination of good qualities in decay that we observed in the others."[3]

In Terje Mærli's Norwegian 1981 adaptation the blackness is retained in Knut Brovik, who has grey hair and beard, black suit, white shirt, and black tie. His Ragnar has brown, long hair, brown suit, white shirt. Not unlike Solness in appearance, he seems to represent a youthful version of the master builder. Kaja, brown-haired, wears a brown blouse with white collar and a black skirt. Aline is very much as described by Ibsen.

In Michael Darlow's BBC production from 1987, Knut Brovik has a pale face, white hair and white large whiskers, glasses, black frock coat and black stock with white spots. Ragnar is dark-haired rather than blond. Kaja has blond hair with a plait surrounding her head and a long lilac dress. Loose sleeves and long aprons mark all three as workers. Darlow's Aline has brown hair, like Kaja with a plait surrounding her head. As prescribed, she wears a black dress.

Ibsen's Halvard Solness strikingly contrasts with his four 'slaves.' He is

> *a somewhat elderly man, healthy and vigorous, with close-cut, curly hair, dark moustache, and dark, thick eyebrows. He is dressed in a grey-green jacket, buttoned up, with high collar and broad lapels. On his head he wears a soft grey felt hat [...].*

Agewise between Knut and Ragnar, Solness is apparently dark-haired and, unlike his four subordinates, in good health. There is potency in his colouring and hair. His clothes strengthen this impression. Dressed like a mountain walker, he is a man of the open air. But the high collar of the buttoned-up jacket warns us that he represses something. Eventually, we learn that he has strong feelings of guilt for his reckless way of treating his fellows. Inside his robust façade, he harbours a "frail conscience." Mærli's Solness is strikingly monochrome. He has a handsome face, thin brown hair and brown moustache. He wears a reddish brown, three-piece suit, white shirt and brown tie. Darlow's Solness is a forceful, grey figure. Looking rather like a troll, he has grey curly hair, bushy eyebrows and a grey beard and moustache. He wears a grey suit, grey waistcoat, white shirt, and a dark red tie with white spots.

The setting for Act I shows in front *"a plainly furnished office in* SOLNESS" *house"* and behind it *"the drawing office."* Apparently without any windows, the rooms have an imprisoning quality. The stage directions for Act II indicate that, as in *The Wild Duck*, the work area and the home are under one and the same roof, separated by an invisible *"wallpaper door."* Solness has sacrificed other people, especially his wife, to make a career for himself as a master builder. He complains of never having had a home. The hidden passage between work room and home, which realistically seems of little significance, indicates Solness' inability or unwillingness to keep the two areas separate as well as his pretense that they are.

Similarly, he pretends that Kaja is merely his clerk when other people are around. Even so, he "*strokes her hair gently*," while Knut and Ragnar Brovik are still behind the open door leading to the neighbouring room. When they are gone, he is more daring:

> SOLNESS. [...] persuade him [Ragnar] to stay on in his good position here with me. Because then I can keep you too, dear Kaja.
>
> KAJA. Oh, yes, how wonderful it would be if it could work out like that!
>
> SOLNESS *takes her face between his hands and whispers.* I can't be without you, you see. I must have you here with me, every single day.
>
> KAJA *shivering with excitement.* God! Oh God!
>
> SOLNESS *kisses her hair.* Kaja, – Kaja!
>
> KAJA *sinking down before him.* Oh, how kind you are to me! How incredibly kind!

At this point both we and Kaja believe what Solness says. We may wonder whether his behaviour towards her is typical of him or, which seems more likely, determined by the fact that his wife is next door. Kaja responds so positively to his advances that we must ask ourselves whether there is a liaison between the two.

Later in the play, we learn that whereas Kaja is in love with Solness, Solness is merely pretending love for her. He is eager to keep the talented Ragnar Brovik as a draughtsman. By responding to Kaja's love for him, Solness can keep her. And by keeping her, he can keep Ragnar. Kaja serves his purpose.

Solness behaviour towards Kaja may be compared to his behaviour towards Hilde ten years earlier:

> HILDE. [...] You took me in both your arms and bent me backwards and kissed me. Many times.
>
> SOLNESS. Oh, but my dear, good Miss Wangel – !
>
> HILDE *gets up.* You're not going to deny it?
>
> SOLNESS. I certainly will!

Solness here suggests that what Hilde describes is something that has happened merely in her mind. But very soon he offers another explanation: "I must have wanted it – wished it – desired it." He now seems to play with the idea that Hilde has, somehow, sensed his feelings for her, has sensed that he desires her. And since to Solness' "frail conscience" what happens in the mind is not essentially different from what happens in reality, he is now ready to admit:

> SOLNESS *impatiently*. Oh well, yes, damn it – then I did it, too!
>
> HILDE [...] You confess?
>
> SOLNESS. Yes. Anything you say.

Is there any relationship between the Solness-Kaja situation just referred to and the Solness-Hilde situation of the past? The situations differ clearly in that Hilde, who is now twenty-three, was thirteen at the time. But since Kaja is of about the same age as Hilde, "*of twenty some years*," and as idolatrous of Solness as she is, we may well assume that she would have reacted exactly as Hilde, had Solness met her when she was thirteen.

In his presentation of the Solness-Kaja sequence, Darlow, who follows Ibsen closely, does not indicate any connection with the Lysanger episode. The end of the quoted passage is presented as follows:

> KAJA. God! Oh God! *She closes her eyes and leans her head against his breast.*
>
> SOLNESS *kisses her hair, whispers*. Kaja, Kaja!
>
> KAJA *drops on her knees, her face against his R, ringed hand*. Oh, you're so kind to me! *Kisses his hand twice.* So wonderfully kind!

Mærli combines the two Kaja-Solness sequences. Already before Solness arrives, Kaja has closed the door to the drawing office. Seeing him enter, she takes off her green eyeshade and fashions her hair. Solness, noticing that the door to the drawing office is closed, comes up to her, kisses her on the cheek, and desirously presses her breasts. She responds immediately. In a close-up we see her voluptuously kissing him. While Ibsen and Darlow suggest no more than idolatry on Kaja's part, Mærli shows a strong sexual component. The intention is possibly to indicate Solness' hypnotic power over Kaja and suggest a connection with the sexually charged Lysanger episode. But the presentation implies rather that Solness and Kaja have a fully established liaison. Seen in this way, Solness is lying to Doctor Herdal when he denies that he has a sexual relationship with Kaja. And as a result, he appears more callous and depraved than Ibsen's Solness when he dismisses Kaja in the presence of his wife and then refers to her as "that poor little fool."

Mystery is brought into the play when Hilde Wangel appears:

> SOLNESS. [...] Some day, youth will come knocking on my door –

HERDAL *laughs.* Well, for heaven's sake, what of it?

SOLNESS. What of it? Why, that will be the end for master builder Solness.

There is a knocking on the door L.

SOLNESS *starts.* What's that? Did you hear anything?

HERDAL. It's someone knocking.

SOLNESS *loudly.* Come in!

HILDE WANGEL *comes in through the hall door.*
She is of medium height, of slender and supple build, slightly sun-tanned. Dressed in tourist costume, skirt hitched up, open sailor collar, small sailor hat, knapsack on back, plaid in strap, long alpenstock.

Even more than Solness, Hilde is a robust, open-air contrast to the four sickly slaves. There is nothing buttoned-up about her. Her costume makes her at once a tourist, a sailor, a mountaineer, and a child, presumably not so different from the girl Solness met ten years ago. Hilde is obviously a mover, a free explorer.

Mærli's Hilde has brown hair, which she loosens up soon after she has arrived, brown coat, white blouse, brown checkered waistcoat, brown skirt, blue-and-white woollen shawl and beret, knapsack. Darlow's Hilde has blond, long hair, a light brown two-piece walking dress, the skirt of which is hitched up for hiking, checkered tie, brown beret, knapsack and alpenstock. Both directors refrain from Ibsen's sailor-cum-child connotations; Mærli's blue-and-white beret seems rather linked with sky and clouds – especially in view of her tendency to worship those who dare climb high. Her brown dress links her with Solness' red-brown suit. Darlow adds a masculine tie to her costume, a sign of emancipation.

While Mærli's Hilde makes a realistic appearance, entering from the darkness outside, Darlow's enters as a shadow in a mystical haze, an entrance that slightly recalls that of his Solness in the beginning. Crosscutting between the shadow of Hilde and close-ups of Solness, Darlow indicates that we now share his subjective vision of her. The haze returns several times later, each time serving to create an atmosphere of unreality.

This is created also by means of non-diegetic music. Hilde's and Solness' lyrical dreams about castles in the air are accompanied by their musical equivalence: the voice of a high soprano. At the end of Act II, the high female voice – the aural equivalent of bright light (synesthesia) – accompanies the light surrounding Hilde, while somber instrumental music sets in as we see Solness, surrounded by blackness, walk toward the grey veranda with its ominous long shadows, foreshadowing his death.

The most striking aspect of Mærli's production are the many mirror sequences and sequences visualising Solness' thoughts and feelings, both pronouncedly cinematic devices.[4]

Mærli opens his performance with a dream sequence, which is partly a flashback, partly a flashforward. An initial frontal close-up of Solness followed by a dissolve informs us that *he* is the dreamer of the subsequent images. We see people running to a burning house – Aline's family home – with water buckets in a vain attempt to quench the fire. Aline, in her nightgown outside in the cold winter night, is in a panic. Via a dissolve from her screaming face to the bedroom curtain, the camera pans to Solness in his bed watching, in what seems to be a nightmarish daydream sequence, his blue-toned alter ego standing beside the bed. Indicating self-confrontation, the shot initiates the series of mirror sequences later in this version. It also initiates the sequence of blue-toned shots that follow immediately: a coffin that is carried out of a church with a funeral wreath on its wall (the wreath for the topping ceremony turned to funeral wreath); Aline in mourning crape; a wintry funeral procession; another close-up of Solness, this time in semi-profile and, superimposed on it, the play title in huge letters, identifying him as the master builder. The sequence makes it clear that Solness is (day)dreaming about his own funeral. After this, a pan around Solness' living room and office, his subalterns lined up along the walls, all of them in frozen stillness looking accusingly at Solness.[5] The camera lingers on some of the key victims: Kaja, Old Brovik, and a man whose face is streaked with blood – apparently one of the men who had been killed in connection with the roof-topping ceremony, a man who foreshadows Solness' fate at the end of the play. The dream images are accompanied by music: drum beats – Solness' beating heart – during the self-confrontation and somber strings in the funeral sequence changing into more worrying, insistent sounds in the accusation sequence, Solness' uneasy conscience made audible. A shot in normal light shows Solness waking up as we hear the clock strike – while Aline, in a separate bed, is still asleep. He gets up and, as though recalling the alter ego of his dream, watches himself in the bedroom mirror.

Unlike Ibsen, who only gradually reveals to us that Solness suffers from a frail conscience, Mærli immediately informs us of his troubled state of mind. Moreover, like Ingmar Bergman in the initial nightmare sequence of WILD STRAWBERRIES, a likely source of inspiration, Mærli forewarns both Solness and us of his imminent death. The initial dream sequence sets the tone for the subsequent action which is regularly interrupted by interiorised sequences, all of them related to Solness.

In Act II, Solness tells Hilde about the fire that destroyed Aline's home, indirectly killed their two babies and at the same time enabled him to start his career as a master builder. Although the fire was an accident, he nevertheless feels guilty, since he had secretly wanted it to happen. Mærli demonstrates his guilt feelings in a series of mental images, some of them flashbacks relating to the burning of the old house and to Aline's beloved dolls, some of them flashforwards relating to the new house he has built for himself and her. Via a model of the new house in the sitting room, we enter Solness' mind. Instead of having the passage, in Act II, where Aline tells Solness about her doubts concerning their new house take place in the sitting room, as Ibsen and Darlow have it, Mærli situates it in the new house, which is symbolically white, inside and outside. Bathing in an unnatural, overexposed light, the couple, dressed in close-to-white clothes, are in a room that is almost devoid of furniture. Unlike the situation in their present bedroom, it contains only one double bed. Sitting in front of a mirror near this bed Aline expresses her doubts about the new home, the home they are now inside. Sitting behind her on the bed, Solness is seen in the mirror, small and 'squeezed' between the real Aline and her mirrored self.

The sequence has its counterpart in the castles in the air sequence of Act III. Solness now finds himself in the same white room together with Hilde. Hilde, standing in front of the mirror in which she and Solness are seen, demands her kingdom and her castle. By situating this passage in the new house, Mærli clarifies that Solness now sees Hilde rather than Aline as his partner in the new home. The dream of castles in the air with a firm foundation is visualised.

These imagined mirror sequences are preceded by a number of real ones. I have already mentioned the first one, showing Solness examining his face in the bedroom mirror. The second is found when Knut Brovik asks Solness to give his son Ragnar a chance as a designer. During this controversy Solness is looking at himself in a mirror, while Brovik is sitting in the background. The arrangement, indicating interiorisation, underlines the fact that Ragnar is now in the same position as Solness once was. When hearing about Ragnar's situation, Solness is, as it were, experiencing his own anew. When the conflict culminates, we see Knut 'squeezed' between Solness' real and mirrored selves, an arrangement meaningful also because it brings the two men, whose fates run parallel,[6] visually close together.

Later in the act, Hilde indicates her propensity for nocturnal dreams without specifying their nature:

SOLNESS. Do you often dream at night?

HILDE. Gosh, yes. Nearly every night.

SOLNESS. What do you mostly dream about?

HILDE. I shan't tell you tonight. Some other time – perhaps.

In Ibsen's version, Solness at this point *"stands by the table downstage,"* Hilde somewhere else in the room. Mærli places her in front of the mirror. In it she can see herself and, in the background, Solness. Both the dreamer and the person dreamed about are inside the frame of the mirror. Solness' second question is answered visually for us. It is noteworthy that what Hilde sees – dreams about – is not Solness' real self but his mirrored self.

In Act II there is another, less obvious mirror sequence. Hilde tells Aline about Solness' climbing of the church tower in Lysanger. Aline refuses to believe her, claiming that Solness gets dizzy even on his own balcony. When this exchange takes place, we see Solness and Aline in the foreground and Hilde, mirrored, in the background between them, an arrangement indicating that Hilde is wedging her way in between the married couple. Her mirrored self hangs on the wall like a relished painting.

At the end of Ibsen's play, Aline, Doctor Herdal, a number of ladies, presumably Aline's female friends, Ragnar and Hilde have gathered on the veranda for the roof-topping ceremony. When Solness has put the wreath on the tower of his house and can be seen waving his hat, Hilde triumphantly cries: "For now, now it is finished!"[7] She snatches Aline's white shawl from the Doctor who is carrying it.[8] Waving it about, she shouts: "Hurrah for the master builder!" Up to this point the situation is very similar to what happened ten years earlier, when Solness put the wreath on the spire of the Lysanger church. Hilde had then waved a flag so violently that Solness had "almost turned dizzy." Now she repeats that action with the shawl, and this time he does turn dizzy, and the dizziness proves fatal:

MRS SOLNESS *and the* LADIES *simultaneously*. He's falling! He's falling!

MRS SOLNESS *staggers and falls back, fainting. The* LADIES *catch her amid cries and confusion. The* CROWD *in the street breaks down the fence and storms into the garden.* DR HERDAL, *too, hurries down there. Short pause.*

HILDE *stares fixedly upwards and says as if turned to stone. My* master builder!

RAGNAR *supports himself tremblingly against the railing*. He must have been smashed to pieces. Killed on the spot.

ONE OF THE LADIES *while* MRS SOLNESS *is carried into the house*. Run down to the doctor –

RAGNAR. I can't move a step –

ANOTHER LADY. Call down to someone, then.

RAGNAR *tries to shout*. How is it? Is he alive?

A VOICE *from down in the garden*. The master builder is dead.

OTHER VOICES *nearer*. His whole head is crushed. – He fell right into the stone-pit.

HILDE *turns to* RAGNAR, *and says quietly*. Now I can't see him up there any longer.

RAGNAR. This is terrible. He hadn't the strength after all.

HILDE *as if in quiet, bewildered triumph*. But he got right to the top! And I heard harps in the air. *Waves her shawl upwards and cries with wild intensity*. My – *my* master builder!

Writing for the stage, Ibsen largely had to resort to teichoscopy in his ending. To disguise Solness' fall, he also placed some *"large old trees"* in front of the new house. In a screen performance the fall could easily be shown. But it would be rather pointless, since the fall is a given, whereas the reactions to it are not. These we need to see.

When Solness greets the crowd, notably Hilde, by swinging his hat, a pronouncedly male gesture, she returns his greeting by waving the shawl, a markedly feminine attribute.

Since Hilde has urged Solness to climb the tower, she is directly responsible for his fall. The festive builder's wreath is turned into a funeral wreath,[9] the white "bridal veil" that she snatches from Aline – Hilde asserts that Solness is now *her* master builder – becomes a "winding-sheet."[10] For Solness, whose conscience is "frail," cannot wholly rid himself of his wife, his past, his guilt. He grows dizzy and falls, a victim to what Hilde has called a "dizzy conscience."

At the end two strongly contrasting visual images are imprinted on our brains via Hilde and Ragnar: Solness, triumphant, high up on the tower, and Solness, defeated, deep down in the quarry. Hilde sees only the former, Ragnar only the latter. *He* cannot accept a triumphant Solness, since his ambition is to replace the master builder. *She* cannot accept a defeated Solness, since only a triumphant master builder makes his death and her life meaningful. How *we* as readers interpret Solness' end has to do with our attitude to this highly controversial protagonist, to the significance of his double movement at the end, and to the ethical conflict underlying the play, the conflict between Nietzschean individualism and Christian altruism.[11]

In addition to Hilde's and Ragnar's reaction, the end describes the reaction of Doctor Herdal, Aline and the ladies surrounding her – the old and mighty generation – as well as that of Ragnar's comrades, the young revolutionaries who come storming into the garden as soon as Solness' death has been proclaimed. With two groups and four individuals, Ibsen provides a many-faceted ending, difficult to accommodate within the small screen.

Darlow, as usual closely adhering to Ibsen's text and conventionally synchronising his camera to Ibsen's cue designations, shows all the people indicated in the text in his ending except the revolutionary young men. Like Mærli, he also abstains from displaying what may be considered their homes, the *"low, dilapidated little houses"* in the street outside Solness' domain. These would be poorly visible on the small screen.

We see an excited Hilde looking upwards at the dark back of Solness who, silhouetted against the sun, puts the wreath around the spire, waves his hat – and looses his foothold. Darlow then cuts back to Hilde waving the shawl she has snatched from Herdal. A high angle long shot shows the ladies surrounding the fainted Aline. Ragnar comes into picture a couple of times. The closing frame shows Hilde, in medium close-up, waving the shawl. Behind her the grey veranda fades out to blackness. Then a triumphant, shadowy Solness on top of his tower fades in. The picture is frozen. Paradoxically, the vision of the victorious master builder, which is exclusively Hilde's, is shared by us.

Darlow's ending is as varied acoustically as it is visually. It is accompanied by a medley of diegetic and non-diegetic sounds: shouting as Solness is climbing; a shrill electronic sound as we see him at the top; shrieking as he falls; the crying of seagulls in the stillness after he has tumbled down; and harp-like piano music when Hilde says that she has heard "harps in the air."

Mærli solves the problem of how to get Ibsen's crowded ending into the small screen by pruning the dialogue, by omitting Aline's female and Ragnar's male friends and by focusing strongly on Hilde. He concludes his performance by showing an excited Hilde, in her white blouse, sidelit by the setting sun, looking upwards. Behind her in the shade stands Kaja, a pale Munch figure in black dress, a black kerchief around her head, her hands crossed over her breast. Unlike Ibsen's Kaja who stays with the dying Knut Brovik and is consequently not present in the ending, Mærli's Kaja could evidently not resist the temptation of seeing Solness again. She is in mourning not only because of what has overcome her prospective father-in-law and herself but also, like her mental kindred spirit Aline, in anguished anticipation of Solness' death. The camera pans right. From here until the end, Hilde alone is in picture. Solness' reaching the top is registered solely through her facial expression and her triumphant words, whispered as though she is talking to herself. Abstaining from the shawl, Mærli can ignore Ibsen's rather artificial need of Doctor Herdal. He simply has Hilde wave ecstatically with her white-sleeved arm when Solness reaches the top. When he falls, she slowly lowers her arm. Ragnar's "killed on the spot" hardly seems to penetrate her mind. In the final shot we see half of her face, a tear running down her cheek, lit by the evening sun. The shot is frozen. Solness has for ever got under her skin.

During Solness' climbing we hear the somber droning of 'viking' horns mingled with the faint ringing of a bell, paganism versus Christianity. The music rises to a high, climactic pitch at Hilde's "now it is finished!" Solness has reached the top. Then it regresses to somber notes as he is falling. There is a moment of stillness, the stillness of death, followed by Hilde's final triumphant words.

8   *Little Eyolf* (1894)

Little Eyolf, it has been said, is, next to *Rosmersholm*, Ibsen's "most pronounced chamber play." Even more than the other play, it is a conversation piece.[1] These criteria, and its limited number of characters, make it fit for the small screen.

Alfred Allmers has married Rita not out of love but for "the gold and the green forests," that is, for money and comfort. She, on the other hand, is jealously in love with him. There is, in other words, egotism on both sides. They have a crippled son, Eyolf, whom they have cared little about, Allmers because he has been busy thinking about his great work on "Human Responsibility," Rita because she only has eyes for her husband. Lured by the mysterious Rat Wife, Eyolf falls into the water and drowns. Allmers reminds Rita of how Eyolf was crippled. When he was still a baby, Rita had lured Allmers to leave him on a table to make love to her. The child fell from the table and became crippled for life. Since he has never been able to swim, he drowns. Rita, Allmers concludes, is responsible for Eyolf's death. She refutes his version, arguing that by letting himself be lured by her, he is as responsible as she.

Next to this main plot, revolving around the married couple, there is a subplot. Allmers and Asta, who are very attached to one another, think that they are half-brother and half-sister. When the play opens, Asta has just discovered that they are not. She informs Allmers about this. He wants her to stay with him and Rita, but realising that there is now nothing to prevent her from luring Allmers away from Rita, Asta decides to escape with Borghejm, whom she does not love and whose adoration of her echoes Rita's of Allmers. Asta and Borghejm could be seen as representing a more honest, realistic and healthy alternative to the tainted bond between Allmers and Rita.[2] Yet Asta's decision to marry Borghejm although she is still in love with Allmers combined with her remark that she is fleeing both from Allmers and from herself indicate rather that she is going to repeat Allmers' mistake of marrying for the wrong reason.

The action of the play *"takes place on* ALLMERS' *estate, out by the fjord, some twelve miles from the town."* Act I shows

> *A handsome and richly decorated garden room, full of furniture, flowers and plants. In the BG, open glass doors leading out to a veranda. A broad view over the fjord. Wooded mountain ranges in the distance.[...] In the FG L, a larger table with armchairs around it. On the table is an open travelling bag. It is early summer morning and the sun is shining warmly.*

The room indicates the opulence of the Allmers. The idyllic indoor comfort, further emphasised by the friendly light, contrasts with the wilderness outside the windows, the mountains from which Allmers, as his travelling bag bears witness, has just returned. Nevertheless, the open glass doors suggest a harmonious relationship between exterior and interior, between nature and culture.

After Eyolf's drowning, Act II shows a very different scenery, reflecting the married couple's guilt feelings:

> *A small, narrow glen in* ALLMERS' *forest down by the shore. Tall, old trees to the L lean over the place. Down the slope in the BG a brook gushes, losing itself among the stones at the edge of the forest. A path winds alongside the brook. To the R stand only a few trees, through which the fjord can be seen. In the FG can be seen the corner of a boathouse, with a boat drawn up. Beneath the old trees on the L there is a table, with a bench and a few chairs, all made of slender birch trunks. It is a heavy day, pregnant with rain, and with drifting clouds of mist.*

The sky is low, visibility impaired. Allmers, now in a low position by the shore, is pondering the meaning of what has happened. Since he is obviously sitting with his back partly turned to the audience, it would be difficult to see that he is staring *"abstractedly"* out over the water. After a while he is ready to go out in the boat, either to search for Eyolf's corpse or to join him by drowning himself. But Asta prevents him from going.

Act III seems a synthesis of the former acts. As in Act II, we are outside; and as in Act I we are high up:

> *A scrub-covered[3] mound in* ALLMERS' *garden. A steep precipice with a railing in the BG and a flight of steps on the L leading down. A broad view over the fjord lying deep below. A flagstaff with lines but no flag stands beside the railing. In the FG on the R is a summer-house, covered with creepers and wild vine. A bench outside it. It is late summer evening with a clear sky. Dusk is falling.*

The high position and the clear sky ensure survey. Topography and weather indicate that the ending should be taken seriously. The unweeded garden supports Allmers' remark that he and his wife, leaving the idyllic and luxurious life behind them (the summer-house),[4] have "a hard day's work" ahead of them. Rita orders Borghejm to raise the flag half-mast, as she has earlier asked Asta to provide Allmers, who has not changed his clothes, with the black bands of mourning. She herself has changed into *"dark clothes, with a black veil over her head."* Is Rita concerned with appearances? Are these social, culture-bound signifiers merely indications that she is more active and down-to-earth than her husband? Or do they metaphorically tell us that she mourns the loss of Eyolf more deeply and feels more responsible for it than he does? A performance of the play will decide in which direction we should seek the significance of the costumes.

The plot is further complicated, allegorised, by the fact that little Eyolf relates both to Asta and to Allmers. Late in the play we learn that when they were very young, Asta sometimes dressed up in Allmers' best clothes. Rather than indicating lesbianism on her part or homosexuality on his[5] – such psycho-sexual interpretations unduly limit the thematic field – this crossdressing reveals her anxiousness to satisfy his narcissism. It would help him to see her as the younger and better part of himself.[6] Similarly, Eyolf persuades his mother to dress him in a *"suit cut like a uniform,"* because he wants his father to see him in it. Being a cripple, Eyolf compensatorily, and absurdly, wants to climb mountains, as Allmers has just done, to swim and to become a soldier. All these desires illustrate Allmers' dilemma.[7] The discrepancy between Eyolf's desires and his ability to make them come true mirrors Allmers' central problem. Eyolf is as unfit for climbing mountains as the narcissistic Allmers is for finishing his *magnum opus* on "Human Responsibility." Or for living according to the rules he would like to set down in his book, judging by its title. When they first appear, Allmers is significantly *"leading* EYOLF *by the hand."*

Conventionally, we expect the mother to care more for a child than the father, not least when the child is a cripple. This pattern seems reversed in the beginning of the play. In retrospect, we understand that Rita's rejection of Eyolf is based not only on her guilt feelings but also on her identifying him with "big Eyolf," Allmers' pet name for Asta, Rita's rival for Allmers' love. Eyolf's fall from the table coincided with the sexual intercourse of his parents. For Allmers sex thereafter became traumatically linked with guilt. From that moment he apparently avoids sleeping with his wife. His impotence vis-à-vis her is "retributional."[8]

Generically, *Little Eyolf* is difficult to pinpoint. For, granted that Allmers is the protagonist, "the distress [...] of one who ardently feels the need of a sorrow he is incapable of feeling makes a very curious dramatic situation, belonging to that no-man's land between tragedy and farce."[9] Not surprisingly, Allmers has not only, as here, been characterised as a man whose insight is disproportionate to his feeling. He has also been moderately praised for his striving to overcome his own deficiencies,[10] as well as blamed for surrounding his pitiful self with a pretentious aura.[11] Whatever interpretation we choose, it is obvious that Allmers is a very passive protagonist, a dreamer rather than a doer. In this he is a representative modern protagonist. Rita is *"a pretty, rather big, full-bosomed, blond lady of about 30."* Asta, on the other hand, is *"slim, of medium height, with dark hair and deep, serious eyes. 25 years old."* The contrast is not so much one between age, stature and power as one between body and soul, the body craving satisfaction, the soul abstaining from it.[12]

The most mysterious character in the play is the Rat Wife, herself "not unlike a rat in her quiet movement and grey hair."[13] The Rat Wife, so called because she relieves people of their rats by luring the animals into the sea, has a mission in the Allmers household. Not unlike Solness' "helpers and servants," she comes "in response to Rita's unexpressed summons to rid the house of the little creeping creature that infests it."[14] As the "materialization of the side of Rita that wants to be rid of the poor crippled child,"[15] the Rat Wife incongruously combines a *"flowered dress"* and *"a big red umbrella"* – indicating enjoyment of life and love – with *"a black poak bonnet and cloak."*[16] Compare Rita's *"light-coloured morning dress"* in Act I and her black veil and dark clothes in Acts II and III.

Nowhere do eyes and eye movements play such a central role as in *Little Eyolf*,[17] where at the end of Act I we get the following:

> BORGHEJM. Do you believe in evil eyes, Mrs Allmers?

> RITA. Yes, I'm now beginning to believe in evil eyes. Particularly in children's evil eyes.

Rita refers, of course, to the eyes of little Eyolf. But her statement is contradicted by the facts. Eyolf's eyes, the reader has already learned, are *"beautiful and intelligent."* The eyes of his father are also described in positive terms; they are *"gentle."* Even more positive is the description of Asta's eyes; they are *"deep, serious,"* whereas the eyes of the Rat Wife are *"sharp penetrating."* Unlike those of the other characters, Rita's eyes receive no general description. But at the end of Act I we get a very significant instant description of them, when she claims Alfred for herself *"with flashing eyes,"* a literal repetition of the Rat Wife's glance when she tells Eyolf about her power to drag living creatures into the depths of the sea. It is obvious that Ibsen has carefully selected and distributed his acting directions with regard to the characters' eyes. Unlike the others, Rita is 'eyeless' – until the momentary expression of her eyes is described, linking her with the Rat Wife. We can now, already at the end of Act I, sense that the evil eyes, far from belonging to Rita's child, Eyolf, belong to herself – as Rita discovers toward the end of the play when the dead Eyolf's "open eyes" keep haunting her. But who are we? Obviously the readers, not the spectators. For how could Ibsen's interactive eye pattern be communicated to a stage or screen audience?

The most controversial part of the play is the ending. Ibsen, Valency finds, unconvincingly "brought the play to an end with the traditional [...] scene of repentance and reformation."[18] Other critics have opted for the idea that Ibsen deliberately created a question mark ending – as he had earlier done in *A Doll's House* and *Ghosts*. Whether or not Ibsen believed in his characters' reformation,[19] it is clear that most modern critics do not. The following may be considered a representative standpoint:

> There is nothing to indicate that Allmers is able to love anything other than his idea of himself, or that Rita's passionate sexuality, hitherto so resentful of the two Eyolfs, will achieve successful sublimation because she lets the urchins live in little Eyolf's rooms [...]. The play closes on another fiction, another illusion.[20]

In line with this is the assurance that "a romanticized Allmers and a happy ending are burdens that no production [...] can hope to survive."[21]

Turning to the TV versions of *Little Eyolf*, we note that while Michael Darlow's British 1982 production has the characteristics of a TV-adapted stage performance, Magne Bleness' and Eli Ryg's Norwegian productions, from 1968 and 1983, respectively, are more televisual. Bleness' version, being made at an early date, is in black-and-white. The other two are in colour. Another difference is that while Bleness and Darlow retain Ibsen's complete dialogue, Ryg makes substantial omissions. Contrary to what one might expect, Darlow's production is some twelve minutes shorter than Ryg's. It says something about the difference in tempo, which is obviously much faster in the British version. It is difficult to say whether this difference in screen time is caused by individual differences between the two directors or by a difference in national temperament and, as a result of this, in national styles of directing and acting.

Ibsen sets the action in a period corresponding to the date of the play, the early 1890s. Bleness and Darlow adjust to this. But Ryg sets the action in a period corresponding to the date of her production, 1983. Both choices may be defended. Bleness and Darlow could argue that if you wish to keep Ibsen's dialogue virtually intact, as they obviously do, it is logical to adjust visually to his choice of period. If you do not, there is a danger that you create a clash between the verbal and the visual elements of the play, that characters in twentieth-century clothes speak like nineteenth-century people. Ryg, on the other hand, could argue that since Ibsen meant his play to have an impact as a contemporary play, you must update it to provide present-day viewers with his intended sense of immediacy. Dressing the actors in nineteenth century costumes means turning *Little Eyolf* into an 'historical' play, that is, creating a distance between the materialised events and the audience.

The controversy is, in fact, insoluble. Both parties could argue that, in different senses, they are faithful to Ibsen's text. One alternative favours coherence between the verbal and the audiovisual elements of the play, the other correspondence in intended effect. Bleness and Darlow could argue that 'historical' costume and scenery do not detract from the themes of the play; these are as valid to a western audience today as they were a hundred years ago. Ryg could argue that turning the play into a contemporary drama will help the viewers to see how the themes of the play are still extremely relevant. The Bleness/Darlow alternative may be called an indirect approach. Assuming that the viewers can see the eternal and universal 'forest' behind the historical 'trees,' it is well suited for the selective audience of the theatre. Ryg's approach is, arguably, more suitable for a mass medium like television. There is no doubt that her alternative is the more cumbersome one for a director. Having updated the play, she was forced to make substantial cuts in the text. Relocation involves considerable adaptation. The question is where you draw the line.

A more relaxed behaviour between the sexes is what we would expect from Ryg's version. Indeed, the clothes of her characters are informal. So are their way of addressing each other. While Ibsen's Borghejm, for example, addresses Asta with the formal "De" or "Fröken Asta" (Miss Asta), Ryg's Borghejm uses the intimate "du" and drops the title. However, there are certain elements in the play which could not easily be updated and which therefore seem at odds with Ryg's modern setting. The contrast between rich and poor, which becomes especially prominent at the end of the play when the opulent Rita and Allmers decide to devote themselves to charity, certainly applies less to present-day Norway than to that of a century ago. (A relocation of the play to a third-world country would have solved this problem.) Similarly, Allmers' excuse that he married the wealthy Rita in order to help his young 'half-sister' Asta sounds rather hollow when placed in a present-day welfare-state context.

Bleness' early version, not surprisingly, today strikes one as being quite conventional. The director not only reproduces the dialogue faithfully, including its ah's and oh's. (He only modernises some obsolete words.) With few exceptions, he also adjusts to Ibsen's stage and acting directions. The great number of close-ups is indicative of the time of production. Apart from being a characteristic of the small screen, close-ups may have seemed especially appealing to early TV directors involved with plays written for the stage, since they emphatically set a screen version apart from a stage version.

Bleness' most obvious deviation from the text is his change of setting for the last act. Possibly for practical, economic reasons it is set, not in the Allmers garden but, like Act I, in the garden room. As a consequence, the hoisting of the flag at the end is omitted.[22]

Darlow's production reveals its stage origin in several ways. The scenery is decidedly the simple, stylised one of the stage. Great distances between the characters, who often move around, necessitate long shots. And notably Allmers speaks with a very loud voice inimical to the small screen. Although both the distances and the loud speaking *could* be directorial devices, indicating separateness between husband and wife and Allmers' rhetorical mind, it is more likely that both are spill-overs from the earlier stage performance.

Each act is preceded by film shots, with the act number superimposed, showing the fjord landscape which forms the background of Ibsen's setting but which is difficult to reproduce like this on TV. The scenic shots end with a high-angle close-up of clear water, in anticipation and a reminder of Eyolf's fate. On the soundtrack we hear part of the First Sea Interlude ("Dawn") from Benjamin Britten's opera *Peter Grimes*, a bleak high flute suggesting the chilly grey light of dawn over a desolate seascape – is it Norwegian or Scottish? – and the ever-present menace of the sea.[23] The actual play opens with Rita unpacking Allmers' portmanteau in the foreground as Asta enters in the background. The focus is thus on Rita.

Darlow's version is based on Meyer's translation, which as usual is a terse, at times rather free rendering of Ibsen's text. A few comparisons with Ellis-Fermor's translation, more faithful to the source text, may be illuminating. Early in Act I Rita calls the telegram that has just arrived from Allmers "quite short and cold." Asta's comment on this is that Allmers is "so quiet about everything." Already here Rita's critical and Asta's conciliatory attitude to Allmers are indicated. This contrast is blurred when Meyer has Rita more matter-of-factly characterise the telegram as "short and to the point" and Asta more negatively describe Allmers as "secretive." A few lines later Rita says that when Allmers appeared the night before, he looked "transfigured." The word has a religious ring that suits Allmers' high-flown ideology better than Meyer's more ordinary "transformed." Further examples will be given in connection with the ending of the play.

Unlike Ibsen, Darlow places the fjord in Acts II and III not in the background but in the 'auditorium.' This has the advantage that the faces, looking at us, are clearly visible. At the opening of Act II, we can see how Allmers' face is marked by apathy stemming from despair. And at the end of the play, Rita's and Allmers' faces will reveal to what extent they themselves believe in their new project.

Ibsen has a habit of making his characters use the name of the addressee very frequently even when there are only two people on the stage. Since in these cases there could normally be no misunderstanding who is being addressed, this kind of namesdropping seems superfluous. When retained on the screen, as in Darlow's production, it rings extremely unnatural, theatrical.

In Ryg's updated production Allmers' rhetorics are considerably toned down. Many of his extravagantly idealistic lines have been omitted. Instead the sexual element is foregrounded. At one point Allmers and Asta, in a close-up two-shot, are nearly kissing. And Asta and Borghejm actually do kiss one another.

The studio-built decor is stylised, simple. Act I shows a bare, formally furnished room. We see two concave, brown-yellowish sofas on either side of a small, round, brown table and in the background a centrally placed door. On either side of the door a chair. This is a room radiating the chill characteristic of the Allmers household. Act II shows a hurdle, preventing a view of the fjord behind it. In front of it a sandbox with a few toys, reminding the characters of little Eyolf. This set visualises how Rita and Allmers in vain try to shut themselves off from what has happened out in the fjord and how they are imprisoned with their thoughts concerning the 'owner' of the sandbox. Act III is set in a large, grey, unfurnished, rather messy room with a view over the water, a room corresponding to Rita's and Allmers' attempt at the end to begin a new life, starting from scratch. As appears from this, Ryg abstains from the mimetic paraphernalia of Ibsen's stage settings, while developing their symbolic aspects in her own way.

Her performance opens and closes with the same somber, electronic music. This may be associated both with "the luring game" the Rat Wife, as Pied Piper, practises – characteristically the music is also heard when Eyolf follows after her – and with "the funeral bells" that haunt Rita after Eyolf's death. More generally, it seems to illustrate the dark undercurrents underlying seemingly friendly relations.

Bleness opens his performance by showing a plant in the window and a tree trunk outside – a shot contrasting what is being cultivated inside with what seems dead outside, warning us of Allmers' failure to make "the seeds of nobility" in little Eyolf "flower." Bleness then pans to the travelling bag. Rita, in the background, approaches it. She is unpacking Allmers' trousers and blank – unwritten – papers, when Asta enters.

Darlow's Rita, in a yellowish white, embroidered blouse and light grey skirt, sensually sniffs at Allmers' clothes as she unpacks his bag. Asta, in a strict, white blouse and grey skirt, enters in the background. From their appearance – both brown-haired and similarly dressed – we would conclude that the two women have more that unites than separates them.

Ryg opens with a pre-title sequence. Eyolf enters Allmers' study. Allmers, sitting at his desk, immediately leaves it and starts to play with his son. A little later we see him playfully entering the living room as a 'horse' with Eyolf on his back. The pre-title sequence seems to prefigure Allmers' transformation – his decision to become a father rather than merely a teacher for Eyolf – by *showing* that he has changed, whereas the text merely has him *talk* about his change. Viewed in this way, Ryg uses the pre-title sequence to characterise Allmers, a problematic protagonist, more positively than Ibsen does. As a result we are inclined, at the end of her version, to believe that Allmers may indeed change his life. However, this does not explain why the pre-title sequence is kept out of focus. The reason for this, I assume, is that it visualises not the real father-son relationship but Allmers' strained attempt at this point to establish such a relationship, his wishful thinking. Viewed in this way, the sequence only elaborates on the critical attitude to Allmers found in the text.

The play proper opens here, too, with Rita keeping herself busy with Allmers' portmanteau. But unlike Darlow, Ryg places Asta rather than Rita in the foreground. She has Asta first eavesdrop on Rita's jealous inspection of Allmers' clothes, then kiss Rita on her cheek. Rita, taken by surprise, is trying to cover up her rummaging. In short, Ryg, unlike Darlow, immediately makes us sense the tension between the two women, their rivalry for the man represented here by a piece of property, the portmanteau, and the clothes in it.

Somewhat less than Darlow, Ryg stresses the outward similarity between the two women. Rita has blond, pinned-up hair and wears lilac pants and a pink, low-necked silk blouse. Asta has brown, loose-hanging hair, a dark-pink blouse and white pants. Surprisingly, Asta who represses her sexuality looks more sensual than Rita who affirms it. Unlike Bleness and Darlow, Ryg immediately creates a dramatic situation by having Rita, in the background, search Allmers' clothes, while Asta, in the foreground, secretly watches her before she enters.

It is a telling opening also in the sense that in Ryg's production, Asta is even a dramaturgic rival of Rita. Especially in the sequence in Act II where she and Allmers recall their paradisaic youth together in Eyolf's sandbox, Ryg has them virtually relive this situation. The sequence ends with a kind of *pietà* grouping, indicating perhaps that Asta is now mothering a 'child' she has lost. A little earlier, when sewing the mourning band onto his lapel, she had cut the thread, the 'umbilical cord,' with her teeth.

The central problem with regard to the Rat Wife is whether to present her as a realistic old woman or as a figure of Death. Ibsen does both. When Eyolf finds her Mopsemand first "horrible," then "beautiful" – as proof of his ambivalent attitude to death – the reader can easily accept this contradiction. To retain it a director would have to conceal the dog from the viewer.

Bleness' Rat Wife is a friendly old woman, dressed according to the acting directions (although we cannot see, of course, that her umbrella is red). Since her Mopsemand, seen in close-up, would seem to most viewers a

rather ugly pet of a bulldog, Eyolf's finding him beautiful appears rather ab-
surd.

Darlow's Rat Wife, too, is a friendly old woman. Appearing in black and
violet and carrying an umbrella of the same somber colouring, she is clearly
a figure of Death. Her dog – this too a bulldog pet – presents the same problem as that of Bleness'.

By contrast, Ryg's Rat Wife is middle-aged, heavily made up and
dressed in a brown-and-white, patterned, loose-fitting long garment – not
unlike an animal hide – on top of a dark skirt; she carries no umbrella. When
she first appears and addresses the four characters, we see only the back of
her head and their reactions to her sudden appearance. This device is not
only suspense-creating; it also suggests that the Rat Wife is primarily a
mythic figure.[24] The dog is this time a rather sweet-looking pet. As a result, it
is hard to understand why Eyolf finds it "horrible."

The crisis of the play occurs when Allmers reminds Rita of how Eyolf
was crippled:

ALLMERS. [...] It's your fault that he [Eyolf] became – what he was! It's your fault he
couldn't save himself out of the water!

RITA *defensively.* Alfred! You shouldn't give me the blame for that!

ALLMERS *more and more beside himself.* Yes, yes, I do! It was you who left that tiny child
unattended on the table -

RITA. He lay there so comfortably among the pillows. And slept so soundly. And you
had promised to look after the child.

ALLMERS. Yes, I had. *Lowers his voice.* But then you came, you, you – and lured me in
to you.

RITA *looks defiantly at him.* Say rather that you forgot the child, and everything else.

ALLMERS *with suppressed fury.* Yes, that's true. *More quietly.* I forgot the child – in your
arms!

RITA *outraged.* Alfred! Alfred, – that's vile of you!

ALLMERS *quietly, clenching his fists against her.* In that moment you condemned little
Eyolf to death.

RITA *wildly.* You too! You too, – if that's true.

ALLMERS. Oh yes – call me to account too, – if you wish. We are both guilty. – And so
there was retribution in Eyolf's death after all.

Ibsen's acting directions indicate that Allmers delivers an attack on Rita characterised by a discrepancy between the (unfair) verbal accusation and the repression of the feeling that goes with it. In Rita, who is strong enough not to project her guilt onto Allmers, there is no such discrepancy. Nowhere in the play is the ethical distance between them more clearly revealed.

Bleness monotonously shows the whole passage in close-ups. Allmers, in a high position, attacks Rita in a low one. And since his Rita is not favourably portrayed, the ethical implication of the text at this point seems muddled.

Darlow climactically builds the sequence in the sense that he has Allmers approach Rita, until they are so close that when he delivers his main attack, he can accusingly point his finger to her body – after which she does the same to him. Paralinguistically, however, there is little variation.[25]

With Ryg that is different. She starts the sequence by showing Allmers' back in the foreground and Rita sitting close to the hurdle in the background, a suggestive shot both because the accuser comes over as big and the accused as small but also because we do not see the face of the accuser, only of the accused. When Allmers delivers his surreptitious attack – "in your arms" – with a raised, aggressive voice, we see their faces close to each other. After Rita's counter-attack, reflection sets in as Allmers, now in a calmer voice, contemplates the role of retribution.

Ibsen closes his play as follows:

[...] ALLMERS *walks over to the flagstaff and hoists the flag to the top.* RITA *stands by the summerhouse watching him quietly.*

ALLMERS *comes back to her.* We have a hard day's work ahead of us, Rita.

RITA. You will see, – a Sunday stillness will fall on us now and then.

ALLMERS *quietly, moved.* Then, perhaps, we shall sense the visit of the spirits.

RITA *whispers.* The spirits?

ALLMERS *as before.* Yes. Then perhaps they are around us, – the ones we have lost.

RITA *nods slowly.* Our little Eyolf. And your big Eyolf, too.

ALLMERS *gazing ahead.* Perhaps now and then – on life's way – we shall still catch a glimpse of them, as it were.

RITA. Where shall we look, Alfred – ?

ALLMERS *fastens his eyes on her.* Upwards.

RITA *nods in agreement.* Yes, yes, – upwards.

ALLMERS. Upwards, – towards the mountain tops. Towards the stars. And towards the great stillness.

RITA *holds out her hand to him*. Thanks.

It is noteworthy that Ibsen has Rita use two expressions: "stillness" (stilhed) and "now and then" (en gang imellem) which are later repeated by Allmers. This verbal echoing underlines their unanimity. Moreover, Rita's "søndagsstilhed" (Sunday stillness) – the word has immanent, religious connotations – suggestively relates to Allmers' "den store stilhed" (the great stillness), his hope for a peaceful hereafter. Meyer retains the repetition of "now and then" but opts for variation with regard to the more important "stilhed," which is rendered first as "calm," then as "silence." He has Rita speak of "a long day" rather than "a hard day's work," which of course meaningfully contrasts with the "Sunday stillness." Similarly, Allmers' general expression "på livsvejen" (on life's way), by Meyer rendered as "on our way," points forward to "den store stilheden" (the great stillness) just as life for everyone is followed by death.

The ending suggests that if Allmers' lofty ideas about human responsibility are combined with Rita's practical altruism, they can begin a new and meaningful life together. Little Eyolf has not died in vain. However, since Rita's and Allmers' 'conversion' occurs at a very late stage and is badly prepared for, it is far from convincing. A director of the play can either leave the ending as it is – in which case it will seem highly ironical in its discrepancy between what the characters and the viewers believe – or try to refashion it so that Rita's and Allmers' plans seem more credible.

Bleness, as always following Ibsen's acting directions faithfully, shows Rita and Allmers in close-up at the end – except in his last shot, where the choice of camera distance prevents the viewer from seeing if Rita holds out her hand to Allmers. Surprisingly, the director abstains from this very significant concluding gesture.

Having hoisted the flag, Darlow's Allmers, in his grey three-part suit with a black band on his arm, in the background, approaches Rita, in mourning, standing by the railing in the foreground. After he has joined her, we see them in medium shot, he to the left looking upward to the stars, she to the right looking downward to the earth. Archetypally, an image of male and female attitudes, of yang and yin, their position connotes separation rather than unity. And although Rita touches Allmers' hand with hers, she immediately withdraws it and continues looking away. As a result, her gesture seems extremely hesitant, more consoling than confirming. There is little hope in this ending.

Ryg's ending, omitting most of Ibsen's lines, shows Allmers, in dark brown trousers and jacket, left standing next to Rita, in a red-brown dress, right, both in medium long shot, facing the camera:

> ALLMERS *looks upwards, slightly to L.* Perhaps now and then we shall catch a glimpse of the ones we have lost. Let us look upwards, Rita, towards the great stillness. *Looks down, then straight ahead.*
>
> RITA *takes his hand.* Thanks.

Many of Ryg's omissions apparently serve to play down Allmers' romantic idealism, hardly palatable to a modern audience. As a result, Allmers becomes more our contemporary, more acceptable in her version than in those of Bleness and Darlow. Yet Rita, even here, refuses to obey him when he suggests that they look upwards. On the other hand, Rita not only "*holds out*" or touches Allmers' hand. She takes it. The way Allmers is outlined and the way the ending is recreated, there is the glimmer of a hope in this conclusion.

Of the three productions we have examined, the one that deviates most from Ibsen's text is to my mind the most successful. Unlike Bleness and Darlow whose versions are hardly TV-friendly – Bleness because his production is an early one, Darlow because it is stage-based – Ryg has created a *Little Eyolf* suited to the screen. Whether or not we agree with her interpretation, this is laudable.

PART TWO – STRINDBERG

9   *The Father* (1887)

If the question of paternity were the central issue of Strindberg's *The Father*, the play would be hopelessly dated now science is able to establish fatherhood. But far from being a problem play, *The Father* is, as Strindberg's subtitle explicitly states, a "tragedy,"[1] which among other things means that it is the protagonist's experience of the issue rather than the issue itself that is at stake. Admittedly, it takes today more of an effort to suspend our disbelief in the necessity of the ending than it did a hundred years ago. The proof of this is that *The Father* can hardly be relocated to the 1990s. What was a contemporary drama has in this respect become an historical play.[2] Yet the mere fact that the play is still widely performed shows that its combination of "psychic murder" and "psychic suicide" captivates modern audiences.[3]

Long considered a naturalistic drama, *The Father* is actually "an attempt to blend subjective and naturalist styles."[4] The three-act play is set in *"the living room of the* CAPTAIN's *house."* There is an irony in the fact that what is, by definition, a room for the whole family[5] is here a very masculine room, indicating the Captain's representative role as *paterfamilias*. The lighting strengthens the impression of subjectivity; as Brandell points out, "there is constantly twilight or night" in this living room seemingly lacking in windows.[6] The sense of imprisonment is increased by the fact that one of the doors, being a wallpaper-covered door, is not made visible until late in the play.

The Captain's military profession is advertised in the *"uniform coats"* hanging by the door, while the *"weapons on the walls: guns and hunting-bags"*[7] reveal that he is also a hunter – another pronouncedly male occupation. What is more, the guns-cum-hunting-bags function as icons of the male sexual organ in this play about male impotence.[8] Both the *"leather-covered couch"* and the *"secretaire,"* which is "the financial centre of the house,"[9] carry masculine connotations. These are further strengthened by the fact that when the play opens, only men appear in the living room, all of them with exclusively male professions.[10] The Pastor's pipe-smoking and the Captain's spurs,[11] turning him into a 'cock,' are also gender-characterising; at the end of Act II, the Captain verbalises this visual imagery when he states that men have deteriorated from "cocks" to "capons." The women's domain is, naturally, the kitchen where Nöjd is said to be "waiting for orders." The expression is suggestive in its indication that the women are behaving like officers, marauding from the kitchen into traditionally male territory.[12] Correspondingly we witness, as the play enfolds, how the male

parlour is gradually being invaded by the women and how the Captain finally falls victim to their cunning 'disarmament.'

In his stage directions Strindberg also calls for "*a large, round table with
newspapers and magazines*" in the living room. A symbol of family unity, the
table is apparently used as the Captain's private desk. There are no books on
it. For, as we later learn, the Captain has not received the books he has or-
dered over the last two months – because of Laura's meddling.

When the curtain rises, the Captain and the Pastor – "church and military
power united"[13] – "*are sitting on the couch,*" acting as accusers of the abuser of
sexual ethics (Nöjd):

> The CAPTAIN *in undress uniform, with riding boots and spurs.*[14] *The* PASTOR *in black, with
> white neck collar, without lappets; smokes a pipe.*

Why does Strindberg inform us about the men's costume, whereas he denies us such information with regard to the women, where it may seem
more called for? The reason, I believe, is that he wants to indicate that the
men, unlike the women, have public as well as private roles. Strindberg always admired Shakespeare's ability to describe both the public and the domestic life of his heroes. Unlike Shakespearean drama, *The Father* shows
only one setting, a domestic interior. This makes it difficult to demonstrate
the public aspect. Nevertheless, Strindberg found a way to indicate this aspect in his description of the Captain's and the Pastor's costumes, which are
both half-public, half-private.

The play opens with an episode, relating to the orderly Nöjd, which is a
little drama in itself. We are immediately introduced to an intricate situation
which moreover is said to have universal application. Rarely has a dramatist been able to involve his audience so quickly in the action unfolding before their eyes.

The Nöjd 'play'-within-the-play[15] dramatises the Captain's (Adolf's)[16]
and the Pastor's (Jonas') attempt to make Nöjd confess that he has made
Emma, a local servant girl, pregnant after having falsely promised to marry
her. (The accusation is apparently based on Emma's testimony.) Consequently, they claim, he must take the economic responsibility for the child
upon himself. Nöjd refuses. According to him, Emma has had intercourse
with several men in the relevant period. It is therefore, he reasons, far from
certain that *he* is the father of the expected child. What makes Nöjd's argu-
ment so provocative is the fact that he does not limit himself to his own situation. Instead, he sees his predicament as an illustration of a general law of
nature:

> CAPTAIN. Once and for all: are you the father of the child or not?

NÖJD. How is one to know?

CAPTAIN. What do you mean? You don't know?

NÖJD. No, that's something one can *never* know. [my italics]

And again:

PASTOR. [...] Don't you think it's dishonourable to leave a girl destitute like that with a child? Don't you think so? Eh? Don't you find behaviour like that ... well, eh ...?

NÖJD. I would, if I knew I was the father of the child. But you see, Pastor, that's something one can *never* know. [my italics]

Nöjd's Swedish pronoun – the folksy "en" (one) – is suggestively vague. It may be taken to mean: nobody can know. But Nöjd being male, it may also be interpreted as: no man can know. There is here at least an indication that the biological difference between the sexes inevitably means that women are more knowledgeable than men about the connection between their sexual partners and a resulting conception. What applies to Nöjd applies to all men: the Captain, the Pastor – and the male part of the audience. While a woman can always / usually / often / sometimes be certain of whether or not a particular man is the father of her child, a man can never be certain.

Obviously, there were – and perhaps still are[17] – situations where neither the man nor the woman could / can be certain, and since Emma seems rather promiscuous, this is in fact the situation that applies here. The conclusion the Captain eventually arrives at shows that Nöjd's generalising, gender-differentiating statement has had an impact on him:

CAPTAIN. [...] The boy most likely isn't innocent; we can't know that, but one thing we know: the girl is guilty, if you can speak of guilt at all.

Moreover, Nöjd's dilemma causes him to think of the not altogether different circumstances surrounding Laura's pregnancy. Just as Nöjd has shared Emma with Ludvig, so the Captain may have shared Laura with the doctor who treated her in the period when Bertha was born. When the Captain repeats Nöjd's statement about the uncertainty of fatherhood to Laura, he provides her with a weapon which she is soon to make use of in her struggle to secure Bertha for herself.

If Nöjd makes the Captain insecure with regard to his own fatherhood, he makes the Pastor insecure with respect to the faithfulness of the Pastor's wife:

NÖJD. I was at it, sure enough, but Pastor, *you know yourself* that doesn't mean something has to come of it. [my italics]

Although Nöjd might here be referring either to a sexual aberration or, on the contrary, to sexual impotence on the part of the Pastor, he is more likely referring to an affair, without consequences, on the part of his wife, since this interpretation agrees with the Captain's reference to the Pastor's cuck-oldry at the end of the play.

Nöjd resorts to yet another generalising statement that will prove of great consequence in the main plot:

> Nöjd. [...] if the girl doesn't *want to*, nothing happens. [my italics]

Will-power stands central in *The Father* – as in many other plays by Strindberg.[18] Nöjd's statement, which introduces the concept of will in the play, may seem highly partial. It excludes, for example, the possibility of rape. Nöjd's one-sided version may be attributed to the fact that he feels a grudge against Emma. But in a wider context, the will-power ascribed to Emma prepares for the Pastor's statement about how Laura has "always been fierce about getting her own way." More generally, it is the first sug-gestion in the play that the weaker sex is actually the stronger one in the sense that women are more able than men to assert their will – by resorting to stratagem.

Although Nöjd is an actual name, and a typical Swedish soldier's name at that, there can be no doubt that the name was selected primarily for its symbolic value. Meaning 'satisfied,' the name indicates one side of the Cap-tain, the other being suggested by the name of his second orderly: Svärd – this, too, a soldier's name, meaning 'sword.'[19] The names indicate how the Captain, with regard to the opposite sex, vacillates between an accepting at-titude (Nöjd) and a protesting one (Svärd).

Once we realise how intertwined the Captain and Nöjd are, the latter's greeting and leave-taking of the former becomes highly suggestive. The al-most identical, religiously coloured entrance and exit lines read: "God save you, Captain." Only in retrospect, when we are aware of the Captain's pre-dicament, do we grasp the full meaning of these polite phrases.

It should be clear by now that the Nöjd-Emma subplot not only prepares for the Captain-Laura main action, it also serves as a generalising statement about man-woman relations.

One problem facing the translator of the opening is how to deal with Nöjd's manner of speaking. In the source text there is undoubtedly a con-nection between his plain way of expressing himself and his natural, animalist view of sex. The following brief speech may serve as an example:

> Nöjd. Ja, nog var jag sta... (I was at it, sure enough...)

Nöjd here expresses himself in a folksy, somewhat corny way. His phrase seems like a thinly disguised euphemism for 'I fucked her all right.' This phrase has been rendered as follows:

> Well, sir, it's true, I did go with her... (Sprigge)

> Well, of course she and I... (Watts)

> Well, I did go with her... (Meyer)

> Well, I had her all right... (Johnson)

> All right, I had the girl... (Carlson)

> Well, sure I know I got it off with her. (Sprinchorn)

Via Nöjd Strindberg, in 1887, is more laconically outspoken in sexual matters than his translators. If Nöjd mirrors an attitude to sex that is *socially* determined, his creator mirrors one that seems *nationally* determined. Most of the renderings just quoted strike one as being overly prudish. There is reason to suspect that the translators have adjusted less to the idiom of the lower class target lingo than to the speech habits of the expected target recipient: the bourgeois reader or spectator. It is symptomatic that it is only the most recent translation which deviates from the pattern, presumably in an attempt to update the play.

Kenneth Ives' 1983 BBC production is preceded by a short introduction by the translator of the play, Michael Meyer, who states that *The Father* "provides profound and understandable reasons for Laura's behaviour" and that "far from being an anti-feminist piece," it "emerges as a cry for understanding and for freedom" – for Laura, that is, as a suppressed woman in a male society. Whether based on genuine conviction or a desire to prevent the female part of the audience from turning off the TV or switching to another channel, Meyer's characterisation differs radically from the traditional view of *The Father* as a highly subjective drama, in which practically everything is seen from the Captain's male point of view.[20] What concerns us here, however, is not whether we find Meyer's characterisation valid or not. It is rather the phenomenon as such, that is, the fact that a viewer of this version is provided with an interpretation of the play which, one may assume, is in agreement with the performance that is to follow. Yet it is hard to see that Meyer's support for Laura is brought out in Ives' rather traditional production.

Ives follows Meyer's translation almost to the letter – although he allows himself some cuts in the last two acts. For example, in the Captain's catalogue aria of women who have sinned against him, the reference to the woman who gave him "ten years of disease" in return for the love he gave her is omitted. This reference to a venereal disease was apparently considered morally unsuitable for a British mass audience. On the other hand, passages that are hardly intelligible to such an audience have been retained. When the Captain in his straitjacket keeps repeating "Omphale," few spectators will realise that he is referring to the Lydian queen who kept Hercules as a slave, dressed him in women's clothes and placed him at the spinning wheel, while she took over his lion's pelt and his club. Similarly, many spectators would fail to grasp the Captain's implicit comparison between his own fate and that of Samson (Judges 16.19). Important as these references are – Strindberg uses them to universalise the theme of the war between the sexes – they are obviously rather superfluous if they only reach a fragment of the audience.

Closely connected with the marital strife is the religious issue. Although nothing is stated about Laura's faith, her brother is a Lutheran pastor and the women surrounding her subscribe to various faiths: spiritism, Methodism, Baptism, Salvation Army. The Captain, on the other hand, is in Meyer's rendering a "freethinker." This is important for it means that, unlike the women, he does not believe in life hereafter. Lacking their faith, the child is his "idea of immortality." When learning that the child may not be his, his substitute faith is destroyed. He now has nothing to live for.

When Ives substitutes "agnostic" for Meyer's somewhat obsolete "freethinker," he obscures the religious conflict which would have appeared much more clearly had he chosen 'atheist' instead. The stronger term explains why the Pastor can describe the Captain as "a tare among our wheat" – a reference to Mat. 13.25 – and why he can turn away from him.

Ives' version comes close to filmed theatre. He restricts the action to the one room prescribed by the author and often resorts both to long shots and long takes. Ives' living room is rather murky and quite English with its brown wainscoting which, incidentally, prevents the inclusion of the typically Scandinavian wall-papered door. By placing the sofa upstage rather than to the right as Strindberg has it, Ives in the opening contrasts a small Pastor in the background, close to the entering Nöjd and a large Captain in the foreground far away from Nöjd. The grouping corresponds to their different roles with regard to the servant, one conciliatory, the other authoritarian.

The relationship between the Captain and Nöjd is underscored by their outward appearance: their dark blue uniforms look very similar, and both of them are dark-haired and wear whiskers. Ives clearly indicates that Nöjd's predicament is in fact the Captain's by framing the latter when Nöjd refers to the uncertainty of fatherhood. Unlike the spectator of a stage version, the screen recipient is in this way provided with a clue as to what this overhearing is all about.

In the dark room the Captain's uniform often looks quite black, not very different from Laura's black dress with its silvery trimmings. The similarity underscores the battle that goes on between them. Since not only the Pastor but also the Nurse is in black and the Doctor in dark brown, there is a certain somber unity of colouring, slightly and temporarily deviated from only by young Bertha.

Unlike Ives, Bo Widerberg in his 1988 Swedish version thoroughly adapts the play text. Words and passages that would be difficult for the audience to grasp are either omitted or replaced by more intelligible alternatives. The mythological, biblical and literary references – Hercules, Samson, Shylock – are done away with. Much of the imagery, being the least natural part of the dialogue, is left out. On the other hand, the director adds, as in his *Wild Duck* production, much small talk as well as two leitmotifs relating to the season represented in the play: Christmas.

Widerberg even changes the play title slightly. *Fadren* is actually an old-fashioned form of what in present day Swedish is 'fadern.'[21] Widerberg not only updates the play when he calls it *En far* (*A Father*). He also particularises it. In his psychologising version we deal with an individual rather than with a representative of the male species.

A comparison between Strindberg's and Widerberg's handling of the opening speeches is illustrative. In Strindberg's version they read:

CAPTAIN *rings.*

ORDERLY. What do you command, Captain?

CAPTAIN. Is Nöjd out there?

ORDERLY. Nöjd is waiting for orders in the kitchen.

The Orderly here uses the general verb "command" (Sw. befaller) the first time and the military-sounding noun "orders" (Sw. order) the second time. Anticipating the central conflict of the play, Strindberg reverses the expected situation: the true officers are the women.

Widerberg omits this opposition in his rearrrangement of the sequence:

ORDERLY *knocks on the door.*

CAPTAIN *shouts.* Yes!

ORDERLY *in.* Nöjd is here now.

CAPTAIN. Who?

ORDERLY. Nöjd.

CAPTAIN. Oh yes, damn it. Hell. Where is he?

ORDERLY. In the kitchen.

Focusing on the psychology of the protagonist Widerberg, unlike Strindberg, makes it immediately clear that the Captain shies away from the problem of unwanted parenthood. Both his forgetfulness of Nöjd and his manifest displeasure indicate his inclination to repress the problem of fatherhood. Excelling in swear-words his Captain is, in line with this, anxious to demonstrate his virility.

Widerberg's Captain is dressed in an authentic Swedish uniform, blue with yellow stripes. In addition, the director provides him with black gloves. Later we see Laura and Bertha daub his hands with some ointment. In the context of the performance – at an early point the atheistic Captain mockingly spreads his arms in cruciform – this may be seen as a sign of stigmatisation: the Captain as 'Christian' scapegoat. More esoterically, it could be seen as a reference to Strindberg's psoriasis,[22] a visual reminder of the close identity between the protagonist and his creator.

The clapper of horse-hooves outside followed by a trumpet signal informs us that the Captain is a cavalry officer. He and the Pastor, both ruled by women, smoke compensatory cigars. There is no wall-papered door and the living room is provided with windows; but it is already dark outside them. Widerberg's Captain is slender and fairly short, hardly a military type, whereas his Pastor is both literally and figuratively a round character.

The performance opens *in medias res* with roaring laughter by both men, raising our curiosity. Presumably Nöjd's situation has caused them to exchange some male jokes about sex. This note of initial masculine joviality is clearly designed to contrast with the undermining of male bondedness that is soon to take place. It also markedly contrasts with the ending.

Act II closes with the Captain throwing a burning lamp at his wife. As a result, the Doctor declares him insane. In Act III.4 he instructs the Nurse how to put the straitjacket on the Captain. It is, in view of this, rather surprising that the two men dare to leave the Captain alone at the end of Act III.5. One would expect the Nurse to remain in the room. But Strindberg wanted Bertha, whose entrance is as poorly motivated as the Nurse's absence, to be alone with the Captain so that his rights to 'his' child could be further undermined. What we get is:

> CAPTAIN. [...] If I don't eat you, you will eat me, and you have already shown me your teeth! But don't be afraid, my beloved child, I won't hurt you! *Goes to the weapon collection and takes a revolver.*
>
> BERTHA *tries to escape*. Help, mother, help! He wants to murder me!
>
> NURSE *enters*. Mr Adolf, what is it?
>
> CAPTAIN *examines the revolver*. Have you taken the cartridges?

To Lamm it is clear that the Captain's intention at this point is not to kill Bertha but to commit suicide.[23] But this hardly agrees with his reproachment of the Nurse at the end of the Scene:

> CAPTAIN. Why didn't you let me kill the child? Life is a hell, and death a heaven, and children belong to heaven!

With such a view, the Captain could certainly argue that killing Bertha "won't hurt" her. Yet in the just quoted passage Strindberg does not indicate how the Captain intends to use the revolver, thereby creating a moment of intense suspense.

A director could here follow the text and leave the question open or indicate that the Captain's intention is to kill Bertha. The suicide alternative suggested by Lamm is hardly possible, since that would make Bertha's reaction incredible.

Both Ives and Widerberg deviate from Strindberg's proxemics in the passage but in totally different ways.

Ives' Captain does not move away from Bertha. Instead, he suddenly and surprisingly – we have not seen it before – puts the revolver to her temple, without firing. Scared, the girl rushes away from him. In the next shot we see him putting the revolver into his own mouth and discharges it only to discover that it is unloaded. Ives suggests in other words, not very convincingly, that the Captain first intends to kill Bertha but suddenly changes his mind and tries to kill himself.

More imaginatively, Widerberg in his child-centred version – the similarity to his *Wild Duck* production is in this respect striking – has Bertha enter only to see the Captain asleep at the table. She exits and re-enters, this time with a Christmas star in her hand. She puts it at the top of the Christmas tree – although the Nurse had earlier made it clear that this is the task of the master of the house.[24] After the Captain's cannibalistic outburst, she encouragingly and consolingly suggests they play the traditional Swedish game in which, guided by the words 'bird,' 'fish' or 'in-between,' you must look for something that has been hidden high, low or in-between. Bertha, who has the Christmas star in mind, ironically guides the Captain to the revolver hanging high up on the wall. Despite her warning he grabs it, cocks it and looks at Bertha, only to discover that the cartridges have been removed. Meanwhile Bertha, crying for help – the director significantly omits her reference to murder – disappears under the table. Very subtly, Widerberg motivates the girl's scared reaction without making it clear if the Captain intends to shoot her or himself. Angry that the Nurse has hidden the cartridges, the Captain begins to rummage in one of the drawers, finds them and sits down on the floor. Lining them up in a row he says: "There they are." The Nurse, turning herself into his loving 'mother' of yore, agrees: "There they stand so nicely." Suddenly the Captain has become a little child playing with tin soldiers. The passage paves the way for the next sequence, where Strindberg has the Nurse make the Captain believe that the straitjacket is a body garment.

For his ending Strindberg has the Captain, in his straitjacket, suffer a stroke. Assembled around him are the Doctor, the Pastor, Laura and the Nurse. Finally

BERTHA *enters L and runs to her mother*. Mother, mother!

LAURA. My child! My own child!

PASTOR. Amen!

Laura has reached her goal. Her emotional claiming of her child pounds home the point already made in the opening of the play. Bertha is indeed *her* child since, the play claims, we can only know who is the mother of a child.

Ives' ending is stiffly conventional. After a two-shot of the Doctor scrutinising one of the Captain's eyes – rather than his pulse, as Strindberg has it – before making his diagnosis, Ives cuts to a long shot of the group assembled around the victim lying on the floor. The angle is low as if the group is seen from the overmastered Captain's point of view. Bertha enters from the background. Mother and daughter embrace. The final shot is a close-up of the consciousless Captain.

Widerberg, as before, focuses on the family triangle in the ending. The Doctor and the Pastor are seen only briefly, and their formal speeches are replaced by Bertha's desperate pleading. She is asking her father to forgive her because she has been lying to him, a highly ironic touch since her lie has been harmless and, presumably, well intended. In extended shots, we see her hysterically crying as she, guilt-ridden, tries to establish contact with her father, who speechless keeps staring at her. As the Captain, offscreen, cries out for Bertha, we see Laura in vain trying to calm her down by holding the Christmas star, his attribute, in front of her like a talisman. She then puts it on top of the tree. The final shot shows her arm stretching out for her daughter. But she never reaches her. The frame is frozen – whereas the crying continues. It is a powerful concluding image, showing the separation – rather than the union as Strindberg has it – between mother and daughter, and the child as an *ongoing* victim in the battle between the parents.

10 *Miss Julie* (1888)

In his famous preface to *Miss Julie*,[1] Strindberg pleads for plays that are not longer than what people can endure when they are presented without intervals. He also advocates that plays be presented on "a *small* stage" with "a *small* auditorium" attached to it, so that "the subtler reactions" can "be mirrored in the face rather than in gesture and sound." Intended to promote his own Scandinavian Experimental Theatre – with its small cast and one realistic setting, *Miss Julie* fits both Strindberg's naturalistic ideas and his financial needs at the time – this pleading now reads like a remarkably apt description of the desiderata for the smallest, most intimate stage in the world: the TV screen. Indeed, what the playwright considers the normal playing time for *Miss Julie*, "one and a half hours," corresponds to what many would consider ideal for television drama.

Miss Julie demonstrates how Julie, daughter of a count, left alone with the people of the manor house on Midsummer's Eve, has sexual intercourse with her servant Jean, who is unofficially engaged to the cook, Kristin. Feeling dishonoured after this act of 'bestiality' Julie, encouraged by Jean, commits suicide.

Although it is not explicitly stated in the text, the play is set in Sweden of the 1880s, more specifically *"in the* Count's *kitchen."* It is

> *A large kitchen, the roof and side walls of which are concealed by drapes and borders. The rear wall rises at an angle from the L; on it, to the L, are two shelves with utensils of copper, iron and pewter. The shelves are lined with scalloped paper; somewhat to the R three-quarters of the big, arched exit port, with two glass doors, through which can be seen a fountain with a Cupid, lilac bushes in bloom, and aspiring Lombardy poplars. To the L on the stage the corner of a big tiled stove, with a section of the overhead hood. To the R, one end of the servants' dining table, of white pine, with some chairs. The stove is decorated with birch-leaves; the floor strewn with juniper twigs. On the end of the table is a big Japanese spice-jar with lilac blossoms. An ice-box, a sink, a washstand. Above the door a big old-fashioned handbell and to the L of this the mouthpiece of a speaking tube.*

The setting visualises the two clashing yet connected themes: class polarity coupled with sexual attraction. The stage is split both vertically and horizontally into a light exterior above-upstage (the domain of the masters) and a shaded interior below-downstage (the domain of the servants). There is also a contrast between the simple pine of the servants' table and the noble Lombardy poplars in the garden. At the same time, there is a link between the lilacs on the kitchen table and the lilac bushes outside, suggesting not only that the servants steal from their masters but also that the two groups share the same sexual needs (lilacs as aphrodisiacs). The combination of Cupid, lilacs and phallic-shaped poplars speaks for itself.

To a Swede, the birch leaves in the kitchen indicate that it is Midsummer, Midsummer Eve being the one day in the year when "all rank is laid aside," when masters and servants come together – and when drinking and love-making are carnivalesque.

Especially toward the end of the play, the unity of place receives thematic significance. As Julie sees all possibilities to escape thwarted, the kitchen is turned into a prison from which there is only one release: death.[2]

If the Swedish two-hour production, directed by Keve Hjelm, seems cinematic by being shot on location, it is theatrical in barely taking the spectator outside the prescribed kitchen. Obviously referring to Alf Sjöberg's prize-winning film adaptation of the play, Hjelm declared that he did not believe in "cinematic escapes." The action should be kept inside the kitchen, he said, or the concentration is lost.[3] Shot in an authentic seventeenth century environment – Löfstad castle, far to the south of Stockholm – Hjelm's kitchen is a large, white-washed room with adjoining dining room for the servants; even Jean's room can be seen in the background. A significant departure from the play text is that the spatial high-low dichotomy is missing, even reversed. Hjelm's kitchen is located upstairs. When Julie first enters the kitchen, we see her along with Jean from the window above the entrance. The choice of an authentic location apparently forced the director to sacrifice a visual aspect of the thematically important class struggle. Since it is a very spacious, light and neat kitchen, and since the glimpses we get of the park outside are extremely brief, there is no significant contrast, as in the text, between interior and exterior.

Both the need to set himself off against the film and the desire to concentrate may account for the fact that even the "Ballet," separating the pre-coital from the post-coital part of the play, is excluded. Along with Jean and Julie we merely see, through one of the kitchen windows, how the people are approaching. Then the picture of them is frozen for a few seconds. In the next shot Julie enters the kitchen from Jean's room. Like Strindberg's "Ballet," the frozen picture, much like a curtain, serves to indicate that time is passing – while the inclusion of a clock in the kitchen, showing 9 p.m. in the beginning and 2.30 a.m. after the intercourse, pinpoints the fact that the screen time does not coincide with the illuded time.

In the stage-based South African version of *Miss Julie*, directed by Bobby Heaney, the play is relocated from Sweden a hundred years ago to contemporary South Africa. Shot on location, like Hjelm's version, the performance visualises a Boer plantation, where Julie, the white daughter of the owner, has sexual intercourse with the black servant John on New Year's Eve. Like

Hjelm, Heany does not emphasise the spatial high-low dichotomy mirror-ing the social stratification. But unlike him, he resorts to "cinematic es-capes" to the exterior surroundings of the manor house, in the wake of Sjöberg's film. His handling of these sequences, unlike Sjöberg's, is heavy-handed, suggesting that what is fit for the big screen is not necessarily suit-able for the small one.

While Strindberg's Jean has learned his refined manners by going to the theatre, John has learned his by watching television. When he and Julie, mo-mentarily, contemplate escaping together since "there will always be barri-ers between us as long as we remain in South Africa," John suggests they go to Mozambique. But by the time Julie's father returns – by car, we only see his legs as he is stepping out of it and walking up the stairs inside the house – this plan has already been given up.

Heaney's version is above all an interesting example of how the theme of class struggle that has lost much of its impact in most western countries, can become a burning issue when coupled with racial segregation. In the South Africa of the 1980s, the transposition from social to racial segregation, using black rather than white actors for the roles of the servants,[4] must have seemed urgent. Only in this way could the play be truly provocative. In Heany's version, the racial conflict stands central, and the servants have here more stature and gain more sympathy than is usually the case. In Julie's line, "It must be terrible to be poor," the last word is replaced by "black." John fears what will happen "if a white woman is seen drinking with a black man." And Christine tells John that he is "all right for us black people." On the other hand, in Julie's climactic diatribe against Jean – "I'd like to see your whole sex swimming in a sea of blood" – "sex" is not re-placed by "race."

Released at a time when apartheid was still in force in South Africa, the presentation of the play was shocking to many South African viewers, aware that in *their* country Julie's intercourse with John was a crime for which you could be taken to court.

Instead of visualising the environment around the kitchen, Hjelm shows us almost every part of the kitchen itself in two sequences which are contrastingly related to one another. The first one coincides with Julie's en-trance. As one critic observed:

> In the beginning the cameras walked around the marble column in the middle. They caught hold of a mortar, boots, lilacs, fire-wood bin, stove. They seemed as curious as alien, gentle eyes and registered reality, while they did not seem to take an interest in finding a totality.
>
> In the same nervous and fractured fashion Miss Julie must have experienced this reality [...].[5]

The second sequence occurs when Kristin is left alone. Hjelm turns her pan-tomime into an exceedingly long sequence, in accordance with the author's assurance in the preface that Kristin "does not hurry as if she were afraid the audience would become impatient." We follow Kristin as she is pouring water into a copper kettle, washing up, drying dishes, putting a wine glass on the table. Moreover, we share her visual point of view as the camera pans around the kitchen, picking up the corkscrew, the mortar, the boots, the speaking tube, the bell, the window, the fire-wood bin, the ice box. This is Kristin's world, where there is much to be attended to.

Once we see the connection between the two sequences, we realise why the first is erratic, fragmentary, whereas the second is exceedingly slow, ca-ressing the various objects, as it were. Two contrasting characters, two tem-peraments are reflected in these camera movements, one belonging in the kitchen, the other an outsider.

Strindberg's characters are of different ages. In the list of dramatis perso-nae it says that Miss Julie is 25, Jean 30 and Kristin 35. Jean is, in other words, not only socially but also agewise placed between the two women. Hjelm's characters, on the other hand, seem to be of much the same age. With him, a beautiful blond Julie is pitted against an attractive, blond Kristin. The cook's plaited hair-knot has its noble counterpart in Julie's plaited 'crown.' Be-tween these Nordic types we find a fiery Jean, black-haired, black-eyed, black-moustached, presumably as attractive to the female part of the audi-ence as Julie is to the male part of it. In a play where the sympathies seem fairly evenly distributed between these two, Hjelm has obviously found it significant that this distribution is reflected also in the outward appearance of the characters.

This does not, as one might think, mean that Hjelm is paying extreme at-tention to the faces of the characters. Around 1970 it was normal in Sweden that about 70 percent of the shots in a TV play were in close-up or medium close-up. Hjelm reduced this figure in his *Miss Julie* production to about 50 percent. In this way more attention could be paid to the bodies, so that the erotic charge of the play could be transmitted.

Heany visually strengthens the social bond between John and Christine vis-à-vis the white, blond and blue-eyed Julie by casting black actors in these parts.

Strindberg gives few indications about the characters" costumes. Kristin wears in the beginning "*a light cotton dress and a kitchen apron,*" which she later takes off. At the end she appears "*dressed for church,*" "*carrying a psalm book in her hand.*" Jean first appears "*dressed in livery,*" later in "*a black frock coat and a black top hat.*" Toward the end Kristin, who wants to take him to church, provides him with "*a false shirt front and a white tie,*" which he finally exchanges for his livery when the Count addresses him via the speaking tube. Of Julie we merely learn that at the end she appears "*dressed for travelling and carrying a little bird cage.*"

Kristin's change from everyday costume to Sunday apparel indicates her changed attitude to Julie. Supported by her Christian faith, the cook suddenly sits in judgement of her mistress. Jean's change of costume indicates a circular development from servant to equal and back to servant. Whereas a director can find guidelines for these two, s/he must invent a costume for Julie when she first appears.

Much like Sjöberg's stage and film Julies, Hjelm's is dressed in an elegant long white dress with thin black borders, indicating both her – pretended? – innocence and her desire to "fall." Corresponding with her costume there are white lilacs on the kitchen table. At the end Julie puts on a blue velvet travelling dress. Blue for her romantic mind? Or her longing for heaven? Kristin combines these two colours in her white-and-blue checkered cotton dress. Jean wears a flashy red-and-black livery, stressing his fiery nature; the associations are with a nineteenth-century soldier or a matador.

Heaney initially dresses both Christine and John in neat but proletarian grey. By contrast, Julie first appears in an elegant and sensual black dress, a broad pearl collar around her neck. Contrasting with this aristocratic costume is her travelling dress at the end: a modest and everyday blue blouse, covered by a black leather jacket, and blue jeans. The jacket has the texture and lustre of human skin. Combined with John's white shirt, it contradicts the racial dichotomy applied by the surrounding society.

Like Strindberg, Hjelm opens the play with Jean entering the kitchen, where Kristin is standing by the stove. Carrying the Count's riding boots, Jean "*puts them down on the floor where we can see them,*" the text says. Reminding us of Jean's subordinate position in relation to the Count – we will soon see him brushing them – the boots above all indicate the Count's constant presence in the kitchen to the spectator and in the minds of the three characters. While this device is easy to realise in a stage version, it is largely lost in a TV presentation with its constantly changing images. Rather than respectfully putting the boots down, Hjelm's Jean throws them down. The camera then pans to the kitchen window and zooms in on the park outside. Dance music is heard. The credits announce: August Strindberg. There is an extreme frontal close-up of Jean, providing a link between the name of the author and the male character. Next a long shot of Jean in profile in his room, where the ominous bed can be seen. Jean leaves the room, enters the servants" dining room and stops before a picture of Oscar II, king of Sweden 1872-1907, serving both as an indication of the period in which the action takes place – the title is visualised together with this shot – and of Jean's concern with the aristocracy, his dream of a social career.[6] Jean continues into the kitchen, and the dialogue, which has been interrupted by the intermediate credit shots, is picked up.

In Heany's version, the shot succeeding the title frame shows the flames of an open hearth. At the same time we hear John state that "she's gone crazy again tonight." The visual image, suggesting that Julie is "on heat," corroborates his statement. Later Julie puts her hands so close to the open fire that she nearly burns herself. Strindberg's acting direction in the hypnosis sequence (see below) is turned into sexual imagery.

But John, too, is "on heat." When Christine lovingly touches his hair, he reacts strongly and tells her that he easily gets worked up. Hjelm's Jean reacts in the same way:

> KRISTIN. You're harder to please than the count when you're in the mood! *Pulls his hair affectionately.*
>
> JEAN *angry.* No, don't pull my hair! You know how sensitive I am.

Jean's reaction at this point, it has been said, reveals that he is sexually aroused by Julie, who is now on his mind.[7] The second time Jean enters the kitchen, after having danced with Julie, he exaggerates his irritation at her in order to oppose Kristin's understandable jealousy.

When Julie enters the kitchen the second time, Jean has just put his arm around Kristin's waist. The rivalry of the two women for the man is firmly established. Hjelm at this point has Jean and Kristin figure in the foreground, their backs turned to the camera, while Julie enters in the background between them. It is an effective demonstration not only of the triangular situation and of Julie's frailty compared with the sturdiness of the servants. It also illustrates her attempt to wedge herself into their relationship.

One of the most spectacular moments of the play is Jean's kissing of Julie's shoe. Unlike a stage production, a TV version can catch the kissing of the shoe in close-up. When preparing himself for the kiss, demanded by Julie, Hjelm's Jean looks as if he wishes to bite his mistress' foot rather than kiss her shoe, a clear expression of his class hatred. Moreover, the close-distance shots effectively set off Julie's attributes – the embroidered lace of her petticoat, her elegant shoe – against Jean's: the plain rag-rug on the kitchen floor.

As soon as Heany's Julie has arrived in the kitchen, she exposes her legs, pretending to fasten her shoe-buckles. She has John kiss her bare foot rather than her shoe. She repeatedly keeps her face close to his. Rarely raising her voice, she addresses him in a huskily seductive way. The sexual theme is more blatantly demonstrated than in Hjelm's and Strindberg's versions.

A further step in the seduction is the 'speck' scene:

They turn in the doorway. JEAN *is holding his hand to one of his eyes.*

JULIE. Let me see what you have in your eye!

JEAN. Oh, it's nothing – just a speck – it'll soon be gone.

JULIE. It was my sleeve that brushed against you; just sit down, and I'll help you. *Takes him by the arm and makes him sit down, takes hold of his head and tilts it back; with the tip of her handkerchief she tries to remove the speck.* Sit still, absolutely still! *Slaps his hand.* There! will you obey! – Why, I think you're trembling, you big strong man! *Feels his upper arm.* With arms like that!

JEAN *warningly*. Miss Julie!

JULIE. Yes, *monsieur* Jean?

JEAN. *Attention! Je ne suis qu'un homme!*

JULIE. Will you sit still! – There! Now it's gone! Kiss my hand and thank me!

The speck, whether invented or real, brings the two physically close to-gether for the first time. The sensuality of the scene is further increased when Hjelm has the camera for a moment tilt down to the abdomens of Jean and Julie and by having her take out a handkerchief from under her bra. Ex-treme close-ups of their faces further suggest the intimacy of the situation.

In the text, the intercourse takes place, offstage, in Jean's room next to the kitchen. The reason for this is, of course, that it would have been impossible in Strindberg's time to show the intercourse on the stage. But even if it had been possible, Strindberg might have opted for this solution, since it has the advantage that we do not know who eventually seduced whom, an uncer-tainty which is important in relation to Jean's and Julie's mutual reproaches after this event.

Unlike Hjelm who originally nourished plans of visualising the inter-course but eventually decided not to do so, Heany shows it at some length. We see how John and Julie, drawn to each other, begin to undress in his sim-ple room. The director then crosscuts between their intercourse – they retain most of their clothes – and the crowd of black servants approaching the kitchen. The orgastic groaning of the couple is intertwined with the ser-vants' singing of a dirty song about them. Heany makes it clear that no one seduces the other. The main reason for visualising the sequence, I take it, was to provoke the audience by showing sexual intercourse between a white woman and a black man.

When Julie and Jean, realising that they cannot stay in her father's house after what has happened between them, are about to leave to escape abroad, she brings the cage with the beloved greenfinch with her. Jean protests. When she says that she would rather have the bird killed than left behind, he brutally slaughters it. In a stage performance the slaughtering is usually done in such a way that the audience does not see the bird, only his gesture. Both Hjelm and Heany show the slaughtering of the bird, and in both cases we have the impression, whether true or not, that a real bird is being killed. Our identification with Julie's horror is thereby strengthened. Like Sjöberg, Hjelm indicates the greenfinch's metonymic relationship to Julie by showing it in close-up in front of her face just before it is killed. Heany replaces the greenfinch – alien to South Africa? – with a white dove. John's slaughtering of the bird, Julie's alter ego, is done in a very realistic way. Having stated that "There is blood between us now," Julie squeezes the blood out of the dead bird. We see her blood-stained hand, in close-up, approaching us. She then wipes the blood off on John's white shirt, a gesture marking him out as 'her' murderer. While the colour of Strindberg's and Hjelm's bird relates to Jean and, indirectly, to John the Baptist,[8] the colour of Heaney's bird suggests rather that it represents the white race that Julie is a member of. John's brutal slaughtering of it is in his version an expression of his racial aggression.

To make Julie's suicide credible, Strindberg found it necessary to have Jean hypnotise her. Julie clarifies her state of mind when she tells Jean

> *ecstatically.* I am already asleep – the whole room is like smoke around me ... and you look like an iron stove ... which resembles a man dressed in black, with a top hat – and your eyes glow like coals, when the fire is dying – and your face is a white patch, like ashes – *The sun's rays have now reached the floor and are shining on* JEAN. – It's so warm and good – *She rubs her hands as though warming them before a fire.* – and so bright – and so peaceful – !

What Strindberg had in mind, Sprinchorn argues, is that the spectator at this point "should be aware of nothing but a black, undefined object in the sun and the voice of the transported Julie."[9] Difficult to effectuate on the stage, this solution can easily be applied in a screen version. But neither Hjelm nor Heany opt for it.

Hjelm recreates Julie's vision of Death by showing her raised hands, fingers apart, in the foreground, while Jean, out of focus, is seen in the background. For a moment the viewer, in this shot of internal focalisation,[10] shares Julie's ecstatic point of view. This is true also of Heany's version, but rather than showing Jean's face as a "patch," it is shown from nearby, strongly backlit. The director is suggesting that Julie is blinded by the sun rising behind his head. Julie's imagery is omitted, and her monologue radically shortened to: "You're like a fire. It is warm, good, bright, peaceful."

The greatest problem of the play has always been the ending: Julie's suicide. As Edvard Brandes put it after having read the manuscript:

> You do not kill yourself, when there is no danger in sight, and here there is no danger.
> Perhaps 5 months from now [Brandes is alluding to Julie's possible pregnancy] but
> not this very night.[11]

The more aristocratic Julie is made, the greater is her decline, and the more
plausible seems the sense of guilt leading to the suicide. But to a modern audience, out of touch with the code of honour of the aristocracy of the past,
such a Julie would seem almost as alien as the nobleman – Strindberg's comparison in the preface – who demands a duel or the samurai who commits
harakiri when he has been insulted. With such a Julie we cannot easily identify ourselves.

If, on the other hand, the historical and social aspect is played down, if instead more general traits in her character are emphasised, Julie becomes
more relevant, more acceptable, more plausible to us – except in the ending.
For such a Julie certainly does not commit suicide on the grounds appearing
in the play.

A third possibility is to see Julie, less as an individual than as representing a drive within all of us – the death instinct – whereas Jean represents the
complementary life instinct. While such an allegorical reading of the play
does not seem to rhyme with Strindberg's naturalistic pretensions, it may
well seem meaningful to post-Freudian theatre-makers as a way of solving
the problem of the ending.[12]

In Hjelm's ending the grouping in the hypnosis sequence is reversed.
Part of Jean is now seen in profile in the foreground left, while Julie, turned
away, is seen in the background right in her blue travelling dress. For each
loud ring of the bell, Jean cringes as though struck by a whip. Unlike
Strindberg's servant, he never "*straightens up.*" Julie leaves the room without turning around, "*awake*" but not in a particularly "*determined*" way as
Strindberg would have it to secure the tragedy of the ending, tragedy im-
plying a voluntary choice on the part of the protagonist. Hjelm instead provides a remarkably impersonal, faceless ending, stressing the distance
between the cringing 'slave' in the foreground and the straight-backed no-
blewoman in the background. Jean's remark toward the end of the play that
the bell that brings Julie to her suicide "isn't only a bell – there's someone sitting behind it – a hand sets it in motion" is substantiated in the final frame,
where Jean's hand is shown in relative isolation in the foreground to indicate that it is not only *his* hand but also the Count's and, in the last instance,
the anonymous hand of society, or even of Fate, that is responsible for Julie's
tragic end.

In Heany's ending Julie and Jean exchange a tender kiss before she exits flashing a hunting knife. The knife was seen in an early close-up showing it slicing a cucumber. As in Strindberg's text, an everyday tool, in this case Christine's knife rather than Jean's razor, becomes a lethal one. The final shot shows John, in a gesture of revolt throwing the Count's riding boots on the ground much as Hjelm's Jean had done in the beginning of his performance.

Given the different social contexts at the receiving end – Swedes used to much more modest social and racial differences than South Africans – the sexual relationship between Hjelm's Jean and Julie necessarily seems much less dangerous to a Swedish audience than the one between Heany's John and Julie does to a South African one – even after the abolition of apartheid. Ironically, the social issue of the play, based as it is on a pronounced class society, is nowadays best retained in certain non-Swedish productions.

Some critics complained about the slow tempo of Hjelm's production, the playing time being about half an hour longer than what is normal on the stage – despite the elimination of the "Ballet" – and twice as long as Heany's version. But by and large the transmission was well received. A Danish critic even declared that "the Swedish TV production of this masterpiece made in a way an even greater impression than a stage production can effect."[13]

11 *The Stronger* (1890)

Strindberg's monodrama *The Stronger*, subtitled "A Scene," describes the random meeting of two actresses who are rivals for the same man (Bob).[1] The meeting takes place in a café on Christmas Eve. In the course of the short play, both the recipient and the single speaker, Mrs X, married to Bob, discover that the silent character, Miss Y, has been – and perhaps still is – Bob's mistress. Strindberg has designed the two ladies as professional parallels and as social contrasts. Mrs X is employed at the Grand Theatre, where Bob has an important position, and she has three children in her marriage with him. Miss Y is unmarried, has no children and is no longer employed at the house in question.[2]

Impressed by the French *quart d'heure* plays, Strindberg wrote *The Stronger* for the Scandinavian Experimental Theatre he was trying to launch at the end of the 1880s, and it is likely that he intended not only the part of Mrs X but also that of Miss Y for his own wife, the Finno-Swedish actress Siri von Essen. In performances in Sweden, Siri could play the speaking part, in performances in the other Scandinavian countries, she could do the silent one. More important than this practical consideration, perhaps, was the experimental nature of the play, which may well have been written to demonstrate that the monologue need not be excluded from naturalist drama. In the preface to *Miss Julie*, written only a few months before *The Stronger*, Strindberg notes:

> Our realists today condemn the monologue as implausible, but if I motivate it, I can make it plausible and use it to advantage.[3]

The criticism of the play text and of performances based on it has focussed on the question of how the title should be interpreted. Who is the stronger? Strindberg was himself divided on this issue. When commenting on the play in the Danish paper *Politiken* on January 24, 1889, that is, a few weeks after it was written and sixteen days before it was staged, he remarked that "the heroine does not say a word."[4] A few days before the opening of the play he gave his wife Siri, who was to play the first Mrs X, written instructions on how she should act the part. Mrs X, he now declared, is "the stronger, i.e. the softer. For the rigid person breaks, whereas the pliable one bends – and rises again."[5] Compare this to Mrs X's line close to the end of the play: "You couldn't learn from others, you couldn't bend – and therefore you broke like a dry reed – but I didn't!"

For a long time most critics have been inclined to link the title with the speaking character, Mrs X. But in more recent productions the silent Miss Y has frequently come over as the stronger person. At times the strength has been so evenly distributed between the two women that spectators could arrive at different conclusions.[6] It has even been suggested that the title refers, not to any of the women but to the absent man they are rivals for. In a Swedish production from the mid-1970s, clearly influenced by Per Olov Enquist's *The Night of the Tribades* (1975), a play based on *The Stronger*, this interpretation was turned upside down when the two women appeared to form a kind of sisterhood against the man they were competing for. One critic even went so far as to claim that the Miss Y of this much-praised production was silent because she dared not say what she wanted to say, namely that she was in love, not with Bob but with Mrs X. Underlying this lesbian version was the idea that the central and powerful position of the absent man in *The Stronger* is merely an expression of Strindberg's (male) wishful thinking, based on a fear that he (as a male) will be removed from the centre to the periphery by the females. As a result of this feminist reinterpretation, the relationship between the two women became exceedingly complex. In addition to being rivals for a man and for attractive roles at the playhouse he is running, they were shown to be sisters in need, both of them highly dependent on the same man, representing male society.

Having determined the question of strength, a director of *The Stronger* must, among other things, decide how to deal with Miss Y's silence, how to dramatise it. The handling of her muteness will by necessity depend on the overall interpretation of the play and of the relationship between the two women. What kind of silence is it? Is Miss Y mute because – to paraphrase Mrs X – she has nothing to say? Or is she mute because Mrs X's stream of words does not give her much chance to say anything? Is her refusal to speak an expression of her attempt to keep her relationship to Bob a secret to Mrs X, feeling that whatever she would say might reveal her? Does it express a hostile attitude to Mrs X or merely an honest one, something like: Why should I pretend that we are friends, when we know we are not? Is it perhaps motivated by a hope that Mrs X will get weary of her, Miss Y's, unresponsiveness and leave her in peace? Or is it a way of making Mrs X insecure? Is it a relaxed or a tense silence, a genuine silence or the silence of someone playing a part? There are certainly many possible explanations for Miss Y's silence. Some of them will give rise to more inspiring directorial solutions than others.

Once the director has decided on the significance of Miss Y's silence, s/he can proceed, together with the actress playing the part, to establish Miss Y's appearance (make-up, costume), gestures and mimicry. His/her choice of actress for the part is likely to be determined both by the actress' appearance and by her expressiveness. Whether we see Miss Y's influence on Mrs X as a result of hypnotic power or, more interestingly, of Mrs X's guilt feelings vis-à-vis her, Miss Y must have a strong radiance - or the performance will lose its balance and tension. This dramaturgic reason excludes to my mind the possibility that a performance of *The Stronger* in which the silent character comes over as the decidedly weaker of the two women can be successful.

Those who witnessed the first performance of *The Stronger* did not find that Strindberg had provided a credible motivation for Miss Y's *continuous* silence, which they found unnatural. In this respect the play was not a convincing *tranche de vie*. Today we may not value verisimilitude as highly as did the naturalists a century ago. Nevertheless, Miss Y's prolonged silence presents a problem to any stage director who decides to do the play realistically. Strindberg sensed this himself when he provided her with some stage business. The *"half-empty beer bottle"* in front of her – a pronounced masculine beverage – indicates that she will now and then take a sip, presumably not from the bottle but from the glass Strindberg took for granted or forgot to include in his stage directions.[7] She will also read *"an illustrated paper, which she exchanges for others from time to time."* When Mrs X, displaying the tulip-embroidered slippers she intends to give her husband as a Christmas present, ridicules his manner of walking and speaking, Miss Y laughs first *"aloud,"* then *"uproariously."* While Mrs X takes this as a sign that Miss Y is enjoying the little 'play' she is performing with the slippers, the sensitive recipient suspects that Miss Y is laughing because, being his mistress, she has often seen Bob in slippers. Moreover, as is later made clear, Miss Y, unlike Mrs X, is very fond of tulips.

Strindberg's rather sparse acting directions for Miss Y have usually been supplemented by others. She has, for example, been seen smoking a cigarette or, in Denmark where this is also a female custom, a whiff. She has been seen striking a match, lighting the cigarette / whiff, watching the match burn until it is extinguished, etc.[8] Such supplementary activities are hardly necessary in TV versions of the play, where the constant change of close-ups keep Miss Y offscreen much of the time, so that we are less aware of her unbroken silence. The verisimilitude is here, in other words, facilitated thanks to the medium.

Toward the end of the play, Mrs X tells her rival: "To judge from certain signs you have already lost him [Bob]." Her exit line reads: "Thank you for teaching my husband how to love! – Now I'm going home to love him!" Assuming that Mrs X is here speaking the truth, several critics have taken these lines at their face value and concluded that Mrs X departs triumphantly. However, there is no proof in the play text that she is right in her assumption that Bob has broken with Miss Y. On the contrary, there is reason to believe that her statement, far from being based on facts, is merely an expression of wishful thinking. Mrs X had earlier made it clear that she values her profession as an actress higher than her position as wife and mother. Her decision at the end to go home and (make) love (to) her husband - both meanings are suggested by the Swedish original - therefore seems based on the cynical consideration that this is the only way in which she can secure attractive parts for herself at the theatre. The relationship to Bob is primarily a means to reach the desired end. Whether the same holds true for Miss Y we do not know. A director must decide whether the two women in this respect are contrasts or parallels. When seen as contrasts, the compromising, down-to-earth Mrs X is pitted against the rigid, idealistic Miss Y - much the way Jean is pitted against Julie in *Miss Julie*. When seen as parallels, Mrs X's characterisation of Miss Y to a great extent applies to herself. If the play is performed in a very stylised fashion, Miss Y may even be seen as "a subjective character, a projection of Mrs X's fear of what might happen if her husband Bob would decide to leave her."[9] It is, however, doubtful whether such an abstract idea can be successfully transmitted to an audience.

In his text Strindberg not only prescribes near-silence for Miss Y. (As we have seen, he permits her to laugh a couple of times.) He also indicates several pauses, inserted mostly to make Mrs X's discoveries about her own position more credible.

Although intended for the stage *The Stronger* is, arguably, even better suited to television, where Miss Y's continuous silence, as we have already noted, seems less implausible,[10] and where her facial expressions, notably in close-ups, will suggest the thoughts and feelings of the silent character.

Let us now see how three TV directors have encoded the two parts in the play. The first two productions, directed by, respectively, Hans Dahlin and Gunnel Broström, were broadcast by Swedish television in 1960 and 1978, the first in black-and-white, the second in colour. Since Gunnel Broström plays the part of Mrs X in Hans Dahlin's production, there is an obvious link between the two performances. The third production, directed by the well-known Andrzej Wajda, was transmitted by Polish television in 1991. Wajda's version, even when we exclude the initial, added scene, is a little longer than the other two. The reason is that he makes more use of pauses than his Swedish colleagues. His Miss Y is also on-screen more frequently than Dahlin's and Broström's, and she is more in close-up. Both circumstances contribute to giving her more of a profile than her Swedish counterparts.

Dahlin's and Broström's versions adhere very closely to the play text. But because we deal with a TV rather than a stage production, the environment is not stylised as suggested by Strindberg but realistic. Both versions are set in an authentic-looking fin-de-siècle café, but whereas Dahlin's café is empty except for the two ladies – thereby underscoring Mrs X's opening line "How do you do, dear Amelie! – Here you're sitting alone on Christmas Eve, like a poor bachelor." - Broström settles for one half-filled with people.

In appearance both Dahlin's and Broström's women are striking contrasts. Their Mrs X is tall and blond, their Miss Y small and dark. In agreement with theatrical tradition, Dahlin's Mrs X wears a hat and dress of a slightly lighter and more feminine design than his Miss Y. Broström's Mrs X is grey-eyed and wears a green dress with a matching green hat. Her Miss Y is brown-eyed and wears a black dress with a matching black hat. In both performances, optimism and hope seem pitted against "mourning," life-affirmation against life-denial.

Both Dahlin's and Broström's Mrs X, though chatty, make a fairly balanced impression. They utter the final words of the play – "Thank you, Amelie, for all your good lessons. Thank you for teaching my husband how to love. Now I am going home – to love him." – in a rather triumphant way. Having overcome the shock the revelation of the husband's adultery a few minutes earlier caused them, they have recovered their initial calmness. Their behaviour demonstrates that Mrs X is indeed very flexible and in this sense the stronger woman.

But in his handling of Miss Y, Dahlin differs from Broström. Whereas her Miss Y shows little variation in mimicry – most of the time she looks merely sad – Dahlin's Miss Y reacts more noticeably and more variedly to Mrs X's monologue, for instance in the following passage:

> And then I know, you see, that he's faithful to me; yes, I know that! For he told me so himself ... what are you giggling at? ... that when I was touring in Norway that nasty Frédérique tried to seduce him – just imagine how infamous! *Pause.* [...] Luckily Bob told me about it himself so that I didn't have to hear it from others! *Pause.* But Frédérique wasn't the only one, you know!

Here the word "giggling" – or "grinning" (Strindberg's word "flina" covers both the more harmless and the more contemptuous meaning) – is an implicit acting direction for Miss Y, who knows that Bob is anything but "faithful" to his wife. Miss Y is triumphant at this point. But when Mrs X shortly afterwards informs her about Frédérique, Dahlin's Miss Y turns sour. Aware that Bob has lied to his wife about his relationship to her, Miss Y, there is no reason for her to believe that he has told his wife the truth about Frédérique. More clearly than Broström's, Dahlin's Miss Y, in other words, indicates that she suddenly realises that Bob has betrayed not only his wife but also his mistress, i.e. herself.

When, toward the end, Mrs X accuses Miss Y of making everything "worthless and sterile," Dahlin's Miss Y has a contemptuous smile on her lips, whereas Broström's shows a sorrowful, guilt-ridden face – as though her expression confirms the truth of Mrs X's accusation. Similarly, when Mrs X declares that Miss Y in all likelihood has lost Bob, Dahlin's Miss Y smiles ironically – signalling to the spectator that Mrs X is wrong in her assumption – whereas Broström's is rather noncommital. As a result of this difference in reactions on the part of Miss Y, we get the impression that whereas Dahlin settles for a balanced situation between the two women with regard to strength, Broström indicates that Mrs X is indeed right when she ascribes the role of the stronger to herself. As we shall see, Wajda opts for the opposite solution.

In Wajda's adaptation, where the time of transmission, Christmas Day, apparently was selected with a view to the time of the play, the setting is a coffee room next to a TV studio. The action is moved from the 1890s to the 1990s. And, as already indicated, it opens with a directorial addition. We witness how Mrs X in a very sugary sequence, sitting on a sleigh in a spangled, white-and-grey "gown," spangled white headgear and a snow-white muff, sings the Polish version of the German hymn "Stille Nacht, heilige Nacht," while soap bubbles representing snow flakes are falling around her.

The panning camera now and then includes a Christmas tree in the frame. Time and mood are established. What we witness here is a variation of the play-within-the-play. *We* see what, hypothetically, millions of Polish TV viewers would see at Christmas: literally soap for the masses. When the show is finished, the TV crew responsible for it is seen with their equipment. The singer takes off her white gown, revealing her ordinary clothes underneath it: a white blouse and black pants. The TV crew admiringly accompanies her away from the studio. She is obviously a star.

Suddenly she sees Miss Y sitting alone in the coffee room. She stops, sits down next to her and launches into her monologue, which Wajda cuts here and there. He omits, for example, Mrs X's rather literary metaphors, thereby making her less inventive but more realistically credible than Strindberg's character.

Unlike Dahlin's and Broström's couples, Wajda's Mrs X is very similar to his Miss Y. Both are of about the same height, blond, grey-eyed, dressed in black (Mrs X) and very dark blue (Miss Y), with almost identical white blouses.[11] It is as though Wajda has expanded upon Strindberg's idea that Mrs X has borrowed virtually everything from Miss Y. He turns the married woman into a replica of the unmarried one, suggesting perhaps that the man, Bob, is actually attracted to a synthesis of the two: the independent strength of Miss Y and the flexibility of Mrs X.

In the course of her monologue, Wajda's Mrs X becomes more and more highly strung, indicated not least by her smoking one cigarette after another. His Miss Y listens calmly, intently and not without sympathy to what Mrs X has to say. The situation is not unlike that of a therapist listening to a patient.

The final lines, preceded by a long pause, are spoken by a Mrs X who by now has collapsed and started crying. The facial expression of Miss Y at this point is an intriguing mixture of integrity, superiority and compassion. Their contrasting attitudes indicate, perhaps, that Bob has not broken with Miss Y and that Mrs X now recognises this. Her "Now I am going home – to love him," spoken in tears, is no more than a desperate attempt to convince herself that she can keep her husband, or get him back, in a deeper sense. A more satisfactory interpretation, to my mind, would be that Bob has indeed broken with Miss Y but that she, being the stronger woman, is able to cope with the situation, feeling some consolation, perhaps, in the fact that she has a fellow victim in Mrs X. As the latter exits to find a substitute for her husband in her lapdog and in the consolation from the people surrounding her, Miss Y shows her an enigmatic Mona-Lisa face with the shade of a triumphant smile around her mouth. After which she exits through a very long corridor – alone.

In retrospect we realise that the TV transmission opening Wajda's production is highly ironical. Not only does the show about a peaceful, harmonious Christmas form a stark contrast with Mrs X's desperate situation at the end. Confronted with Miss Y's complete silence, the words about a "still night," far from signifying a blessing, become a threat.

Unlike Dahlin and especially Broström, Wajda combines his many close-ups with a great number of pauses. As a result, he manages to illuminate the psyche of both women in a more penetrating way. While *their* versions remain quite theatrical – this is especially true of the way in which Dahlin's Mrs X expresses herself – *his* is televisual not only in its selected environment but also in demonstrating that, more than the stage, the screen can substitute mimicry for words. What is enunciated in Wajda's captivating presentation, for good reasons dedicated to Ingmar Bergman,[12] is merely a part of the screen drama. The rest is visual "imagery" made prominent through silence.

12 *A Dream Play* (1902)

Both with regard to play texts and play performances, we speak of various -isms, meaning sometimes a particular style, sometimes a particular period, usually both. But the fundamental choice for both playwrights and play directors is not whether to settle for naturalism, expressionism, absurdism or any other -ism of this kind. The fundamental choice with regard to stage performances is "whether the stage should be consciously preserved as a stage [...] or whether it should be presented as something that it is not."[1] The choice, in other words – also with regard to the screen – is between the two basic -isms: illusionism and non-illusionism.

This choice becomes especially problematic when we deal with a play which imitates the nocturnal dream to evoke the feeling that life is a dream – as is the case with *A Dream Play*. Shortly after he had completed the play, Strindberg, inspired by Plato and Schopenhauer, wrote in his diary that it is doubtful whether the world "exists at all – for it is really only a dream picture." In a note he added: "Consequently my Dream Play is a picture of life."[2] Viewed in this way, the much debated question of who is the dreamer of the play[3] – the author, the recipient, Indra or Indra's Daughter – can be answered quite simply. What Strindberg is presenting is a picture of life recognisable to anyone who shares his view that it is dreamlike.

Since the whole play is conceived as a simile, the fundamental question for a director is whether the dream aspect (the signifier) or the life aspect (the signified) should be stressed. If the dream aspect is overly emphasised, we end up with distortion of what we normally call reality. If the life aspect is overly emphasised, the dreamlike feeling – life experienced as unreal – is weakened. The stage history of *A Dream Play* demonstrates how directors have struggled to find a balance between these two extremes.[4] Generally speaking, we may discern a German tradition, in the wake of Max Reinhardt's famous 1921 production, stressing the dream aspect and a Swedish tradition, following Olof Molander's equally famous 1935 production, stressing the life aspect. Reinhardt sought to recreate an inner reality. Molander strove to find a balance between outer and inner reality. Reinhardt's approach may be termed 'expressionism,' Molander's 'semi-realism' – in agreement with Strindberg's own term "half-reality."[5]

In *A Dream Play* human life is described as a constant oscillation between hope and fulfillment, illusion and disillusion. The characters, synecdochically representing mankind, are in this sense all "such stuff as dreams are made on."[6] Their hope, usually expressed in the form of endless waiting for something better, is always thwarted. The only hope that ulti-

mately remains is the hope that this life is but a dream and that death signifies the awakening to a better existence.

The slender story line, patterned on the life of Christ, is exceedingly simple. Indra's Daughter descends to (the Castle of) Earth, where she is reincar-
nated as the Glazier's daughter with the 'Christian' name of Agnes.[7]
Gradually, she is made aware of human misery. The nadir is reached when
she experiences the most intimate kind of human relationships, marriage, as
an imprisonment. She now longs for freedom and prepares for her return to
her Father in heaven. At the end we witness her death-by-fire when she enters the burning castle, a symbolic ascension.

As a character-narrator, that is, "both mediator and object of our vision,"[8]
the Daughter is an unusual protagonist – especially in view of her divine origin. Unlike the traditional outsider, she is more knowledgeable than the
people she is visiting. She can see a meaning in their suffering – even if she
cannot explain it, since her explanation would be incomprehensible to
them.

As Szondi has noted, the Daughter's "epic separation from mankind" –
and we may here think both of the people on the stage and in the auditorium – is indicated by the alienating third-person form of her recurrent "det
är synd om människorna,"[9] a phrase meaning not only "human beings are
pitiful" but also "human beings are sinful" – a fundamental ambiguity necessarily lost in translation.[10] In the course of the play, on the basis of the
Daughter's earthly experience, the emphasis is transferred from the former
to the latter meaning.

The dreamlike nature of the play is mirrored in the outward structure.
The traditional division into acts and scenes is lacking; nor is there any list of
dramatis personae. Scenes and sequences are indicated only by means of
blank spaces or asterisks. In the ms. notes, however, the play, here called
"The Growing Castle," is divided into three acts and fourteen scenes:

Act I	Scene	1	Outside the castle I.
		2	The Officer's room in the castle.
		3	The Mother's room.
		4	The theatre corridor I.
		5	The Lawyer's office.
		6	The church.
		7	Fingal's Cave I.

II	8	The Lawyer's home.
	9	Foulstrand.
	10	Fairhaven.
	11	By the Mediterranean.

III	12	Fingal's Cave II.
	13	The theatre corridor II.
	14	Outside the castle II.

The Prologue, describing the Daughter's descent to Earth, is still lacking in the first edition of the play. As a result she appears as totally human in the first scene. But already in the following scene, the reputation of her divine status has spread:

> MOTHER. Oh, it's Agnes? You know what they say? ... That she's the god Indra's daughter, who has asked to come down to earth to feel what human life is really like ...

Being a play about the plight of mankind, the settings for *A Dream Play* are not geographically specified. (Scene 11, usually referred to as the Coalheaver scene and often omitted in production, is in this respect the only exception.) Yet in Molander's many productions of the play, highly important for Ingmar Bergman, most of them were given a definite Swedish *couleur locale*. However, in his Swedish TV production of the play, from 1963, Bergman, like Strindberg, on the whole abstains from geographically localised settings.

It may seem surprising that Bergman's first performance of *A Dream Play* – he has produced it four times – was done, not for the stage but for TV. With its many scenes and thirty-six actors and actresses, it differs from all the other plays in this book in its 'Shakespearean' size and may in that respect seem unsuited for the small screen. Bergman's performance of this play was indeed the largest production undertaken so far by Swedish television.[11] On the other hand, the dreamlike quality of the play seems better suited to the screen than the stage. "No Swedish drama of supreme dignity," it was said in response to the performance,

> can be better suited to the special possibilities offered by television. The play should flow on like the dream itself, where the scenery changes enigmatically. Ingmar Berg-

man applied this device. We did not notice when we moved from the theatre corridor to the Lawyer's office.[12]

Indeed, one of the problems when staging *A Dream Play* is how to make the scene shifts swift and smooth. In that respect a film or TV version can suggest the dream quality of the play much more convincingly than a stage version.

As in his later productions of *A Dream Play*, Bergman omits Strindberg's *Prolog im Himmel*, which he dislikes because "it destroys the strange, bizarre self-evidence of the play opening."[13] By this he presumably means that the dreamy, fairy-tale quality of the play must affect us from the very beginning. The Prologue does not have that quality.[14] Taking his cue from the play's reference to the Poet as "a dreamer," Bergman replaces the objective, supernatural aspect of the play – the Daughter's descent to and ascent from Earth – by the subjective idea that the whole play is a dream dreamt by its author, Strindberg.[15] Strindberg's *Dream Play* opens, after the Prologue, with a scene representing an earthly paradise:

> *The backdrop represents a forest of gigantic hollyhocks in bloom; white, pink, purple, sulphur yellow, violet; over their tops can be seen the gilded roof of a castle with a flower bud resembling a crown uppermost. Beneath the foundation walls of the castle, heaps of straw are spread out covering cleaned-out stable litter.*

Along with Indra's Daughter, just born into life, and the Glazier, her earthly father, we see the growing castle, symbol of Life, surrounded by the colourful variety characteristic of life. But the beautiful flowers are rooted in – draw their life from – manure, just as human souls cannot exist in life without bodies. One colour is lacking: the heavenly blue. At the end of the play, when the Daughter is ready to return to her celestial domicile, we find

> *the same scenery as in the first tableau. But the ground at the foot of the castle is now covered with flowers (Blue monkshood, Aconite).*

The celestial blue has replaced the initial variety of colours. Paradise has been relocated from earth to heaven.

The first speeches of the play proper concern the castle:

> DAUGHTER. The castle's still growing out of the earth ... Do you see how much it has grown since last year?

> GLAZIER *to himself.* I've never seen that castle before ... have never heard that a castle grows ... but – *To the* DAUGHTER *with firm conviction.* Yes, it has grown two ells, but that's because they've manured it ... and if you look, you'll see that a wing has shot out on the sunny side.

This is at once fairy tale and dream. Like Christ, the Prologue has informed us, the Daughter has descended to Earth, to be reborn there as a child of man. As a divine creature and a child, she is not someone we can easily identify with. It is rather the grown-up Glazier who in the opening scene fulfils this function. Like him, we have never heard that a castle can grow.[16] And we understand him when he benevolently plays into the hands of the Daughter. The dialogue continues:

> DAUGHTER. [...] Tell me, father, why do flowers grow out of dirt?

The choice of "dirt" is striking. The word, emphasised by the Daughter, has a negative ring. The Glazier answers her question in a surprising way:

> GLAZIER *devoutly*. They don't thrive in dirt, and so they hurry as fast as they can up into the light to bloom and die!

This is a poetical, metaphoric answer pointing, as the paralinguistic acting direction indicates, in a religious direction. Interestingly, the Glazier answers the Daughter as though her question had been differently phrased, with an emphasis on the dynamic verb "grow" rather than on the static noun "dirt." We tend to think of flowers as static. Here they become dynamic. The reason is, of course, that metaphorically they stand for human beings. *We* are the ones who do not thrive in sinful life on Earth, who long for light and purity beyond life. The basic theme of the play is intoned in this imagery. More specifically we witness, in the course of it, how the Daughter grows up until, at the end, she is ready "to bloom and die," to return to heaven.

Bergman's TV version opens with white text – "Ett drömspel af August Strindberg" (A Dream Play by August Strindberg) in the playwright's own handwriting – on a black background. In the next shot we get a quotation from Strindberg's "Explanatory Note" to the play superimposed on the face of the author. In this first shot, containing the statement that "one consciousness remains above all of them [the characters]: the dreamer's," the director makes it clear that Strindberg is the dreamer of the black-and-white "dream" we are about to see.

Strindberg's face dissolves into a cloud. Out of this cloud Indra's Daughter emerges. We see her approaching a barred something in the foreground. Since we, as spectators, are found on this side of the bars, the impression communicated is that *we* are inside a prison. This is in agreement with the central idea of the play that all mankind is imprisoned in life – and that the Daughter, the Christ figure, has come to set us free. In this way Bergman draws us into the action, breaks down the barrier between screen and offscreen, creates a *theatrum mundi*. These initial shots are accompanied by music – a mixture of harmonies and disharmonies – ending with what sounds like a knell as the Daughter opens the gate and enters the Prison of Life. Bergman's Daughter is significantly blond, 'haloed,' and she wears a white, high-collared dress, indicating her pure, innocent, divine nature.

Bergman thus immediately clarifies that his performance is not an objective, divine report about the sad state of mankind but a subjective experience of life on the part of the author, whose alter ego in the play, we later discover, is the Poet. This is indicated especially at the end, where the Poet enters a cloud which dissolves into an extreme close-up of Strindberg's face. The creator of the world, Indra, is replaced by the creator of the play, Strindberg, whose face frames the performance. However, by opening the play with a *theatrum mundi* effect which makes the viewer part of the action, Bergman provides a link between the author and the audience. Strindberg becomes a *pars pro toto* for mankind. His 'dream' becomes our 'dream.'

Returning to the opening scene, we note that Bergman abstains from a direct view of the castle and, since his version is in black-and-white, omits the flowers and the colour symbolism they represent. Bergman's Glazier, a 'prisoner' in his striped shirt, in accordance with his profession carries a huge window-pane on his back in which the castle that he and the Daughter are watching is reflected, so that we, too, can see it. The *theatrum mundi* idea is maintained. *We* see what *they* see – with a difference. Since the castle *we* see is a reflection, we see merely "through a glass darkly" (1 Cor. 13.12), to quote a well-known Bergman film title. In this way the Daughter's Platonic remark later in the play that "the world, life and human beings are [...] only phantoms, appearances, visions" is visually underscored. Moreover, this arrangement enables us to see the faces of the two characters, their reactions to what they are watching – a situation that is difficult to handle in the theatre when the castle, as Strindberg suggests, is placed upstage, so that the characters must turn away from the audience when looking at it. As always with Bergman, it is not the object seen that is important but the reaction to it, as reflected in the human face.

The prison imagery is retained in Scene 2, where the Daughter telling the Officer that he is "a prisoner" in his rooms is visualised in the form of huge shadows on the wall behind him of what is obviously a barred window.

The transition to Scene 3 is indicated as follows by Strindberg:

Voices are now heard from behind the screen, which is immediately drawn aside. The OFFICER *and the* DAUGHTER *look in that direction, then freeze their gestures and expressions.*

In Bergman's TV version this transition is done more smoothly. The Daughter consolingly puts her hand on the Officer's shoulder. As the offscreen voices of his parents are heard, he turns his face, now lit up and in close-up, to the camera. There is a dissolve, indicating that we are sharing his memory, to a medium two-shot of his Father and Mother, both dressed in black and sitting together in a sofa. After a close-up of them, his face frontal, hers in profile, asking forgiveness of each other, Bergman tilts down to their hands which, their wedding rings clearly visible, 'embrace' each other. This image of communion and good intentions is immediately upset when the Mother wants to give the silk scarf she has received from her husband to their servant. The scene ends with the Mother putting her hand on the Officer's shoulder, as the Daughter had done earlier.

One of the most obvious dream effects in the play is Strindberg's use of a technique related to the cinematic dissolve. Several of the decor elements in Scene 4 (Theatre corridor) return in new configurations in Scenes 5 (Lawyer's office) and 6 (Church). The most important of these elements is the *"door with an air hole in the shape of a four-leaf clover."* In the Theatre corridor it is an enigmatic door:

> OFFICER. [...] I've looked at that door two thousand five hundred and fifty-five times without understanding where it leads to! And that clover leaf that is to let in light ... for whom is it to let in light? Is there anyone inside? Does anyone live there?
>
> DOORKEEPER. I don't know. I've never seen it opened ...
>
> OFFICER. It looks like a pantry door I saw when I was four [...] the pantries were always in the entrance with bored round holes and a clover leaf!

In the Lawyer's office the door is *"part of a cupboard containing documents."* In the church it is a door that *"leads into the sacristy."*

In all cases, the door is the entrance to a private, secret room. When the door in the Theatre corridor is eventually opened, the representatives of humanity all declare that there is "nothing" behind it. But the divine Daughter indicates that they are unable to comprehend what this "nothing" signifies.[17]

The enigmatic door is clearly a door separating this life from what comes after it. This explains why the representatives of mankind are unable to see anything behind it. Along with the Officer they can only hope that it is a pantry door hiding something good, that there will be pie in the sky by and by. The holes in the door, which provide light and air, enable us to breathe in this vale of tears and give us hope for a better hereafter. The four-leaf clover, which promises fortune, has its counterpart in the Officer's waiting for Victoria, for victory, success. But just as his red roses are doomed to whither until only the thorny stems remain, so the four-leaf clover is 'transformed' into a cross in the Church scene.[18] The search for happiness in this life gives way to the awareness that suffering is the meaning of life.

This symbolism is continued when the self-occupied Officer, who has done nothing to deserve a doctor's degree, is crowned in the Church scene with the academic laurel, symbol of victorious achievement, whereas the altruistic Lawyer, who has devoted his entire life to helping his fellow-men, is denied it. Recognising the Lawyer's vicarious role, the Daughter places a wreath that is "more becoming" to him on his head: *a crown of thorns.*"

Bergman introduces the Church scene with a shot of the crucified Christ. As Chopin's *Funeral March* is intoned,[19] the academic procession passes under the crucifix. Between two rows of men, in tails and Swedish doctor's hats, the newly laureated Officer and Schoolmaster return to their places, while the Lawyer, facing the camera, is approaching the laurel wreath held up to him by two anonymous hands in the foreground. From his fumbling with his braces, we conclude that he is afraid of dropping his trousers – a nightmarish addition by Bergman. When he approaches the laurel wreath he begins to smile hopefully. Suddenly the wreath is lowered. The music stops and is replaced by the tolling of bells. There is an extreme close-up of the Lawyer's suffering face, his glance turning down. We then see him in a long shot by the organ with his back turned to us, as if he is put in the corner. The Daughter comes up to him and places the crown of thorns on his head.

Even more than Strindberg, Bergman counterpoints the academic ceremony and what it represents – the celebration of science – with religious signifiers standing for very different values.[20]

In Scene 8 (The Lawyer's home) the Lawyer and the Daughter experience the agonies of marriage. A hairpin, discovered on the floor, becomes a metaphor for marital relations:

> LAWYER. [...] It has two prongs but is one pin!
>
> There are two, but it's one! If I straighten it out, it is one single piece! If I bend it, there are two without ceasing to be one. That means: the two are one! But if I break it – here! Then the two are two! *Breaks the hairpin and throws the pieces away.*

When he was young, Bergman saw one of Molander's productions of *A Dream Play*. The hairpin sequence made an indelible impression on him:

> It was the first time I had experienced the magic of acting. The Advocate held a hairpin between his thumb and forefinger, he twisted it, straightened it out and broke it. *There was no hairpin, but I saw it.*[21]

However, what is magic on the stage is not necessarily magic in a close-up medium. In Bergman's TV version the hairpin, because it is seen at close distance, is very real.

At the end of Scene 9 (Foulstrand), visualising life as purgatory and inferno, various characters voice their suffering. The scene ends as follows:

OFFICER. We are to be pitied – all of us!

ALL *raise their hands toward heaven and utter a cry of pain resembling a dissonant chord.*
Oh!

DAUGHTER. Eternal One, hear them! Life is evil! Human beings are to be pitied!

ALL *cry out as before.* Oh!

Bergman abstains from this collective expression of suffering. The dissonant vocal chord is replaced by dissonant music accompanying a sequence
of close-ups of the characters who have earlier voiced their torment:

CU of OFFICER *looking L.* We are to be pitied – *With a deep sigh.* all of us. *Dissolve to*

CU of DAUGHTER *frontal. Quick pan to*

CU of POET *frontal. Dissolve to*

CU of OFFICER *looking R. Dissolve to*

CU of SHE *frontal. Pan L up to*

CU of HE *frontal. Dissolve to*

CU of QUARANTINE MASTER, *his hand to his blackened face, flames behind him. Dissolve to*

CU of PENSIONER. *Dissolve to*

ECU of DAUGHTER, *in misty light, her lit eyes looking upwards.* Eternal God, hear them.
Life is evil. Human beings are to be pitied.

All of the faces, except the last, are shaded, more or less – a visual indication
that mankind is not only pitiable but also sinful. The use of dissolves and
pans, rather than cuts, increases the feeling of a common plight. Significantly, the Daughter is shown twice, first as one of the group of human
beings, then as a divine figure.

Strindberg's Foulstrand, in the foreground, includes a view of its paradisaical opposite, Fairhaven, in the background:

*The back of the stage is a beautiful shore with trees in foliage, piers decorated with flags to
which white boats are moored; some with sails hoisted, others not. Small Italian villas, pavil-
ions, kiosks, marble statues can be seen among the foliage.*

It is as though part of the torment of those who dwell in Foulstrand consists
in having Paradise within reach without being able to get there – an extreme
version of the play's leitmotif of frustration.

Strindberg's distant shore would obviously not be visible on the small
screen. Instead, Bergman shows us a screen-filling picture of the lovely

shore with the text "Fairhaven" underneath, so that we realise that it is a photo. When the photo is lowered, we discover that it is part of a newspaper called *The Morning*. Behind it we see the blackened – sinful – face of the Quarantine Master. By showing Fairhaven in front (the photo) and "Foulstrand" behind it (the blackened face), Bergman reverses Strindberg's arrangement – while retaining its meaning: the longing of those who suffer for another, better existence when we awaken, in "the morning" from the nightmare of life.

In Scene 11 (By the Mediterranean), Strindberg forcefully pits against each other the most extreme example in the play of (social) injustice, the Coalheavers' slavery, and the sanctioning of this injustice:

> DAUGHTER. Hasn't anyone thought there are secret reasons why it [life] should be as it is?

The scene opens:

> To the L in the FG can be seen a white wall, over which fruit-bearing orange trees stick out. At the back, villas and a casino with a terrace. To the R, a large pile of coal with two wheelbarrows. At the back to the R, a strip of the blue sea.
>
> Two COALHEAVERS, naked to the waist, black on their faces, on their hands, and on the other exposed parts of their bodies, are sitting in despair, each on a wheelbarrow. The DAUGHTER and the LAWYER appear at the back.
>
> DAUGHTER. This is paradise!
>
> FIRST COALHEAVER. This is hell!

As the stage directions indicate, "paradise" is placed downstage left and upstage, "hell" downstage right. When the Daughter enters, she sees only the lovely part of the setting left. The First Coalheaver's protesting remark could be addressed either to the Daughter or to his fellow sufferer, the Second Coalheaver.

Bergman opens the scene by showing a group of rich, leisurely people, all dressed in white, in Fairhaven. The faces of the Daughter left and the Lawyer right, both in profile, move into the screen in the foreground, so that the attractive background motivates her smiling remark about paradise. Both of them are dressed elegantly, making them part of paradisaical Fairhaven. As the camera tracks out, vertical bars appear in the foreground. The Daughter turns her head to a frontal position. There is a cut to the two Coalheavers behind the bars, dressed in dirty clothes and with sacks covering their heads. The First Coalheaver addresses his mate: "This is hell."

We notice how Bergman, while shrinking the space to fit the small screen, places the Coalheavers behind bars. Within the Prison of Life, where everyone is doomed to dwell, there is a second prison for the proletariat. Bergman omits the Daughter's sanctioning of the injustices in life and instead makes her side with the socially suppressed. Strindberg ends the scene:

> DAUGHTER *covers her face and leaves*. This is not paradise!
>
> COALHEAVERS. No, it's hell, that's what it is!

In Bergman's version this becomes:

> *ECU* DAUGHTER *frontal*. This is not paradise.
>
> *MCU* FIRST COALHEAVER. No, it's hell. That's what it is.
>
> *ECU* DAUGHTER *frontal, tears running down her cheeks*.
>
> *CU* SECOND COALHEAVER, *slow fade-out*.

Bergman's concern for sound appears most notably in Scene 12 (Fingal's Cave II). From inside the cave, the Daughter and the Poet watch a ship in distress. The crew, hoping to be saved, sing a "Christ Kyrie":

> POET. Now they're calling [...]! But no one hears!

Ironically, when the crew see Christ walking on the water, they scream "out of fear of their saviour." The Poet, indicating that the crew about to be shipwrecked represents humanity, remarks: "Scream when they're born, and scream when they die!" From beginning to end, life is suffering.

While Strindberg, as the acting directions indicate, has the crew scream, Bergman opts for muteness. We see the crew screaming, but we do not hear them.[22] In this way we, the TV audience, are meaningfully included in the Poet's remark that no one hears. We too turn, as it were, a deaf ear to the crew's, our fellow-men's, suffering – as we have done earlier to Ugly Edith when she, in utmost despair, voices a mute scream.

A Dream Play, it is often said, is more cinematic than theatrical. It is true that the screen media enable us to move freely in time and space. The problem of how to create smooth scene shifts, so that the sequence of scenes is experienced as a series of dreamlike images, is here no problem at all – whether the director settles for abrupt changes, cuts, or gradual changes, pans, tilts or dissolves. On the other hand, the mythical or parabolic quality of the play lends itself much better to the stage. With its fifty to sixty characters – Strindberg needed that many to describe the plight of mankind – and with its symbolically significant scenery, the play is hardly suited to the close-up-oriented small screen. And contrary to what might be imagined, even the dreamlike atmosphere is in danger of being lost there:

He who has seen [...] Bergman's own [performance] at the Royal Dramatic Theatre in 1970 could certify that the dreamy quality was managed better on the stage. Why? Was it because colour television had not yet started in Sweden? Or because the many close-ups of faces reduced the possibilities for suggestion via the stage design? Because the electronic cameras demanded so much light that it was difficult to create chiaroscuro? Or because cameras create such sharp images?[23]

To this we may add the most important difference between the stage and the screen. With its confrontation of live actors with a live audience, the stage can, as the screen cannot, create a sense of communion, of sharing something. When this something, as in the case of *A Dream Play*, has to do with the fundamental questions of life, this feeling of communion is all the more important.

Aware of the fact that the stage is able to create a sense of *theatrum mundi* much better than the screen, Bergman chose to accept the limitations of the TV medium and make use of its possibilities. Rather than express, parabolically and directly, humanity's experience of life, his version expresses one individual's, the author's, experience of it. It is questionable whether Bergman in this way creates a convincing *pars pro toto*: Strindberg as a representative of mankind. Rather, he seems to make a statement about his own affinity to Strindberg's view of the world as an illusion, a phantom, a dream image.

13 *Thunder in the Air* (1907)

In 1960 Ingmar Bergman launched his first TV production of a Strindberg play. He chose the chamber play *Thunder in the Air*.[1] The transmission, which took place on 22 January, Strindberg's birthday, and which was simultaneously broadcast to the neighbouring countries, met with great enthusiasm. A Danish critic called it a milestone in the history of the teleplay and even went so far as to claim that not until now, when shown on the small screen, had Strindberg's chamber play fully come into its own.[2]

Eighteen years later the play was again transmitted by Swedish Television, this time directed by Göran Graffman. In the following we shall examine these two productions in relation to the text, the first in black-and-white, the second in colour.

The protagonist in *Thunder in the Air* is an old gentleman with an unhappy marriage behind him. Preparing himself for the final rest, he longs for "the peace of old age." He imagines that he has reached a stage in life where loneliness, as a preparation for the ultimate loneliness, can be calmly accepted. He lives in an apartment house, surrounded by other people. And he has a housekeeper, a young relative, who seems to function as a substitute wife. In short, he leads a life bordering on that of a hermit, a choice indicative of his vacillating attitude to loneliness and togetherness. His habit of strolling "along a broad, tree-lined avenue" is another indication that he cherishes a *flaneur* existence of observation, of non-involvement.

The nameless Gentleman is self-centred and highly subjective. Yet Strindberg disguises this initially by having us share his point of view. For a long time we tend to side with the Gentleman against his wife Gerda – until we discover that he gives controversial reasons for his divorce from her. It is only after we have come to doubt his judgement that Strindberg has the Brother, his closest friend, reveal that neither Gerda nor her new husband, Fischer, are as wretched as the Gentleman would have himself believe. Eventually, the Brother remarks: "You only see things from your viewpoint." Suddenly, we realise that the Gentleman has been an unreliable narrator of his own life story. And that Strindberg has deliberately structured his play in such a way that he is not seen at close range by the recipient until fairly late, at which time his mask of friendliness has dropped, and he reveals his bottled-up aggression toward his fellow-men.[3]

Set on an August evening shortly before the gaslamps are lit, *Thunder in the Air* introduces us to a twilight world – whether we think of the Gentleman's old age as the twilight of life or of his memories as belonging naturally to the crepuscular light.

On the screen the Gentleman's memories could be visualised in the form of flashbacks. But unlike Alf Sjöberg, in his well-known film adaptation of *Miss Julie*, both directors abstain from such excursions into the past, partly perhaps because the memories are rather uneventful.

The setting for *Thunder in the Air* reads in part:

> *The façade of a modern house [...]; above the semi-basement is the ground floor, the large windows of which stand open; four of these belong to a dining room, elegantly furnished; above the ground floor can be seen the first-floor flat, the four central windows of which are covered by drawn red blinds, lit from inside.*
>
> *In front of the façade is a pavement with the trees of the avenue; in the FG, a green bench and a gas streetlamp.*[4]

What strikes the recipient is the unusual – passionate, frivolous – colour of the blinds and the many open windows, indicating that it is a hot summer evening.

Strindberg opens with a nearly empty stage. Only the Gentleman is seen inside the house "*at the table in the dining room.*" Then the Confectioner appears from inside his café with a chair and sits down in front of the house. The Brother, entering from left, goes up to one of the open windows and addresses the Gentleman inside.

Bergman's performance opens with a series of stills. Accompanied by the somber tolling of church bells, there is the iconic photo of a thundercloud with the title of the play, the genre (chamber play), and the name of the author in his own handwriting written into it. The somber cloud dissolves into a low-angle still of a church tower (Hedvig Eleonora in the opulent Östermalm part of Stockholm) with a prominent old-fashioned lamppost in front of it. There is a dissolve to a high-angle photo of a marketplace (Östermalmstorg) taken from the church tower. Then another dissolve to a picture of an avenue with apartment houses and a row of high lampposts in the middle of the avenue. Finally, a dissolve to a row of stately apartment houses behind a line of trees.

Via this authentic material, the play is firmly located in Stockholm at the turn of the century. In the fashion of the biographically oriented Olof Molander – the leading Strindberg director in Sweden for decades – we are introduced to Strindberg's 1907 environment.[5] To those who are familiar with the author's life at that time, Bergman strongly suggests that the Gentleman is Strindberg's alter ego.

As the last still dissolves to a high-angle close-up of a gas streetlamp, the somber tolling of the church bells is replaced by a cheerful waltz played on a piano, Waldteufel's *Pluie d'Or*, prescribed by Strindberg later in the play. The high camera tracks in on the ground floor of an apartment house and pans right. Through the open window, the Gentleman is seen reading a paper. Another pan right reveals him through another window, now with the young Louise next to him serving him after-dinner coffee.

The transference from the initial authentic stills to a studio-built apartment house immediately creates the impression that the building before us, in which the Gentleman lives, is not a real house but an illusory one. In this way, Strindberg's idea of life's unreality is retained. But unlike Strindberg's house, which faces a street, Bergman's seems to face a narrow courtyard, that is, a claustrophobic environment.[6] In the play text, Gerda at one point refers to her marriage, and by implication also to her life, as an imprisonment. Similarly, when the Confectioner comes out of his domicile, which is here below ground level, sighing and wiping his neck, the claustrophobic scenery helps to suggest that he is not so much suffering from the heat as from infernal life.

Unlike the stage, the small screen allows Bergman to focus immediately on one of the central symbols of the play: the gas streetlamp. This lamp clearly relates to the streetlamps we have seen in the stills. All the streetlamps are found in an intermediate area between heaven and earth. But unlike the lamps in the stills which were seen from below, from a human perspective, this one is seen from above, from a celestial one. The still of the church and the tolling of the bells have already provided a religious atmosphere. This is retained when Bergman has the camera lower itself and track in on the house behind the uppermost part of the streetlamp, the lantern. Like another Indra's Daughter, the camera here descends to Earth to visit the House of Life. This is synchronised with the sound effects indicating a similar dichotomy between death and the after-life on the one hand – since the sound of the church bells suggests a funeral – and life (the dance music) on the other.

It is surprising in view of this emphasis on metaphysical aspects that Bergman has not retained the Gentleman's initial stage business as indicated by Strindberg. In the text it says:

> The GENTLEMAN *is seen at the table in the dining room.* [...] *A* YOUNG GIRL, *dressed in light colours, is serving him the final course. The* BROTHER *enters L, and knocks with his walking stick on the window sill.*
>
> BROTHER. Are you finished soon?
>
> GENTLEMAN. I'm coming in a little while.

Not only is the Gentleman being served his *last* course by an angelic figure; he is also being asked if he will be *finished* soon. From the very beginning Strindberg implies that the Gentleman's life is coming to an end. Bergman's

Gentleman, by contrast, is simply reading a paper by his after-dinner coffee. Realistic or practical concerns here seem to have prevailed over metaphoric ones. Graffman ignores the existential overtones of the Brother's speech by changing the line from "Har du slutat snart?" (Are you finished soon?) into the more colloquial "Är du färdig snart?" (Are you ready soon?).

Strindberg pays little attention to the outward appearance of the characters, leaving even the task of clothing them to the director. While Louise in the play text says that the brothers *may* be twins, Bergman strongly suggests that they *are*. His brothers are dressed aristocratically and almost identically: grey top hats and grey frock-coats (the Gentleman's is a shade darker), white gloves, black shoes covered by white gaiters. The sameness is further emphasized by their identical way of walking, as we see them side by side leaving for their evening stroll, one hand carrying a cane, the other a pair of gloves behind the back – a slightly comical touch. The point of this visible identity is that it helps to suggest two attitudes of Man on the threshold of death, one calm (the Brother), the other worried (the Gentleman). Bergman's approach is essentially existential.

As Graffman produced his version in colour, he has a richer palette at his disposal than Bergman. Unlike him, he presents the brothers outwardly as a black-and-white antithesis. His Gentleman, who has spent the summer in the city, who likes the darkness and feels death approaching, appears in a black suit, grey waistcoat, red tie and black shoes, a grey hat in his hand, whereas his Brother, who has enjoyed the light summer evenings in the countryside, wears a white summer suit and a white hat. Only his black hat band and black tie link him with the Gentleman.

Graffman opens his version by non-diegetically intoning the *andante con moto* from Schubert's piano trio no. 2 in E flat major (D929) while showing the Brother walking toward the house. He then cuts to the Gentleman sitting inside it at the dinner table. Movement is contrasted with stasis. Play title and credits are superimposed on a long shot of the house and the characters in and outside it. We note the contrast between the two red-lit windows upstairs – obscured in Bergman's black-and-white version – and the three dark windows on the ground level (the Gentleman, we recall, likes darkness), two of which are open.

Strindberg's text is sometimes puzzling, as in the following passage from Act I:

> *A waltz is faintly heard being played in the apartment on the first floor.*

> BROTHER. Always waltzes, perhaps they run a dancing school, but almost always the same waltz; what's it called?

> GENTLEMAN. My word, I think it's ... *Pluie d'Or* ... I know it by heart...

BROTHER. Did you have it in your house?

GENTLEMAN. Yes! I've had that one and Alcazar...

The Brother's statement about waltzes is puzzling.[7] He cannot mean that one hears nothing but waltzes in the Fischer apartment; for while the Fischers have recently moved into the house, the Brother has not been near it since before the summer. Yet if his remark refers to a more general situation – viewed as an ellipsis for 'you hear nothing but waltzes these days' – why should he immediately assume that there is a dancing school up above? Whatever we make of this speech, the Brother's attitude to waltzes seems to be the negative one of an aristocrat. Characteristically, he does not know the name of the popular waltz.

Unlike his brother, the Gentleman knows the name of the waltz, for his ex-wife Gerda apparently used to play it on the piano.[8] She later refers to the piano still standing in the Gentleman's drawing room as hers. The first indication of Gerda's return, still unknown to the brothers, is by way of a piece of music that the Gentleman necessarily must link with her. The very name of the waltz, *Pluie d'or* (golden rain), seems to imply that it is associated with a happy period or happy moments of his marriage. How does the Gentleman react to the waltz? Does he share his brother's denigrating attitude? His reply, Ewbank notes, "doesn't solve the problem of whether nostalgia or irritation is the emotion here," adding that "the former is more likely." Strindberg provides no paralinguistic indication at this point. The director or actor must consequently decide for themselves on the Gentleman's emotion here. Since Strindberg stresses the Gentleman's – very common – habit of repressing bad memories in favour of good ones, it may seem likely that with the passing of time *Pluie d'Or*, whatever he thought of it at the time, has turned into a treasured memory – just as the ex-wife has become a treasured 'altar piece.'

Whatever his reasons may have been, Max Reinhardt for one, in an early stage production of the play, opted for nostalgia.[9] Bergman shows the two brothers, in a medium frontal shot, sitting next to each other in rather identical positions on the bench. The Brother's first speech is interspersed with affirmative hummings on the part of the Gentleman, who suddenly recognises the waltz, unenthusiastically remarking that he has had it in his house. Graffman, like Ewbank assuming carelessness on Strindberg's part, divides the Brother's speech between him and the Gentleman to make it more logical. When the waltz is heard, we get:

MS *of* BROTHERS, *sitting on green bench in front of house.*

GENTLEMAN, *his arms folded.* Always waltzes.

BROTHER, *looking upwards*. Do they run a dancing school?

GENTLEMAN. It's almost always the same waltz.

LS of house and BROTHERS *on bench in front of it.*

BROTHER. What's it called?

GENTLEMAN. I think it's ... *Pluie d'Or.*

Apparently disturbed by the tune, Graffman's Gentleman then reacts stiffly to it, as though wishing to repress this memory. Unlike Reinhardt, both directors opt for a rather negative reaction to the waltz. But whereas Bergman, stressing the identity between the brothers, can retain Strindberg's illogical text by creating a dreamlike feeling that we are actually experiencing a pseudo-dialogue which in fact is a soliloquy, Graffman, choosing a more realistic approach, both changes the text and the camera distance, incorporating the source of the music – the upper floor – in his second shot. To put it differently: whereas Bergman retains and even amplifies the idiosyncracy of the text, Graffman straightens it out, demystifies it.

Act II opens with Louise playing chess with the Gentleman. When she has to leave, the Gentleman asks the Confectioner to play a game with him, but the Confectioner cannot leave his "saucepans." The Gentleman is left alone for a few moments. Strindberg's text reads:

> GENTLEMAN *alone, moves the chessmen for a few seconds, then gets up and paces.* The peace of old age; yes! *Sits down at the piano and strikes a few chords; gets up and starts to pace again.* Louise! Can't you postpone that with the laundry?
>
> LOUISE *in L doorway.* That's impossible. The washer-woman's in a hurry, and she has a husband and children waiting for her...
>
> GENTLEMAN. Oh! *Sits down at the table and drums with his fingers; tries to read the newspaper, but tires of it; strikes matches and blows them out; looks at the clock. Noise in the hall.* Is that you Karl Fredrik?

In Bergman's version of this largely pantomimic sequence, the Gentleman sits down again at the chess set, his sherry glass next to it. Deep sigh. He moves the chessmen to an opening position. Loud ticking of the grandfather clock. He impatiently drums his fingers against the table, gets up, walks over to the piano, strikes a few keys. The clock is heard loudly. As Louise 'dismisses' him, he walks into his study, which is considerably darker than the dining room, sits down at his desk, puts on his glasses, picks up the evening paper but almost immediately puts it back on the desk. Another clock, ticking faster than the one in the dining room can be heard. The Gentleman, now in close-up, lights a match, blows it out, lights another match, blows it out, takes out his pocket watch, gets up as he hears a noise from the front door and leaves the room.

The position in front of the chess set, indicating the lack of a partner, the listless striking of the piano keys, the interrupted newspaper reading – all these signs in the text of an old man who is bored with his lonely existence are found in Bergman's version too. By having the Gentleman move from one room to another, from one clock to another, Bergman can quite naturally change both the lighting and the sound. Moreover, it is by such realistically motivated audiovisual changes that the Gentleman's increasing anguish is expressed. An acoustic link is provided between the two clocks and the Gentleman's pocket watch.

The climactic moment of the pantomime sequence, indicated by showing it in close-ups, is the lighting and blowing out of the matches. The matches are here comparable to the streetlamps which, as we know, are lit and extinguished daily. Clearly, both the matches and the lamps stand for the flame of life.[10] But in addition, we are here confronted with a picture of Man sensing how his life is passing away, minute by minute, and how death is approaching.

Graffman shows the Gentleman in an extreme high angle shot – obviously chosen to underscore his loneliness – walking around in his dining room as the ticking of the clock and the Schubert music are heard. Moving from the piano to the tile stove, he lights the two candles on either side of the portrait of his ex-wife and child. He then sits down at the table and tries to read the paper. Graffman then cuts to a close-up of his depressed face; he raises his hands and folds them as if praying for an end to his loneliness. Before and after this, Graffman inserts close-ups of Louise, the Postman and the Iceman, all secretly watching him. Together they represent the curiosity rather than the helpfulness of the surrounding world. Graffman seems to imply that "the silent house," representing the world, is full of spying and slander. The characters surrounding the brothers are in his version more negatively delineated than in Bergman's. This is especially true of Louise, who here appears as a calculating and rather artificial young woman, and of the Confectioner's daughter Agnes, who is here gaudily dressed, rather like a streetwalker, obscuring the parallel between the Gentleman and his daughter Anne-Charlotte on one hand and the Confectioner and his daughter Agnes on the other.

The reversal in *Thunder in the Air* comes close to the end of the play when Louise tells the Gentleman that Gerda has gone to her mother in the countryside to settle there with their child. Strindberg's and Graffman's Gentleman receive this message standing by the window outside the house.

Bergman's receives it in the dining room, sitting by the chessboard. His moved reaction is preceded by an exceedingly long pause. When he remarks, relieved, that everything "has sorted itself out," soft non-diegetic music – the celestial *adagio molto* (muted strings and harpsichord) of Vivaldi's "Autumn," the third movement of his *Quattro Stagioni* – lasting until they get seated on the bench outside, begins. The music emphasises the peace that has come over the Gentleman now he knows that his child is "in a good home." As soon as he has told Louise to switch out the lights in the apartment above and lower the curtains there, we see how he himself switches out the lights in the dining room, so that, in a close-up, the portrait of Gerda is blotted out. He then switches out the lights in the hall. Through the darkened hall, the two brothers leave the house. What we witness in Bergman's performance, more extensively than in Strindberg's text, is a symbolic leave-taking from the house, from life. The Gentleman's last weighty line – "And this autumn I'll move out of the silent house." – is ritually dramatised.

At the end of *Thunder in the Air*, we find the two brothers and the Confectioner outside the house. Strindberg does not indicate how they are grouped. Bergman's brothers sit next to each other on the bench to the left, while the Confectioner remains on his chair to the right. Three old men, who have experienced the storms of life, are waiting for the Lamplighter – and for the full moon. This is Strindberg's way of dramatising Man's inevitable waiting for death. The Gentleman's phrasing – "Look! Here comes the Lamplighter. At last!" – indicates his longing for death. Bergman stresses this longing by having him stretch out his arms as though he wanted to embrace the Lamplighter. The Gentleman's desire is fulfilled. Though dressed in black as Death should be, Bergman's Lamplighter has a shining Father Christmas face. Looking upwards to the lantern he is about to light, and to the moon – greeting both, as it were, with a friendly twinkle – he seems to incarnate the wisdom of old age that the Gentleman identifies with "the blind lantern," whose light can be shaded so that it does not shine on the carrier. This is a suggestive metaphor for the idea that the flame of life is hidden – this is the Gentleman's hope – rather than extinguished when we die. The Gentleman's mentioning of the blind lantern coincides with the lighting of "the first lantern,"[11] as he calls the street lantern. As a result, this becomes – in our imagination – a blind lantern, a source of hidden light, of life transcending death.

The Lamplighter's arrival implies that "det börjar skymma," as the Gentleman puts it, indicating not only that "it is beginning to grow dark" but also that his eyesight is failing. The moment of death is close at hand. Bergman's choice of turning out *all* the lights in the apartment house points in the same direction. His version ends as it began with a high angle shot of the lantern in close-up. The lantern, which we saw unlit in the beginning and which has remained so throughout the performance, is now being lit. If we agree that the lighting of the gas lantern at the end of *Thunder in the Air* symbolises the moment of death, then the position of the lantern between earth and heaven is certainly meaningful. In the opening, we discerned two people behind the unlit lantern inside the house. Now, behind the lit one we discern two people walking away from the house, visibly moving offscreen – a visual pun on the euphemistic Swedish expression for dying: "gå bort" (literally: go away). The last we see of the two is their backs, out-of-focus, shadowy.

Graffman, staying more within the limits of the play text, shows a Lamplighter not unlike Bergman's: bearded, dressed in black, with a bowler hat on his head. But while Bergman does not show us the Lamplighter until he is lighting the lantern, and then in such a way that he can focus on his facial expression, Graffman shows us, in a pan, how the Lamplighter arrives behind the two brothers. The Gentleman rather dryly makes his remark that the Lamplighter is at last arriving. Like Bergman, Graffman catches the lantern in a high angle close-up when it is lit but he does so in one static shot, whereas Bergman tilts from a close-up of the lantern down to the face of the Lamplighter, a movement repeating the descending one in the beginning of his performance. From its high angle, Graffman's camera tracks in on the brothers, showing them, in a medium two-shot, sitting on the bench, as the Gentleman, rather prosaically, voices the play's final speech. In a long shot, accompanied by the slow movement from Schubert's piano trio, we finally see the façade of the house, the three men sitting in front of it, and Louise closing the windows and drawing the curtains in the apartment above. The post-credits are superimposed. The ending clearly echoes the beginning.

Despite a pronounced sense for the play as a mood piece, despite some superb acting and despite the asset of colour – which brings out the green (for hope) of the bench and the tile stove and the red (for passion) of the upper apartment and Gerda's corresponding dress – Graffman's version misses much of Bergman's psychologically subtle camera work and suggestive existential overtones. Interestingly, it is the less realistic production that is the more captivating.

14 *The Ghost Sonata* (1907)

With his conviction that "the motif determines the form,"[1] Strindberg in *The Ghost Sonata* has created a drama which is more theme- than plot-centered.[2] Like *A Dream Play*, it is a norm-breaking drama. How could one transpose a drama of this sophisticated kind for a mass medium attuned to more immediately intelligible, realistic fare?

The play, in three parts here called acts, opens on a Sunday morning with a random meeting between the Student and the Milkmaid in front of a house by a drinking fountain. He tells her how on the preceding night he witnessed the collapse of a house and helped to save many of the victims. The Milkmaid remains silent. At his request she gives him water to drink, then disappears. The Student is now addressed by an old man, Jacob Hummel, a cripple sitting in a wheelchair. Hummel has not seen the Milkmaid. The Old Man, who appears quite benevolent, claims that he has saved the Student's father from bankruptcy. He now asks the Student to do him a favour in return. Will he go to the Opera together with the Colonel and his daughter, the Young Lady, who live in the house behind them? In this way he will get acquainted with the Young Lady, whom he adores. During the conversation between the two men, the inhabitants of the house appear in the windows or outside the house, and this causes the Old Man, who knows them all, to comment on them. The Old Man is wheeled out by his servant, Johansson, who returns and now paints a very negative picture of his master. When the Old Man comes back, surrounded by a crowd of beggars, the Student at his suggestion is hailed by everyone for his courage during the preceding night. The Milkmaid again appears, with her arms above her head like a person drowning. This time not only the Student but also the Old Man sees her. He shrinks with fear into his chair.

The same evening, the ghost supper – so-called because the participants "all look like ghosts" – takes place in the Colonel's round parlour inside the house. The Fiancée, the Aristocrat and the Student have been invited. But the Old Man, too, turns up. He has come "to pull up the weeds, to expose the crimes." The Colonel, he reveals, is neither a colonel nor a nobleman but a former servant. He had seduced the Fiancée when she was still engaged to the Old Man. And the Old Man himself, in revenge, seduced the Colonel's wife, the Mummy. The Young Lady is the fruit of this adultery. But now the Old Man in his turn is revealed. He, too, is a former servant. His name is false. He is a liar and an usurer. And worst of all, long ago he drowned the little Milkmaid, because she had witnessed a crime he wished to keep secret. The Old Man must now atone for all this. The Mummy orders him to hang

himself in the closet, where she has been repenting her adultery for many
years. While he does so, the Student in the Young Lady's adjacent hyacinth
room, unaware of what has happened, recites from the *Song of the Sun*, an
old Icelandic poem: "Man reaps as he sows."

A few days later, we find ourselves in the Young Lady's hyacinth room.
In the background the Colonel and the Mummy are sitting silently in the
parlour. Inspired by the beauty surrounding him, the Student gives a lyrical
description of woman, love and existence. The Young Lady explains that
the Cook, who has just appeared, has taken all her strength and that the Student can never have her. In despair, the Student declares that all mankind is
impure and that life is infernal. The Young Lady collapses and dies. Re-
morseful, the Student in a final prayer expresses his hope that she be carried
to a blessed after-life. He recites again the same lines from the *Song of the
Sun*. And the play ends, very spectacularly: "*The room vanishes; Böcklin's*
Toten-Insel *becomes the backdrop*."

The play title has both an exoteric and an esoteric meaning. The exoteric
meaning, related to the main theme, is that since life on earth is a shadow
life, a mirage, it follows that we are all ghosts – whereas those who appear
as ghosts in the play are the truly living.

Esoterically, the title alludes to Beethoven's piano sonata no. 17 in D
minor (op. 31, no. 2), usually called *Der Sturm* (*The Tempest*). In a letter to his
German translator, Strindberg refers to it as the *Gespenster* (Ghost) sonata.[3]

Strindberg presumably also wished to indicate in the title that the structure of the play is somehow akin to that of a sonata. The subtitle "Chamber
Play Opus III" suggests this, especially when combined with Strindberg's
own definition of the term 'chamber play' "the concept of chamber music
transferred to drama. The intimate action, the [...] significant motif, the sophisticated treatment."[4]

In a Prologue written for the opening of his own Intimate Theatre in
Stockholm, where the play was first performed, Strindberg speaks of the
journey that mankind must undertake "from the Isle of the Living to the Isle
of the Dead." He is alluding to Arnold Böcklin's well-known paintings.[5] In
The Ghost Sonata we witness a similar journey. The house we see on the stage
represents the House of Life which at the end vanishes and is replaced by
the Isle of the Dead. Without actually realising it, we have been on our way
to another reality. Along with the Student, we gradually discover that the
house which on the outside looks so attractive, inside is in poor shape. Life
may not be what we had expected, but *amor vincit omnia*. Yet even this
proves to be an illusion: like everyone else, the beloved Young Lady is
tainted by Original Sin ("sick at the core of life"). The stable, attractive house

has proved to be a mirage. The true reality – this is what Strindberg wants us to experience – is to be found in the life hereafter.

The fundamental idea of the play, then, is that life on earth is painful and illusory (dreamlike) and that when we die we are saved, returning from this pseudo-existence to the original one. Only by hoping for this can we endure this life. This ties in with the idea that the living are actually ghosts – as indicated by the cue designation 'The Mummy' and the reference to the "ghost supper."

The Student is "a Sunday child" who "can see what others cannot see." This is indicated by his being a student of languages trying to find the unity behind and beyond the linguistic tower of Babel mankind has erected "to keep the secrets of the tribe." The Student is also the only one who sings in the play, "matching human language with the 'universal language' of music."[6] At the same time he is Everyman, starting out in life enthusiastically but ending it in disillusion. His hope for a better existence in the after-life, justifying the pain of this life, is not just an individual hope but expresses the hope of mankind.

The unity of time and place is loosely adhered to in the play. Act I opens on a Sunday morning, Act II plays in the afternoon and evening of the same day, Act III a few days after Hummel's funeral about a week later.

Every act is spatially linked to the next one. Along with the Student we move from the street (Act I) through the round parlour (Act II) to the hyacinth room (Act III), from wider to narrower space, a Dantean journey in reverse. By synchronising this inward movement with the Student's increasingly negative view of life, Strindberg indicates a connection between life experience and denial of life.

Strindberg's use of space in *The Ghost Sonata* is quite cinematic. "The gradual revelation of the rotten foundations of the house [...] is presented visually by a zoom from act to act towards the center of the house."[7] The spatial reversal in Act III has its counterpart in a reversed point of view: that of the young couple in the foreground replacing that of the aged people in the background.

In his acting directions, Strindberg gives rather sparse and somewhat capricious information about his characters' outward appearance. We lack information about how the Old Man is dressed in Act I and what the Young Lady wears in Act III; at her second appearance, we learn that she *"has changed her clothes"* but we are not informed in what way. In Act I the Colonel appears *"in civilian clothes"*; how he is costumed in the following acts Strindberg does not tell us, but we can assume that he wears his uniform in Act II; here the author could rely on widespread knowledge in Sweden of military fashion around the turn of the century.

The duplicity characteristic of mankind – the attractive social mask hiding the ugly face – is visualised in the *"façade"* of the House of Life. The initial stage directions read:

> *The ground floor and the first floor of the façade of a modern house; only the corner of the house is visible, ending on the ground floor in a round living room, on the first floor in a balcony and a flagpole.*
>
> *Through the open windows of the round living room can be seen, when the blind is raised, a white marble statue of a young woman, surrounded by palms, brightly lit by rays of sunshine. In the window to the L, pots of hyacinths (blue, white, pink) are seen.*
>
> *On the balcony rail at the corner of the first floor a blue silk quilt and two white pillows are seen. The windows to the L are hung with white sheets. It is a bright Sunday morning.*
>
> *In the FG in front of the façade is a green bench.*
>
> *To the R in the FG is a street drinking-fountain, to the left an advertisement column.*
>
> *To the L at the back is the entrance, through it are seen the staircase, the stairs of white marble and the banister of mahogany and brass; on both sides of the entrance on the pavement are laurel bushes in tubs.*
>
> *The corner with the round living room also faces a side street, which is thought to lead inwards towards the backdrop.*
>
> *To the L of the entrance, on the ground floor, is a window with a reflecting mirror.*[8]

The play opens as follows:

> *When the curtain rises the bells of several churches in the distance are ringing. The doors of the façade are open; a* WOMAN IN DARK CLOTHES *stands immobile on the stairs.*
>
> *The* CARETAKER'S WIFE *sweeps the entrance hall; she then polishes the brass on the entrance doors; then waters the laurels.*
>
> *The* OLD MAN *is sitting in a wheelchair by the advertisement column reading a newspaper; he has white hair and beard and wears glasses.*
>
> *The* MILKMAID *enters from the corner with milk bottles in a wire basket; she is in summer clothes, with brown shoes, black stockings, and a white beret; takes off the beret and hangs it on the fountain; wipes the sweat from her forehead; drinks from the cup; washes her hands; arranges her hair, using the water as a mirror.*
>
> *A steamship bell can be heard ringing, and the bass notes of the organ in a nearby church now and then break the silence.*
>
> *After a couple of minutes of silence, when the* GIRL *has finished her toilet, the* STUDENT *comes in from L, unshaven and showing he has not slept. He goes right up to the fountain. Pause.*

STUDENT. *May I have the cup?*

The GIRL *pulls the cup toward herself.*

STUDENT. Haven't you finished yet?

The GIRL *looks at him in horror.*

OLD MAN *to himself.* Who's he talking to? – I don't see anyone! – Is he crazy? *Continues to watch them in great amazement.*

The theme of food takes a prominent place in Strindberg's writings.[9] In *The Ghost Sonata* the blood-sucking vampire has her antipode in the suckling mother. The Old Man and the Cook are the vampires of the play. The opposite, nourishing archetype we find in the character who is but an apparition: the Milkmaid. It is she who represents the nurturing, loving force in life. When Strindberg provides the Milkmaid with white milk bottles, he gives her an attribute which blatantly contrasts with the Cook's "colouring bottle with scorpion letters on it."

The opening continues with the Student telling the Milkmaid that he has "bandaged up injured people and kept watch over the sick all night," thereby clarifying his kinship with Jesus and with the good Samaritan. The explicit reference to the latter is a key to the whole opening scene which recalls the passage in John 4.7-14, where Jesus meets a woman of Samaria at Jacob's well.[10] "Give me to drink," Jesus asks her. "Give me a drink of water," the Student asks the Milkmaid. The antithesis in the biblical text between Jacob's earthly water, which only temporarily quenches the thirst, and Jesus" "living water" which does so eternally is latently present in Strindberg's play in the contrast between the earthly existence on which Jacob Hummel's power rests and the heavenly one to which the Milkmaid belongs and for which the Student finally hopes.   The full significance of the opening does not become clear until we reach the ending of the play:

The YOUNG LADY *has drooped, seems to be dying, rings.* BENGTSSON *enters.*

YOUNG LADY. Bring the screen! Quickly – I'm dying!

BENGTSSON *returns with the screen, which he opens up and places in front of the* YOUNG LADY.

STUDENT. The liberator is coming! Welcome, pale and gentle one! Sleep, you lovely, unhappy, innocent creature, who have suffered guiltlessly, sleep without dreams, and when you wake again ... may you be greeted by a sun that does not burn, in a home without dust, by friends without stain, by a love without flaw... You wise, gentle Buddha, sitting there waiting for a heaven to grow out of the earth, grant us patience in our ordeal, purity of will, that the hope may not come to nought!

The strings of the harp hum softly; the room is filled with a white light.

I saw the sun,
to me it seemed

that I beheld the Hidden,
men must reap what they have sown,
blest is he whose deeds are good;
deeds which you have wrought in fury,
cannot in evil find redress;
comfort him you have distressed
and your goodness is your gain.
No fear has he who does no ill,
Best is to be guiltless.

A wailing is heard from behind the screen.

You poor little child, child of this world of illusion, guilt, suffering and death; this world of endless change, disappointment, and pain! May the Lord of Heaven have mercy on you as you journey forth...

The room vanishes; Böcklin's Toten-Insel *becomes the backdrop; faint, quiet, pleasantly sad music is heard from the island.*

Böcklin's monumental painting *Toten-Insel* shows an isle with high, crater-like rocks surrounding a group of tall cypresses. In the walls of the rocks, there are openings similar to those of sepulchral chambers. On the shore below, centre, there are stairs of white marble; here the recently dead are received. *"A black boat with a black oarsman, carrying a white coffin with a white figure standing next to it"* – Strindberg's stage directions for his unfinished sequel of *The Ghost Sonata*, entitled *Toten-Insel* – approaches the stairs across the still water.

In *The Ghost Sonata* the final projection of this painting forms an antithetic counterpart to the solid façade in the play opening. The marble stairs of the house – the entrance to Life – correspond to those of the isle, the entrance to Death. The windows have their equivalents in the sepulchral openings. The white marble statue inside the house, *"surrounded by palms,"* resembles the erect white figure in the boat, surrounded by the cypresses of the isle – evergreen like the laurels outside the house but with a more "aspiring" shape. The mournful Woman in Dark who *"stands immobile on the stairs"* corresponds to the black rower in the boat. Even the fresh water of the street drinking-fountain, in which the Milkmaid mirrors herself, has its counterpart in the still water around the isle in which the reflection of the white figure in the boat can be seen.

It is from this isle of the blessed that the ghostly Milkmaid emanates. This explains why she wears *"summer clothes"* despite the fact that she was drowned in the winter. And it is to this isle that the Young Lady journeys forth in the final tableau. The house of earthly existence, the Old Man's realm, has collapsed, and in its place we see its spiritual counterpart, "a home without dust," the Isle of the Dead, "the station of rest, or the summer vacation after the first death," as Strindberg calls it in the section called "Higher Forms of Existence: *Die Toteninsel*" in one of his *Blue Books*.[11]

The connection between the beginning and the end of the play is also underlined by the sound effects.[12] When the curtain rises for Act I, we hear the ringing of bells of *"several churches at a distance."* While the Milkmaid washes her hands – an act of purification – and looks at herself in the "fresh water" of the street drinking-fountain, *"a steamship bell can be heard ringing, and the bass notes of the organ in a nearby church now and then break the silence."* By this puzzling combination of sound effects, Strindberg from the very beginning creates a strange and solemn mood. Only in retrospect, when we have witnessed the ending, do we realise their metaphoric significance, do we understand that the ringing of the steamship bell signifies leave-taking from the shore of life and that the organ music is there to help on the last journey.[13]

Johan Bergenstråhle's Swedish TV production, from 1972, opens as follows:

1 *Fade-in to credits* THE GHOST SONATA. Chamber Play by August Strindberg *on patterned wallpaper. Organ music. Dissolve to*

2 *LS of choir dressed in black (six female, four male singers, five on either side of the organ). Organist, his back turned to spectator, conducts with L arm. Organ music and singing in same manner until shot 7.*

3 *Tilt down to* OLD MAN *in light, yellowish summer clothes and hat (with a black ribbon) and black gloves. His face is hidden behind newspaper. Street drinking-fountain in FG. Splashing of water.*

4 *Slow zoom-in on* OLD MAN, *who lowers his paper and looks up, so that his face can be seen. He wears glasses. Splashing of water.*

5 *Section of grey apartment house with high windows, one L with flowers in it (the hyacinth room) and double bay-window R, covered with white curtains (the round parlour). Pan R to*

6 *Open front door with laurels in tubs on either side. Window R of door (*FIANCÉE'S *window). Inside door* DARK LADY *is standing, in black with mourning crape over her face.* CARETAKER'S WIFE *is scrubbing the floor.*

7 OLD MAN *looks up from his paper, then disappears again behind it. High organ notes followed by* a capella *female voices and, finally, a single female voice.*

8 MILKMAID *walks down stately grey staircase from L to R. She wears grey dress and beret and carries milk bottles in wire baskets. Turns L when she reaches ground level. Organ music until shot 12. Footsteps.*

9 *Zoom-in on* MILKMAID *as she walks up to drinking-fountain and puts wire baskets next to it.*

10 MILKMAID *wipes sweat from her forehead, picks up cup, fills it with water from fountain and drinks. Dissolve to*

11 STUDENT *walking down stately grey staircase (identical with that in shot 8) from R to L. He wears Swedish student's cap, black waistcoat and trousers, white shirt with rolled-up sleeves. Footsteps.*

12 MILKMAID *washes her hands in fountain. Behind her a poster, advertising the program at the Royal Theatre, and part of staircase. She leans on fountain with her arms, mirroring her face in water. Splashing of water. Chiming of church bell until shot 15.*

13 STUDENT, *who is unshaven and whose cap is dirty.* May I have the cup?

14 MILKMAID *looks at him frightened.*

15 STUDENT. Haven't you finished yet?

16 OLD MAN, *muttering to himself.* Who's he talking to? *Lowers paper, looks up, turns his head R. To himself.* I don't see anyone. *Turns head back, to himself.* Is he crazy?

In Bergenstråhle's scenographic solution there is no indication, as in the play text, of an inward movement. The whole play is acted out in one huge space, in which the high-low dichotomy is essential. The setting is in itself dreamlike in the sense that we do not know whether it is an exterior (a street) or an interior (a church), whether the prop in the foreground is a street drinking-fountain or a baptismal font. Our first impression, as we see a huge organ with organist and choir, all placed on a raised level in the background and as we hear the music and the singing, is indeed that we are inside a church. In the organ music the director seems to have incorporated Strindberg's ship's bell: the monotonous notes played remind one of the puffing of a steamship chimney. But one may also think of the regular ticking of a clock – relating the sound of the ominous clock in Act II – or the beating of a heart, the Old Man's pangs of conscience. The plaintive, wordless singing from the very beginning intones the mood. We are in a somber world in which humanity is both pitiable and sinful, the central theme of *A Dream Play*, a drama which looms large in Bergenstråhle's *Ghost Sonata*.[14] The sound of murmuring water from the fountain – an unrealistic sound – helps to emphasise the biblical connotations of the "fresh water."

Bergenstråhle significantly manipulates this sound, turning it especially loud when the Milkmaid, the good Samaritan, in a long take, bathes the Student's eyes.

While in the play text we move from (love of) this world to (love of) heaven, from blindness to seeing – at the end we are, as it were, blessed with the Student's second sight – Bergenstråhle makes the heavenly aspect immediately explicit. Instead of a play beginning in a physical reality and ending in a spiritual one – Strindberg's idea – we are faced with a 'medieval,' allegorical construction with heaven above and earth-cum-hell below. The Milkmaid and the Student both enter the ground level (the world) from the organ-loft above (heaven) in virtue of their childlike innocence – much as, in the words of the Student, "Jesus Christ descended into hell. That was his pilgrimage on earth," a line that apparently has been decisive for Bergenstråhle's scenographic solution.

Once we see this, other things fall into place. The dominance of greyness, for example, which indicates not only the drabness of human existence but which is also the colour of stone, stone being the material with which the Old Man, akin to the biblical Tempter, builds his world. When the camera tilts down from the organist, the praiser of God, to the satanic Old Man, it is a clear statement of the metaphysical polarity.

The Old Man appears in yellowish summer clothes, black mourning ribbon and black gloves. This is a non-realistic costume bringing out his corpse-like nature, his pretence to mourn the Consul, whom he has 'murdered,' as well as his feeling cold (the gloves), indicating both his mental coldness and his sense of approaching death. By showing the Old Man first hiding behind his paper, then lowering it so that his face can be seen, Bergenstråhle not only depicts his deceitfulness, he also introduces the central theme of appearance versus reality.[15]

If Bergenstråhle's production is characterised by theatricality, symmetry and a subtle use of colours, Philip Saville's version, transmitted eight years later, is dynamic, cinematic and variegated. Like most BBC directors, Saville relies on Michael Meyer's translation.

Saville's version opens with a pre-credit sequence, based on two events that are related in the play text. The first concerns the collapse of a house; the Student says to the Old Man:

> For example yesterday ... I was drawn to that secluded street where the house was later to collapse. I got there and stopped in front of the building I'd never seen before ... Then I noticed a crack in the wall, heard the joists snapping. I ran forward and grabbed hold of a child who was walking under the wall ... The next moment, the house collapsed ... I was saved, but in my arms, where I thought I held the child, there was nothing...

The significance of this situation does not appear until the end, where the Student tries to save the Young Lady from this sinful world until he discovers that innocence does not exist, not even in her. The death – actually escape – of the Young Lady in other words corresponds to the disappearance of the child. This is partly the reason why the Student at the end speaks of the Young Lady as a 'poor little child, child of this world of illusion.'

As long as the illusory child is merely mentioned – as is the case in the play text – it fully retains its symbolic significance of child of man. When visualised, as in Saville's version, it can no longer be just a child; it must receive a gender. Saville turns the child into a little girl, dressed in blue. Although the link with the Young Lady is hereby provided, via the blue hyacinth associated with her, the universality indicated in the play text – the child as a representative of mankind – is gone.

The collapse of the house is shown in a swift sequence where Saville crosscuts between the collapsing house and the reactions of the people in and around it. In this way he climactically creates suspense, much as in an adventure film.

Then follows the title of the play, in trembling, ghostlike lettering combined with a picture of a nude young girl who seems to come out of the water only to be pushed back into it. This shot relates to the Old Man's crime against the Milkmaid, revealed at the ghost supper: "he was accused of having lured a young girl out onto the ice to drown her, because she had witnessed a crime he feared might get discovered." The shot – out-of-focus, in slow motion – is accompanied by non-diegetic, eerie music. All these unrealistic effects obviously serve to suggest that we are concerned with a nightmarish inner reality: the Old Man's traumatic guilt feelings.

Summarising, we might say that in the pre-credit sequence Saville shows us (a) the Student saving a little girl from being killed, and (b) the Old Man killing a young girl. Innocence saved versus innocence killed is thus established as the central opposition in the production.

Having devoted close to fifty shots to the pre-credit sequence, Saville begins the teleplay proper as follows:

1 *Window with shutters.*

2 Dark Lady *inside shutters. Zoom-in.*

3 *Profile of* Old Man *reading a Swedish newspaper* (Dagens Nyheter). *He wears a black coat and beret.* Milkmaid *approaches from bluish BG with two buckets on yoke. She wears a white-and-yellow 'folk costume' and a white bonnet.*

4 OLD MAN *turns round to frontal position. Zoom-out revealing a barrier behind him. Zoom-in on* MILKMAID *who, now nude, gains superhuman size behind barrier before she disappears L.*

5 *HA CU of drinking-fountain. Reflection of* MILKMAID's *face in the still water.*

6 *Water surface splashes as* MILKMAID *pumps water into fountain.*

7 *LS HA of* OLD MAN *in wheelchair reading paper, plaid over his legs, grey shawl. R FG white-and-red flag of consulate. Stones of small square form circular patterns.*

8 STUDENT, *dark-haired, dressed in white, up to pump and* MILKMAID, *who has put her white bonnet on pump. Blue sky behind them.*

9 STUDENT *to* MILKMAID. May I have the cup?

10 MILKMAID.

STUDENT *to her.* What are you staring at?

11 STUDENT *to* MILKMAID. Am I so repulsive? Oh, I see. I haven't slept all night, so of course you think ...

12 *CU of* MILKMAID, *frontal.*

STUDENT *offscreen.* ... I have been dissipating.

13 *CU of* OLD MAN *with glasses.*

STUDENT *offscreen.* Give me a drink of water, girl – I've earned it. I've been bandaging wounds all night, and tending the injured;

14 STUDENT *alone by pump in BG,* OLD MAN *in FG.*

STUDENT. I was there when the house collapsed yesterday evening. Now you know.

Although Saville by certain captions – *Bagarbod* (Bakery), *Dagens Nyheter* (Daily News), *Kungl. Teatern* (Royal Theatre) – suggests that the action is set in Sweden, there is little else to verify this. Unlike Bergenstråhle's Student, Saville's lacks a Swedish student cap – for natural reasons, since a British audience, unfamiliar with this ethnic phenomenon, would only be confused by an iconic sign of this kind. The Student's deviating all-white costume, apart from indicating his purity, may suggest that he is a kind of Samaritan. The Milkmaid wears what looks like a south German folk costume, and her yoke and water buckets turn her into a Gretchen of the early nineteenth century rather than a German milkmaid of the early twentieth. Of Strindberg's Milkmaid there remains only a maid; an essential aspect of the figure is lost. Possibly Saville has wanted to universalise the play and at the same time indicate the connection with the Samaritan woman fetching water from Jacob's well.

Rather than in a street we find ourselves in a square, surrounded by a barrier; we do not know what is behind it. Does the barrier represent the border between consciousness and subconsciousness? This seems indicated when the drowned Milkmaid grows to gigantic size behind it, thereby visualising the Old Man's growing guilt feelings. The stones of the square, suggesting this grey and hard world, are effectively linked with the Old Man and contrasted with the blue heaven against which the Student and the Milkmaid are silhouetted.

In a stage performance a director can choose between visualising or not visualising the Milkmaid; in the former case we would share the Student's point of view, in the latter the Old Man's. Since Saville's version was made for the screen, he is able to present a third alternative. The spectator alternates between the two viewpoints. But since the Student, as we have seen, takes a very special place, functioning as our guide, it is essential that we immediately can fully identify with him. This possibility is disturbed in Saville's version of constantly shifting optical viewpoints.

Some notable deviations from the play's stage directions may be due to Saville's reliance on a target text. Thus, while Strindberg's Caretaker's Wife is *"sweeping the entrance hall,"* Saville's, presumably as a result of Meyer's incorrect rendering – is *"cleaning the front steps."* And while Strindberg calls for *"a couple of minutes of silence"* before the Student enters, so that the impression that the Milkmaid is, somehow, linked to the Old Man can sink in, Saville, possibly misled by the translator's *"a few moments of silence,"* makes the pause considerably briefer than Bergenstråhle does.

In Act II Strindberg's young couple are seen in the hyacinth room in the background. In Bergenstråhle's version they do not appear at this point; instead, the white marble statue behind the guests, centre, seems to represent their youthful innocence. As in his version of Act I, the arrangement is highly symmetrical. The director alternates between long shots of the five guests and medium close-ups of the speaker, the Old Man.

Bergenstråhle's production was criticised for its use of old-fashioned language. As a matter of fact, its language is varied in a considered way. Thus, when the Old Man adheres to extremely formal language in his monologue – using plural forms of the verbs, for example – it seems to be a sign of how he has learned his speech by heart in advance. His unmasking of the others is in other words carefully prepared. To give his condemnation of them the appearance of objectivity, he speaks like a statute book. When his true self later comes to the fore, he reverts to a plain way of speaking. The monologue is delivered in crescendo, with the right arm raised a couple of times –

in contrast to the organist who raised his left arm? – reminding us of a certain rhetorical dictator, the prime satanic figure of our time.

The emphasis in Bergenstråhle's version falls on the Mummy's speech of contrition ("we are miserable human beings," etc.), delivered with the crucified Christ as background and with a strong back light turning the Mummy's hair into an aureole.

Saville's version demonstrates a very different approach. Unlike Bergenstråhle, he breaks the monologue up into a great many shots, some of which visualise what is on the characters' minds. This is how the Colonel is revealed:

> *CU of* COLONEL *with monocle.* [= mask]
>
> *LS of* COLONEL *naked on stairs, moving away from camera.* [= hiding]
>
> *CU of* COLONEL *looking down.* [= ashamed]

And this is a portrait of the Old Man:

> *CU of* OLD MAN *breathing heavily.* [= guilt feelings, thinking of...]
>
> *LS of* MILKMAID, *nude, swimming by a landing-stage, surrounded by green, coming out of water, approaching camera, happily smiling.*
>
> *CU of* OLD MAN.
>
> *LS of landing-stage, now empty.* [= Milkmaid drowned]

The two sequences are linked by contrasts: the Colonel's feeling of being ashamed of his nakedness versus the Milkmaid's happy acceptance of it (relating her with the nude marble woman); his environment (stone house, stately staircase) versus hers (simple wooden landing-stage, nature); his movement away from the camera versus her approaching it.

More ambiguous is the following sequence:

> *LA CU of* OLD MAN.
>
> *LS of* YOUNG MAN *in grey suit in green meadow.*
>
> *CU of* FIANCÉE.
>
> *LS of* YOUNG MAN *running towards the camera.*
>
> *CU of* FIANCÉE.

The first shot of the Young Man is inserted between close-ups of the Old Man and the Fiancée, the second one between two close-ups of the Fiancée. This indicates that he represents their remembrance of how the Old Man was once an innocent and attractive young man. With this interpretation the shots of the Young Man are flashbacks. Alternatively, they may be seen as 'flashforwards,' visualising the Old Man's dreams of a bright future for the Student and the Young Lady; the shots, it should be noted, accompany his statement about how he has tried to find a friend for her.

During the ghost supper the Old Man is forced to atone for his sins by hanging himself in the closet, where the Mummy has been repenting her adultery for many years. In the play text this atonement begins when the Milkmaid "*appears in the hallway door, unseen by all but the* OLD MAN, *who shrinks back in horror.*" This happens as the Mummy rings for Bengtsson, the only person who knows about the Old Man's crime against the Milkmaid. Bergenstråhle has the Milkmaid appear on the stairs and sink down there as if she were drowning. Saville has her appear at an earlier point, just before the Old Man imperiously strikes the table with his crutch:

1 *LA of* OLD MAN, *a big wall clock behind him with a moving pendulum. Ticking of clock. Shadows. Slow zoom-in on* OLD MAN.

2 MILKMAID *in white dress and bonnet in green meadow.*

3 *Hand of clock. Loud ticking.*

4 OLD MAN *raising his crutch.*

5 MILKMAID *coming out of water, out-of-focus, slow motion. Eerie music.*

6 OLD MAN.

7 *Zoom-in to ECU of* MILKMAID, *coming out of water, hand pulling her down.*

8 OLD MAN *striking crutch on table.*

In the drama text, the Old Man's hubris culminates with his striking of the table which he compares to the striking of the clock, thereby equating himself with Fate. With Saville, on the other hand, the striking of the table is an expression of the Old Man's attempt to repress the painful memory of the drowning of the Milkmaid, visualised in shot 7, which is granted key status by being identical with the title shot. Saville's Hummel is a more active murderer than Strindberg's.

The clock figures prominently in the performance, and the Mummy's stopping of it is with Saville the climax of Act II. The reversal of power is indicated by low-angle shots first of the Old Man, then of the Mummy. She is dressed like a nun to illustrate her 'nunnery' existence in the wardrobe, her many years of penance.

Towards the end of Act III, as the Student speaks his somber monologue, Bergenstråhle has him walk up the stairs, pass in front of the organ and then walk down the stairs left, stopping on the way by a mirror, by the choir and by the crucifix. He has made his pilgrimage through life, and he now repeats it in quick tempo as he summarises his negative experience of it. His movement is a spatial counterpart of the coda-like repetition of earlier motifs that his monologue signifies.

Bergenstråhle's Student does not recite the *Song of the Sun* by heart as in Act II but reads it from a book, as though he were distancing himself from it. His concluding prayer for the Young Lady is omitted; death is no "liberator" in this version.

The performance ends with a long shot of Bengtsson, in black livery and with clasped hands, in front of the death screen – like a priest officiating in front of the altar. The camera tilts up to the choir and the organist; there is white light from above and plaintive singing. The ending is thus a symmetrical reversal of the opening, Bengtsson (the servant) now taking the place of the Old Man (the master); as it says in the play text: "the roles of life alternate."

Saville omits the *Song of the Sun* but retains the Student's prayer. With Bergenstråhle the Student's outburst – "[I saw] a virgin – by the way, where is virginity? Where is beauty? In nature and in my mind when it's in Sunday clothes." – is uttered as he is standing next to the crucifix. By way of contiguity, "virginity" becomes associated with Christ and, obliquely, with His mother, the Virgin Mary.

Saville places the Student next to the nude marble statue as he utters Meyer's rendering of this passage: "Where is virginity to be found? Or beauty? Only in flowers and trees ... and in my head when I am dressed in my Sunday clothes." Since the marble statue represents Eve before the Fall, what is here suggested is rather that innocence cannot be found after the Fall. In the text the implied opposition is: nature (innocence) versus human nature (sin). Meyer obscures this with his free rendering "flowers and trees," which may well have inspired Saville to the Eden-like context in which the Student finds himself at this point.

The play text does not state that the Young Lady is dying, merely that she *"seems to be dying,"* by Meyer tritely rendered as: *"has crumpled in her chair."* What Strindberg is suggesting here is that we, the living, are deluded. Like the characters on the stage, we mistake appearance for reality. As we have seen, the death of the Young Lady is no death at all, only a transformation, a rebirth to the true life. This appears also from the acting direction referring to the Young Lady's manner of 'dying.' *"A moaning is heard behind the screen,"* Meyer translates, but Strindberg's *"kvidande"* could better be rendered as *'whimpering'* or *'wailing,'* that is, a sound suggesting both birth and death.[16] If Saville's rendering of the Young Lady's 'death' seems commonplace, it may have something to do with the difficulty of having the Strindbergian meaning carried over in translation.

Saville ends the play by placing the Student, in white, in front of a red death screen, his back to the camera. There is a dissolve to a painting with a white figure in the centre – as though the Student had entered the picture. A zoom-out verifies that the painting is indeed Böcklin's *Isle of the Dead*, hanging on a wall – as it did in the pre-credit sequence. A sudden crack in the wall causes the painting to fall down. The final shot shows it next to a candelabra on the floor. There is a pan and zoom-in on the little girl in blue whom the Student tried to save from the collapsing house in the pre-credit sequence. The freezing of the frame signals the end of the performance.

By retaining Strindberg's *Toten-Insel*, Saville may seem to follow the play text more closely than most directors. Actually, his ending brings a message very different from Strindberg's. In the text it is the white-shrouded corpse in the boat – reminiscent of the white mourning sheets in the beginning – which represents the recently 'dead' Young Lady; it is she who is taken to a blissful hereafter – at least in the Student's imagination. In Saville's version it is the Student himself who is taken there – while the little girl in blue (representing the Young Lady) remains among the ruins of the collapsed house. Whereas Strindberg holds the possibility open that the idea of a blessed post-existence is not merely another illusion, Saville dismisses it as just that.

Schematically, the differences between the two TV productions may be summarised as follows:

	BERGENSTRÅHLE	SAVILLE
Text	Source text	Target text
Changes	Slight	Moderate
Scenery	Uniform	Varied
Colour scheme	Sparse	Varied
Sound effects	Sparse	Varied
No. of shots	Low	High
Camera angles	Neutral	Spectacular
Flashbacks	None	Many

The major contrast between the two versions is one between homogeneity (Bergenstråhle) and heterogeneity (Saville). The former is in the Swedish Molander tradition of heightened or magic realism, with strong religious overtones and a sparseness of effects. Saville's version – nightmarish, expressionistic, out of touch with recognisable reality – belongs rather in the Reinhardt tradition. It may seem preferable in that it utilises specific possibilities of the TV medium – as Bergenstråhle's does not. But this is a superficial criterion on a par with statements like: radio plays making the utmost use of sound effects are laudable. Or: films with a minimum of dialogue are preferable. Much more important is the question: Are the visual and verbal elements properly balanced? The lack of visual fireworks in Bergenstråhle's production means that the exceedingly compact and polysemic dialogue receives due attention; we are given time to ponder and feel the effect of the words. In Saville's version the visual elements obtrude, attract too much attention, while the verbal ones are harmed by a sometimes defective translation.

What the two directors have in common is their departure from Strindberg's ending, which neither of them apparently found ideologically attuned to our secularised time and/or to their own conviction.

15 The Pelican (1907)

As in *The Ghost Sonata*, the style of *The Pelican* is heightened naturalism bordering on the grotesque. How to recreate this in the realistically oriented TV medium? In the following we shall see how this is done in two Swedish productions, Yngve Nordwall's from 1973 and Vilgot Sjöman's from 1982.

The Pelican, Strindberg writes on the title page of the manuscript, "can either be presented as one long act or as three." Nordwall has chosen the former alternative, Sjöman the latter. The play is not very long, about an hour and a half on the stage.[1] Adapting it for TV therefore need not mean that the dialogue be condensed.

The three acts or scenes are all set in the same drawing room. It creates a sense of confinement corresponding not only to the Mother's guilt feelings – "that's why I am sitting here imprisoned ... and I can't dwell in the other rooms" – but also to the feeling of all the characters that life on earth is a life-time imprisonment. When the Mother, Elise, at the end *"opens the balcony door and plunges out,"* it is, realistically, an attempt to escape the fire in order to save her life. Metaphysically, it is rather an escape from a feared Hell or Purgatory. "I don't want to burn!" the Mother cries. "We shan't burn," her daughter Gerda assures her brother Fredrik. The verbal parallel underlines both the similarity and the dissimilarity between her and their situation. Both lines are omitted in Nordwall's performance. But the escape of the Mother can also be seen as an escape from the earthly prison into death equating liberation. In the opening of the play, her counterpart in some respects, old Margret, states: "soon the hour of liberation is come, not yet though." And when the Mother has earlier contemplated jumping out of the window, after she has looked *"down into the depth,"* suicide has clearly been on her mind. Her escape from the house – from earthly existence – has its verbal counterpart in the Son's concluding monologue, where he in a vision double-projects the voyage out to a lovely island in the archipelago and the hope for a blessed after-life.

Like film, but to a lesser degree, television drama is inimical to an absolute unity of place. Nordwall shows us several rooms of the apartment. In addition to the drawing room we see the corridor, the dining room and the kitchen. But we stay inside the apartment. The sense of confinement is retained.

Sjöman shows us not only different rooms in the apartment. In the pre-title sequence he also displays the apartment house from the outside as well as its surroundings. The sense of confinement is diminished. As a consequence the final 'escape' is less accentuated.

Toward the end of Act I we get an interesting stage direction:

The stage is empty; it is windy outside, howling by windows and in the tiled stove; the rear door starts to slam, sheets of paper from the desk whirl around the room, a palm on a pedestal is shaken violently, a photograph falls from the wall. Now the voice of the SON *is heard:* "Mother!" *Immediately afterwards:* "Close the window!" *Pause. The rocking chair moves.*

There is a natural explanation for the wind. In one of the opening speeches we have learnt that it is "windy" outside. Nevertheless, the Mother has opened a window to get rid of the smell of carbolic acid. Strindberg leaves the stage empty for a little while – while the Mother opens the window in another room. For the reader the opening of the window is explained *after* s/he gets the stage directions just quoted. We are, in other words, offered a supernatural explanation for the wind *before* we are offered a natural one. The same goes for the spectator, although the arrangement is here spatio-temporal rather than purely temporal.

This situation is difficult to recreate on the small screen, where a combination of empty room, long shot and long take would seem very theatrical. Nordwall trivialises the situation by rearranging the sequence. We see the Mother open the window, thereby letting in the wind. The rocking chair does not move. Sjöman, on the other hand, omits the opening of the window and the wind but retains the movement of the rocking-chair, the chair of the 'murdered' husband, a movement that now seems even more supernatural, or subjective, than that of Strindberg's rocking-chair. Whereas Strindberg, as usual, settles for half-reality, Nordwall opts for naturalism, Sjöman for supernaturalism.

Next to the action visualised by Strindberg, Nordwall makes use of a few insertions showing simultaneous actions. In the beginning we get the following passage:

SON. Father wasn't mean ...

MOTHER. Oh no?

SON. Now I think I hear steps of someone outside!

We never learn who is "outside." Is it, as Nordwall shows in a long shot, old Margret who is leaving the house for good? Or is it, as the conversation seems to imply, the dead husband/father who haunts the house, he who once "was moving around down in the tobacco patch, in darkness and rain, howling out of longing for wife and children?" After a moment of perspicacity, the Mother contemplates suicide by jumping out of the window,

but then she changes her mind, when there are three knocks at the rear door. Who is it? What was that?

Nordwall abstains from the three mysterious knocks and cuts instead to the Son-in-law walking out of the house. Like Margret, he is leaving the family to their fate.

In both examples the meaningful idea of the dead haunting the living – a dramatisation of their guilt feelings – is replaced by a more rational, and more trivial, explanation. The possibility to identify with the Mother is diminished. *She* believes in ghosts, *we* know better.

Striking elements in Sjöman's version are the frequent use of sounds – ticking clocks and tolling church bells – and the brief visualisation of things past, two ingredients which seem very Bergmanian. In three of the flashbacks, the dead father appears. In a diary note made while working on *The Pelican*, Sjöman writes:

> Daddy is dead, when the play begins: is never seen!
>
> This works in the theatre: You can talk about a character in such a way that he comes to life. In film this does not work. – And how about TV?!
>
> Suppose I ask Ernst Günther to come and do the father, so that we have visible impressions of him throughout the play?! (After all, Strindberg began writing *The Pelican* with a play about the father: the fragment of *Toten-Insel*!)[2]

In his attempt to satisfy both his medium's need of visualisation and the author's intentions, Sjöman's production is to a certain extent a combination of *Toten-Insel* and *The Pelican*.[3]

The flashbacks of the father are not the only ones. In a couple of others, the Mother sentimentally remembers how she danced with her Son-in-law, Axel, at her daughter's wedding – while the bride, forlorn, stood looking at them. These flashbacks can be combined with the Son's indication that there have been secrets in his mother's marriage. When this is said, Sjöman's Mother and Son-in-law, standing next to Gerda, exchange telling glances, indicating that the Mother, in the words of the director's diary, "has had an affair with her future son-in-law – before she handed him over to her daughter." This is further suggested by Sjöman when he has the Mother run after her Son-in-law with the words "Don't go!", words that in Strindberg's text concern the Son.

The Son's reminding the Mother that she has once wanted to take her life by jumping out of the window prepares for her 'suicide' at the end. Sjöman visualises the suicide attempt of the past no less than three times, thereby indicating both its traumatic nature and the fact that the Mother's sleep-walking existence has to do with repressed guilt. These flashbacks, motivated by Sjöman's unwillingess to accept Strindberg's one-sided depiction of the Mother, illustrate his attempt to "see the course of events from [her] point of view."[4]

In Gerda's single flashback of herself we see her, dressed as a bride, next to her doll's house, a property added by Sjöman that returns in her visualised description of the burning chattels. In both places a music-box tune is heard. Like Ibsen's Nora, Gerda has never been allowed to or dared to grow up.[5]

Strindberg is rather capricious concerning his character's spatial positions. In the introductory stage directions we learn that there are three seating possibilities in the drawing room: "*a chaise longue,*" "*a rocking chair,*" and "*an easy chair.*" When later we hear that "GERDA *sits down in a chair,*" we do not know which chair is meant. Similarly, the acting direction that "*the* SON *gets up from the rocking chair*" is surprising, since we have not learnt that he ever sat down there. All we hear is that he "*gets up*" from the chaise longue. This kind of inadvertencies, lacking with Ibsen, are common with Strindberg. They illustrate both the speed with which he wrote his plays, his unwillingness to make changes in them, and his faith in the power of the actors to complement the text in a meaningful way.

When Strindberg first indicates that the deceased husband has been a business man and later implies that he has been a teacher, he makes himself guilty of a remarkable inconsistency. It is obviously the Son's vision of the approaching summer vacation that has caused this change of occupation. Both professions are thematically so deeply rooted in the drama that it is hard to overcome the inconsistency in performance. Significantly, it remains in both productions.

The Pelican has been characterised as "a drama that still seems modern and yet is not always so, from a linguistic point of view."[6] Some of the words, now obsolete, present difficulties for the recipient of today; these are listed in the word explanations accompanying the play in the new edition of Strindberg's *Collected Works*.[7] What is considered difficult for the reader must be considered doubly so for the spectator, who has little time to ponder what is being said. One would therefore expect that many of the words listed here would have been replaced by others in the TV productions. But while Nordwall updates the dialogue throughout, Sjöman is much more moderate.

More important than this is that the directors omit different parts of the text. The opening of the play is a case in point. With Strindberg it reads:

MOTHER. Shut the door, please.

MARGRET. Are you alone, Ma'm?

MOTHER. Shut the door, please. – Who is that playing?

MARGRET. What terrible weather tonight, windy and rainy ...

MOTHER. Shut the door, please, I can't stand this smell of carbolic acid and spruce twigs ...

Nordwall retains this dialogue more or less. But with Sjöman the dialogue is considerably condensed and becomes in fact a monologue:

MOTHER. Shut the door, please. – Shut the door, please, I can't stand this smell of carbolic acid and spruce twigs ...

This passage causes, as Steene has shown,[8] not only interlingual problems, problems arising when translating from one language to another. It also causes intralingual problems, problems within one and the same language. Few Swedes today know that carbolic acid has anything to do with death.[9] Even so both directors prefer to retain the words "carbolic acid" rather than replace them with, for instance, 'desinfectant,' a word that is more intelligible but too modern in the linguistic context and less meaningful since it is not clearly related to the dead husband / father.

With Strindberg the introductory stage directions read:

A drawing room; door in the BG to the dining room; door to the balcony R in pan coupé.

Chiffonier, desk, chaise longue with crimson shag cover; a rocking chair.

The MOTHER *comes in, dressed in mourning, sits down to idle in an easy chair; listens worriedly now and then.*

Outside Chopin's Fantaisie Impromptu Oeuvre Posthume op. 66 *is being played.*

These stage directions are not complete. Later we learn that there is a *"portrait"* of the husband / father on the wall and a *"tile stove," "a palm on a pedestal," "a photograph,"* a *"table," "a bookcase"* and *"a flowerpot"* in the room.

Strindberg's manner of gradually introducing us to the room – he differs from Ibsen in this respect – means that there is a discrepancy between the reader's experience of the text and the spectator's experience of the performance; what is linear or sequential for the former is simultaneous for the latter. Yet here is an interesting correspondence between Strindberg's text and the screen media, where the properties of a room are usually shown successively, in different shots. For the reader and the TV viewer, the various props do not exist until the dramatist / director chooses to mention / show them.

Strindberg's drawing room has only one real door. (The door to the balcony is not a normal door.) All entries and exits must take place via this door.

Nordwall's opening up to the first speech, lasting 45 seconds, is as follows:

1 *Chopin's* Fantaisie Impromptu *is heard during this and following shots. CU of a silver plate, filled with black funeral candy. A hand picks up one of them. Pan R to* MOTHER, *in mourning and with grey shawl, sitting in an easy chair, covered with a white sheet. Bored she unwraps the black paper and puts the white candy in her mouth. Engagement and wedding ring on her L hand.*

2 MARGRET, *white-haired, in black-and-white dress and white apron, is seen in the kitchen. She walks toward the door in BG. In FG a table.*

3 *Long brown corridor.* MARGRET *enters through the door L in BG and exits through the door on the opposite side. Superimposed text:*

THE PELICAN

BY

AUGUST STRINDBERG

Text remains during the next shot.

4 MARGRET *enters another room. A table covered by a white sheet in FG. Pan with* MARGRET *walking L past a green tile stove in BG and the* SON, *playing the piano in FG. She exits through the door.*

5 MOTHER *in her chair R, in FG a chaise longue, in BG a rocking-chair, all covered with white sheets. In BG a chiffonier. On it a clock with, on either side, white candles in candlesticks.* MARGRET *enters through the door in BG.*

The first, emblematic shot gives the impression that the Mother has been sitting in the same position for hours. Already at this point, her being dressed in mourning informs us that a close relative has died. The funeral candy, a period signifier added by the director, further supports this impression, although we may wonder how many viewers will be acquainted with this obsolete custom. The Mother who consoles herself by eating candy, while her children are starving, initiates the central vampire motif.

The drawing room is provided with three doors, the balcony door excepted. White sheets covering the windows formerly meant that someone had recently died in the house and was laid out there. Nordwall instead shows how the furniture is covered with white sheets. The viewers, not aware of turn-of-the century customs, could misunderstand this as being an indication that the family is either about to move to their summer house or have just returned from there. Or they may interpret it symbolically as the Mother's need to cover up what has happened on the chaise longue in this room.

The Mother's mourning combined with the two rings informs us that she has, probably, recently become widowed. Margret's roaming about serves to introduce us to the apartment and to the Son, whose Chopin *Impromptu* sounds too professional. Not least the low temperature in the apartment should motivate a more fumbling playing.

The corresponding part in Sjöman's performance, lasting close to four minutes, can be transcribed as follows:

1 *Golden text* AUGUST STRINDBERG *on black BG, surrounded by golden, rectangular* art nouveau *frame. The same text arrangement in the following shots. Two light strokes of a clock.*

2 *Text* CHAMBER PLAY *Light stroke of clock.*

3 *Text* OPUS 4 *Light stroke of clock.*

4 *Text* THE PELICAN *Two dark strokes of clock. Croaking.*

5 *Text* ACT 1 *One dark stroke of clock. Croaking.*

6 *Sunset across snow-covered field with high reeds. In BG a tower. Croaking, tolling continues until shot 12.*

7 *Avenue of dark, bare trees. Snow-covered ground.*

8 *A* MAN *dressed in black (the* FATHER*) with black top hat and a thick book under his arm makes way through the snow towards a red-brick church in BG.*

9 *A high red apartment house.*

10 *CU of* MARGRET *behind a window pane. She is looking at a thermometer.*

11 *HA of the red-brick church.*

12 *Drawing room. The* FATHER*, in black dress, rocks in a black, creaking rocking chair.*

13 MARGRET *puts a white cloth on the table. Creaking.*

14 *The* FATHER *up from the creaking rocking chair, locks chiffonier. Ticking of the clock. Portrait of the* FATHER *behind him on wall. While* MARGRET*, in BG, spreads a black cloth on the table, he falls down on the chaise longue in FG.* MARGRET *up to him, supports his head. Zoom-in to CU of the* FATHER*. Dissolve to*

15 *Flames with superimposed white text:* "And God shall wipe away / all tears from their eyes *Ticking of clock, tolling until shot 20.*

16 *White text on black BG:* and there shall be no more / death

17 *White text on black BG:* neither sorrow / nor crying / nor pain

18 *White text on black BG:* for the former things are passed away"

19 *CU of the* Mother, *in mourning, black earrings, red hair, red nails. She keeps her hands pressed together. Track-out. She smooths out the green-yellow cover on the chaise longue in FG, sighs. In another room in BG the* Son *is seen. He walks L. Pan with the* Mother *in FG who walks R. She stops by the chiffonier with its black cloth and white candles, grabs the cloth, winces when* Fantaisie Impromptu *is intoned.*

20 *CU of a piano with music, the* Son's *back in FG. He is playing. Tilt up to a mirror above piano. His head is seen in the mirror. He stops playing, looks up into the mirror.*

21 *CU of the* Mother *in profile. She turns her face to frontal.* Impromptu *is heard.*

22 Margret *in from L in BG room with a white cushion and a red blanket. The* Son, *playing, seen in BG. She puts down her load on the table in BG room and exits L.*

23 *CU of the* Mother, *who is putting funeral cards into envelopes by a lit candle.* Impromptu *played and stopped. Ticking of clock.*

24 Margret *in with a glass of milk, which she puts down on the piano. Touches tenderly the* Son's *shoulder.* Impromptu *played and stopped.*

25 *The* Mother *puts down the telephone and rings off as* Margret *enters in BG with cushion and blanket.* Impromptu *played and stopped.*

The pre-credits are inventively designed as a kind of funeral card. Their *art nouveau* arabesques indicate the date of the play and, more importantly, of the visualised action. Already at this point the sound effects warn of death. Shot 6 provides information both of season and time of the day, soon further specified by the clock strokes. It is three in the afternoon. The day – life – is approaching its end, and it is cold, frigid. This is how the husband/father experiences his situation in the pre-title sequence added by the director, in which an event, merely related in the play, is acted out: the husband's sudden death. The difference of presentation is important. In Strindberg's text we experience his death indirectly, through the other characters, which makes us uncertain as to how precisely it came about. In Sjöman's performance we experience his death directly. This is then how it happened. Presumably, the director's choice is part of his attempt to humanise the Mother.

The sequence, which has quite a bit in common with the opening of Bergman's Cries and Whispers, provides us with a symbolic description of environment and characters. The apartment is situated high up. This information is important since from this we can conclude that the Mother can hardly survive her jump from the balcony at the end. The apartment house is close to a church, just as life borders on death. In there the clock of life is ticking, out there the bells of death are tolling. The death of the Father in the opening corresponds to the death of his children at the end. This is indicated by the fact that his death is accompanied by the same non-diegetic flames which diegetically return in the end. And that we receive the same Bible text in both places.

Like his *Ghost Sonata*, Strindberg's *Pelican* ends spectacularly. Here too the room (rather than house) of life is annihilated and replaced by the Isle of the Dead. In *The Pelican* this does not happen through the collapse of the house but through destruction by fire. And *Toten-Insel* is not visualised but verbalised, in the Son's concluding visionary monologue:

> That's the way life should always be, he [the Father] said, and I think it was he who was the pelican, for he plucked himself clean for us, he always had trousers that were worn at the knees and the velvet collar on his overcoat was threadbare, while we walked about as though we were children of a count ... Gerda, hurry up, the ship's bell is ringing, Mama is sitting in the forward saloon, no, she isn't with us, poor Mama! she is gone, is she still ashore? ... where is she? I don't see her, it is no fun without Mama, there she comes! – Now summer vacation begins!
>
> *Pause. The doors in the rear open, the red glare is strongly visible. The* SON *and* GERDA *sink to the floor.*

It may seem as though the Son's incendiary equals murder and suicide. But in a deeper sense his action is not one of revenge but, on the contrary, of desperate longing for reunion. In his concluding monologue all the voyages to the summer island of his childhood are synthesised and blend with the last voyage from the shore of life to the Isle of the Dead. The final words commemorate not so much a family united in the past – was this family ever united? Rather they voice, as at the end of Bergman's WILD STRAWBERRIES (1957), the dream of a union in the life hereafter. Although it now stands clear that it is the Father who has sacrificed himself for the family, the Mother is not rejected. Both Gerda and Fredrik use the compassionate and forgiving expression "poor Mama." The umbilical cord, Strindberg seems to say, here as in *The Father*, is so strong that the Mother's morals are of subordinate importance. The concluding fire means that the former chill is replaced by warmth. Metaphysically, it is a purifying fire,[10] an earthly Purgatory. "Everything had to burn," says Gerda using a telling past tense as though she had already died, "or we hadn't got out of here!"

In Nordwall's version the Son's vision is recreated thus:

> 1 *ECU of the* SON *with half-closed eyes. Smoke glides across his face.*
> SON *faintly.* That's the way life should always be, he said. I think it was he who was the pelican, for he plucked himself clean for us, he always had trousers that were

worn at the knees and the velvet collar of his overcoat was threadbare, while we walked about as though we were children of a count... *Dissolve to*

2 *Double projection of part of a white steamer, the* CAPTAIN *on the bridge. He rings the ship's bell. (The sound of this is heard, with intervals, even as the post-credits unroll.) After a track-out a* BOY (*the* SON *when young) is seen next to him in school cap, butterfly and light blazer.*
BOY *shouts.* Gerda, hurry up, the ship's bell is ringing, Mama is sitting in the forward saloon. *He leaves the* CAPTAIN.

3 BOY, *up on deck, next to a life-saver, shouts.* No, she isn't with us. Poor Mama. She is gone. Is she still ashore? I can't see her. It's no fun without Mama. *Takes off his cap, waves it, smiling.* There she comes. *Fade-out.*

4 *ECU of the* SON *with closed eyes, enveloped in smoke.* SON *faintly.* Now summer vacation begins.

5 *Slow zoom-out until his and* GERDA'S *heads are seen close to one another, enveloped in thickening smoke. His eyes are still closed, while hers are open. Their heads are hidden in the smoke, which pours forth as the post-credits come up.*

This is the only flashback in Nordwall's performance. The dissolve and double projection clarify that the Son remembers himself as a little boy, dressed like the son of "a count." The ringing of the ship's bell is a sound presumably associated with the tinkling of the fire engine on its way to the burning apartment.[11] The life saver functions as a vehicle between the warning signals of the past and the present.[12] In the final line we are removed from the past and return to the present. Its "summer vacation" is contradicted by the thickening smoke which Fredrik, unlike Gerda, refuses to see. Dreaminess is pitted against clearsightedness. The paradisaical vision is rejected as wishful thinking.

Sjöman, who earlier in his performance made ample use of flashbacks, abstains from this device in his ending. Instead, he spends twice as many shots on this part as Nordwall:

1 *Frontal CU of* GERDA *sitting on the floor, leaning her head against the leg of the table.* SON *faintly.* That's the way life should always be, he said.

2 *Frontal CU of the* SON *lying close to her on the floor, flames behind his head.* I think it was he who was the pelican GERDA *coughs.* for he plucked himself clean for us, he always had trousers that were worn at the knees and the velvet collar on his overcoat was threadbare

3 *Frontal CU of* GERDA.
SON *faintly.* while we walked about as though we were children of a count. GERDA *coughs.*

4 *Frontal CU of the* SON *raising his head.* Gerda,

5 *Frontal CU of* GERDA *opening her eyes.*
SON. hurry up, the ship's bell is ringing, Mama is sitting in the forward saloon. GERDA *closes her eyes.*

6 *Frontal CU of the* SON. No, she isn't with us. *Whispers.* Poor Mama.

7 *Frontal CU of* GERDA.
SON *faintly.* Where is she? Is she still ashore?

8 *Frontal CU of the* SON *faintly.* It's no fun without Mama. There she comes. Now summer vacation begins.
His eyes close, his head sinks back.

9 *Frontal CU of* GERDA *quenching a cough.*
SON *faintly.* It's no fun without Mama.

10 *CU of the* SON *from the side, dying.*

11 *White text on blue-green BG:* "And God shall wipe away / all tears from their eyes

12 *White text on blue-green BG:* and there shall be no more / death

13 *White text on blue-green BG:* for the former things are passed away."

Flames hide the text.

Brother and sister are in complete unison. Sjöman shows this, not by constantly framing them in two-shot but by alternately paying equal visual attention to both of them. Moreover, by having Gerda cough, he can let her be heard even during her brother's monologue. Drops of perspiration are visible on the cheeks of both of them. Caused by the intense heat, they are also 'tears' relating to those mentioned in the concluding biblical text. As such they express the earthly suffering man is relieved of when he dies. It is significant that although the text is identical with that of the opening, it now has a more hopeful background colour.

Unlike the final speech of Strindberg's Son, that of Sjöman's does not express the hope for a better life hereafter: "Now summer vacation begins!" Sjöman instead has the Son die with the line that breathes longing for the Mother. In his diary the director comments on the end: "This sick family! – Well, perhaps this is what we finally will show: the game between children and parents in a neurotic family? When the mother dies, the children wail in the flames: 'It's no fun without Mama ...'."[13] The difference between Strindberg's and Sjöman's ending is a difference in accent. The pregnant and hopeful final line of the drama text, which signifies a breaking out of the closed room, is replaced by a wailing repetition. A psychological perspective is foregrounded at the expense of a metaphysical one. Longing for the Mother, or for the uterus, substitutes longing for life hereafter. Sjöman tries to balance the two perspectives by "meeting" Strindberg, as it says in his diary, in the quotation from the Revelation.

On closer inspection the biblical quotation proves to be an esoteric intertext. Sjöman was well aware that Strindberg, in a letter to his German translator Emil Schering, had suggested that the very words from the Revelation 21.4 which frame Sjöman's production of *The Pelican* might be included "in letters of fire above *Toten-Insel*" at the end of *The Ghost Sonata*.[14]

Like plays, performances are time-bound. Although less than a decade separates the two productions of *The Pelican* considered here, the difference between them can at least partly be explained by a change of *Zeitgeist*. Nordwall's production originated in a left-wing climate, in which social problems were foregrounded. The metaphysical aspect of Strindberg's chamber plays, unpalatable for many in secularised Sweden, was something one preferred not to see. Instead, the plays were interpreted in a Marxist way as attacks on bourgeois society, "hollowed out, decadent and doomed to destruction."[15] Nordwall's performance mirrors this rather narrow, one-sided perspective, stimulated by television's preference for a realistic approach.[16] The suggestive oscillation in Strindberg's play between natural and supernatural, meaningful not least because it activates the recipient, disappears when rational explanations are provided at the expense of supernatural alternatives.

When Sjöman produced his version, the climate had changed. It was not as necessary for him to reject what he calls a "religious reading" of the play. And he could more easily accept the universalist message, succinctly voiced in the Mother's "it's the same in all families." As a result, the family in *The Pelican* could be seen as a *pars pro toto*, not for the bourgeoisie but for humanity.

Even more important, perhaps, is Sjöman's close relationship to Ingmar Bergman who, as the foremost film-maker of his generation, has for a long time played the role of mentor to him.[17] As I have already indicated, some of Bergman's films have a strong affinity to Sjöman's *Pelican* production. This is especially true of AUTUMN SONATA (1978), focusing on a mother's guilt-laden relationship to her two daughters, a theme that may well have been inspired by Strindberg's chamber play,[18] which Bergman has staged twice. In his film, Bergman shows more understanding for the mother than

Strindberg does in his play. In his attempt to justify the Mother in *The Pelican* to some extent, Sjöman has undoubtedly been inspired by Bergman's Autumn Sonata.

EPILOGUE

Ibsen, Strindberg and the Small Screen

Both Ibsen and Strindberg wrote their dramas for a double audience, for readers and spectators.[1] Of Ibsen's twenty-five plays, only six were performed before they were published. The rest were performed *after* publication, most of them within a few weeks or months. All Strindberg's around sixty plays were published before they were staged, and it often took years before they reached the theatre.[2] At the end of the last century, publication was important in Scandinavia since it meant that the plays could reach recipients living far from the few theatrical centres that existed at the time. Publication also increased the possibility of being translated and produced abroad. An important side-effect was that dramatists had a reading audience *before* they had a viewing audience. Ordinary theatregoers as well as directors, actors and critics could react to their texts before they reacted to performances based on these texts. Those who did so consequently experienced the performances as re-recipients. This situation no doubt strengthened the position of the dramatist vis-à-vis the director, who in fact was just beginning to emerge around this time.

When viewing the plays dealt with in this book – all of them modern classics – in their televised form, many spectators would be re-recipients, because they had either read them or seen them on the stage. But undoubtedly a much larger group would consist of first-time-recipients. As far as I know, a measurement of different kinds of recipients in this sense has never been undertaken.

The development in this century has, as we know, favoured the director at the expense of the author, irrespective of whether the plays are published before or after performance, or not at all. With regard to TV productions, the gradual development towards a director's theatre and the concomitant diminished respect for the author's text have gone hand in hand with the development from a theatrical to a cinematic presentation of television drama. By opting for the latter, a director obviously has greater possibilities of putting his/her own stamp on the production.

Adaptation of stage drama for television is as old as television itself. For a long time it was the dominant form of drama on the small screen. Already in 1938, BBC transmitted the first full-scale Shakespeare production. Since television was introduced in Scandinavia much later, it was not until the mid-1950s that teleplays began to be transmitted there.

Like the British, the Scandinavians have naturally been anxious to present *their* domestic classics – especially Ibsen and Strindberg – in the new medium. Unlike Shakespeare, Molière or Goethe – to mention but three national classics – Ibsen and Strindberg wrote in a primarily realistic, at times even naturalist, vein, mirroring late nineteenth-century reality. Moreover, they wrote for a picture frame stage where the presence of the audience, behind the absent fourth wall, was ignored.[3] Both circumstances make many of their dramas well suited to the TV medium. It could in fact be argued, as Williams remarks, that

> the television play was the ultimate realisation of the original naturalist convention: the drama of the small enclosed room, in which a few characters lived out their private experience of an unseen public world. [...] This was a drama of the box in the same fundamental sense as the naturalist drama had been the drama of the framed stage.[4]

For realism in drama Raymond Williams lists three main criteria: a contemporary setting, secular action, and a "socially extended" theme.[5] The last simply means that a realistic play should deal not with kings or nobility but with ordinary people, recognisable to the audience and with whom they can identify. To this we may add a fourth criterion: a realistic drama is written in prose. Unlike Shakespeare's plays, which are more frequently televised than those of any other dramatist, Ibsen's and Strindberg's dramas fulfil these four criteria – if we disregard the fact that, like all plays using a contemporary setting, they have eventually turned into 'historical' plays.

We may even go one step further and note that many of their plays, and nearly all the plays dealt with here, focus on bourgeois families. Since television, with regard to reception, is exceedingly family-oriented, this means that there is no great distance in their case between the screened families and the viewing families, especially since the latter would often belong to the same bourgeois group as their screened counterparts.

This does not mean that the two Scandinavians are identical twins. Apart from ideological differences, notably in their attitude to women, there are also formal ones. Ibsen's plays are nearly all full-length dramas. Strindberg's are of varied length; many of them are one-acters. This makes the Swede's plays more easily adaptable to the small screen.[6] Many of them could be transmitted without being shortened at all. Moreover, the lack of a curtain in Strindberg's one-acters, *Miss Julie* being the prime example, means that the spectator's illusion is never broken, a situation that, if we ignore the in-between spots in commercial channels, has become a convention in screen media. On TV this convention is even extended to the full-length play, where the 'curtain' usually consists of a fade-out lasting only a few seconds.

Although TV versions are usually shorter than stage versions, there is much variation. Thacker's *Doll's House* is thirty-six minutes longer than

Fassbinder's, and Warner's *Hedda Gabler* exceeds Garpe's by twenty-eight minutes. Hjelm's *Miss Julie* is twice as long as Heney's. Wajda's *The Stronger* is seven minutes longer than Broström's, a considerable difference for a *quart d'heure*. It would be rash, however, to conclude from this that there is any correlation between play length and presentational style. Whether a version seems closer to a theatrical or to a cinematic presentation is determined by other factors.

It is not only because of their format that Strindberg's plays fit the small screen better than Ibsen's.[7] When Ingmar Bergman finished his film *Fanny and Alexander* with a quotation from the "Explanatory Note" preceding Strindberg's *A Dream Play*, it is a reminder that what is said there better suits the screen than the stage. "Time and space do not exist" in *A Dream Play*, Strindberg claims – no more than in a dream. No more than in the dreamlike medium called film, one is inclined to add. And when later in the "Note" it says that "the characters split, double, redouble, evaporate, condense, overflow, converge," one is reminded of what modern editing can do to screen characters. In several respects late Strindberg anticipates the feature film.[8]

But Strindberg also anticipates television drama. As early as in the preface to *Miss Julie* he calls for "a *small* stage and a *small* auditorium." What stage could be smaller than that of the TV screen, which auditorium more intimate than that of the living room? The naturalism that Strindberg propagates in his preface suits in fact the small screen better than it did the Intimate Theatre with its 161 seats. Better than on the stage, "the subtlest changes of the soul [are] mirrored in the face" on the TV screen, where a face with a "minimum" of make-up is very close to the natural face.

Formally, the plays dealt with here fall into two different categories. While most of them are illusionistic, Strindberg's *Dream Play* obviously does not belong to this category, and his chamber plays do so only partly. Whatever label we put on these dramas – heightened realism, symbolism, expressionism, absurdism – it is clear that they aim more at a symbolic than at a mimetic presentation of life, more at essentialism than at illusionism. Ibsen's *Master Builder*, which moves from recognisable houses for human beings to metaphoric castles in the air, may be seen as a border case. Not surprisingly, the two dramatists' largely realistic plays have been transmitted more often than the more symbolic dramas – at least outside Scandinavia. It is a moot question whether this is because these plays are better suited to the small screen or to the viewers of the small screen, whether the reason is aesthetic or economic. Most likely, it is a combination of the two.

It is still common to think that productions differ from one another mostly because every director interprets the text in his or her own way. This is a simplification of the matter. Since theatrical production, whether for stage or screen, means team work, it follows that there are many reasons why performances necessarily differ from one another, reasons which may be related to five codes.

The *linguistic code* concerns the dialogue of play and performance text. The dialogue of Ibsen's and Strindberg's plays mirrors the spoken language of a century ago. A director can here choose to let actors and actresses faithfully reproduce words and word forms as written – at the risk of being at times unintelligible and often sounding unidiomatic to his/her audience. The performance threatens in such a case to be no more than a period document. To avoid this, most directors prefer to adjust the dialogue to what the audience would consider normal spoken language – unless, of course, deviations from the norm are deliberately intended. They change certain words, word forms and expressions to make them more intelligible and/or recognisable to the audience. This tendency is especially characteristic of performances made for a mass medium like television.

All the directors discussed here delete some of the dialogue. But the amount varies considerably. Some of them also make significant additions; Widerberg's *The Father* is a good example. The dialogue may be updated, modestly (Ryg's *Little Eyolf*, Nordwall's *The Pelican*) or radically (Widerberg's *The Father*). In Ryg's case, the updating matches the temporal relocation of the play (see below). In Nordwall's and Widerberg's case it occasionally leads to a clash between the nineteenth-century setting and the twentieth-century idiom.

Words may be replaced by images, as Brinchmann does when dealing with Nora's soliloquies in *A Doll's House* or Garpe when she chooses a cinematic approach in parts of *Ghosts* and *Hedda Gabler*.

The transference from source to target text implicates many linguistic problems. The difference between Scandinavian and British forms of address is a case in point. Where Ibsen and Strindberg quite naturally, and psychologically meaningfully, can switch between formal and informal pronouns, the English translator must choose between what sounds natural *or* what is meaningful. Ambiguities, often depending on homonyms, verbal correspondences and imagery, are examples of linguistic phenomena that are notoriously difficult to retain in another language.[9]

The *cultural code* is either spatially or temporally determined, or both. Pre-credits mentioning actors rather than characters is an example of spatial determination. Behind this is the rationale that the actors' names serve to catch the interest of the (domestic) audience for the play that is to follow.

When a play is set in another place and/or in another time than indicated by the dramatist, the cultural code is at work. Purely spatial relocation is rare. Our productions provide no example. At best we may speak of hybrid cases in connection with foreign productions. If we disregard incidental cultural signifiers, notably the names of the characters, Thacker's *A Doll's House* and Ives' *The Father* seem as much set in Victorian England as in Oscarian Norway or Sweden. Purely temporal relocation is more frequent. Ryg's *Little Eyolf* exemplies a deviation from the period indicated in the text. Quite common is the more radical spatio-temporal relocation. Fassbinder's *Nora Helmer*, Safran's *The Wild Duck*, Heaney's *Miss Julie* and Wajda's *Silniejsza* all exemplify this kind of change.

The reason why directors relocate plays – spatially, temporally or both – is obviously that they wish to bring them closer to their audience. This desire, one may suspect, is particularly strong when they are addressing a mass audience. Relocation is of course not unproblematic. The cultural code established in the text will rarely match the one in the relocated performance in all respects. As a result – and this is especially true of the spatio-temporal relocation – the play text has to be adapted quite thoroughly to fit the new cultural code. In some cases – *Ghosts* and *The Father* are obvious examples – the subject matter of the play resists temporal relocation. Even if we agree that syphilis and paternity are not the fundamental themes of these plays, the mere fact that the former can now be cured and the latter easily proved counteracts updating of these plays.

It is evident that many plays contain cultural signifiers of one kind or another: references to national customs, regional folklore, allusions to literature, art, music, etc. In Ibsen's case one thinks especially of the biblical and mythological references.[10] But Ibsen is rather sparse in his use of cultural signifiers compared to Strindberg, one reason no doubt why his plays are internationally more accessible. It is significant that Hedda Gabler plays *"wild dance music"* on her piano, while Gerda in *Thunder in the Air* plays *Pluie d'Or* on hers. More specific than Ibsen, Strindberg similarly in *The Ghost Sonata* calls for white sheets covering the windows of the house and prescribes Böcklin's *Toten-Insel* for the end of it. A director must in each case consider how important these signifiers are in the context of the performance and measure this against their intelligibility. Keep, omit or change, that is the question.

Cultural signifiers can also be added by the director. Moshinsky intones his *Ghosts* with Schönberg's *Verklärte Nacht*, Garpe her *Hedda Gabler* with Beethoven's *Appassionata*. In both cases it is, of course, the emotional impact of the music that matters. But if we recognise the compositions, we discover that the titles are also significant. Similarly, when Bergman opens his *Thunder in the Air* with a series of photos of a city, we realise that we are introduced to the setting of the play that is to follow. Some viewers will, in addition, understand that what is shown here is the part of Stockholm where both Strindberg and Bergman have spent a great part of their lives.

The *medial code* applies generally when, as here, we deal with transpositions of plays, intended for the stage, to the screen. Spatial distribution of the characters (proxemics), their movements and gestures, mimicry and vocal characteristics (paralinguistics) are all determined by the presentational mode: stage or screen. Characters who on the stage can be placed at great distances from each other are often squeezed together on the small screen so that they can be framed either in over-the-shoulder shots or in two-shots. Since distances between characters are often psychologically determined, these changes may affect our interpretation of the characters' relations to each other. Gestures have less relevance on the screen than on the stage, for the simple reason that when screen characters are shown in medium shot, medium close-up or close-up, we see little or nothing of their hands. Mimicry, on the other hand, is extremely important in a close-up medium like television. It can contradict, undermine words and even replace words. The interplay between mimicry and dialogue is one of the most important aspects of television drama.

As the preceding chapters have demonstrated, the *directorial code* is undoubtedly the dominant code. The director decides the appearance of setting and characters (the mise-en-scène), the blocking (the grouping of the actors), the number, length and sequence of the shots, the camera distances and angles, etc. Although actors often come up with ideas of their own concerning appearance, movements, gestures, mimicry and paralinguistics, it is virtually impossible for the recipient of the finished product, the performance, to separate their self-direction from the director's direction.

We all have our individual traits and mannerisms. And there is a limit to what an actor or actress can do to change or suppress these in performance. If we have seen the actress doing X or the actor doing Y in other roles, we are bound to recognise some of their features as being outside the part they are presently playing. Consequently, by the *actorial code* is meant not what the actor contributes to his or her part but, on the contrary, that in him or her which does *not* belong to the part.

These features will often give rise to highly personal – positive or negative – reactions on the part of the spectator. The liking or disliking of certain stars undoubtedly in no small measure has to do not with what they do to their parts but with what they do not do to them. What we like or dislike is, partly, their 'natural' selves. The reason why this aspect has been neglected in the previous chapters is obviously that, being highly personal, it calls for another – empirical – approach than the one applied here.

An important distinction, relating to all the five codes, is that between *obligatory* and *voluntary* differences between text and performance. The fundamental medial difference between stage and screen obviously necessitates numerous obligatory changes, as does the difference between source and target text. The cultural code tends to stretch in the same direction, whereas the directorial code is largely determined by voluntary choices. The discrepancy between role and actor consists of a blend of obligatory and voluntary differences, of what actors can do to their parts and what they cannot do to them.

There are innumerable problems involved in the transposition from drama text to small screen, problems which are often only partly overcome. For every transposition made, the gap between source text and performance increases. Television drama, especially in target productions, by definition reduces the importance of the dramatist in favour of that of the director.

This should not blind us to the fact that the protean and emotive TV medium has added new aspects to drama and drama adaptation, aspects which cannot be disregarded by anyone who feels the need of keeping playwrights of yesterday in rapport with present-day audiences. For it is not, as we still tend to think, as readers of the drama texts or as spectators of stage performances that most people today become acquainted with Ibsen and Strindberg. Even a successful production in Paris, London or New York will attract a far smaller, and socially much less varied, audience than a TV version of the same play. For most people today, an Ibsen or Strindberg play is neither book nor stage performance but TV presentation. Also for this reason we need to pay due attention to what is happening in this intimate form of theatre.

1   Nora (Lise Fjeldstad) in Ibsen's *A Doll's House*. From the Norwegian 1973 production, directed by Arild Brinchmann. Photo: Robert Meyer.

2   Nora (Juliet Stevenson) and Krogstad (David Calder) in Ibsen's *A Doll's House*.
    From the British 1992 production, directed by David Thacker. Photo: courtesy
    BBC.

3 Mrs Alving (Judi Dench) and Oswald (Kenneth Branagh) in Ibsen's *Ghosts*. From
   the British 1987 production, directed by Elijah Moshinsky. Photo: courtesy BBC.

4   Hedvig (Melinda Kinnaman) and Gina (Pernilla Östergren) in Ibsen's *The Wild Duck*. From the Swedish 1989 production, directed by Bo Widerberg. Photo: Björn Edergren.

5 Hedda Gabler (Monna Tandberg) and Jørgen Tesman (Tor Stokke) in Ibsen's
   Hedda Gabler. From the Norwegian 1975 production, directed by Arild
   Brinchmann. Photo: courtesy Norsk Rikskringkasting.

6   Hedda Gabler (Fiona Shaw) and Judge Brack (Donald McCann) in Ibsen's *Hedda
Gabler*. From the British 1993 production, directed by Deborah Warner. Photo:
courtesy BBC.

7   Halvard Solness (Kjell Stormoen) and Hilde Wangel (Minken Fosheim) in Ibsen's
    The Master Builder. From the Norwegian 1981 production, directed by Terje
    Mærli. Photo: courtesy Norsk Rikskringkasting.

8   Hilde Wangel (Miranda Richardson) and Halvard Solness (Leo McKern) in Ibsen's
    The Master Builder. From the British 1988 production, directed by Michael
    Darlow. Photo: courtesy BBC.

9 Rita (Diana Rigg) and Alfred (Anthony Hopkins) in Ibsen's *Little Eyolf*. From the
British 1982 production, directed by Michael Darlow. Photo: courtesy BBC.

10 The Captain (Colin Blakeley) and Laura (Dorothy Tutin) in Strindberg's *The Father*. From the British 1985 production, directed by Kenneth Ives. Photo: courtesy BBC.

11 The Captain (Thommy Berggren) in Strindberg's *The Father*. From the Swedish 1988 production, directed by Bo Widerberg. Photo: Björn Edergren.

12 Julie (Bibi Andersson) and Jean (Thommy Berggren) in Strindberg's *Miss Julie*. From the Swedish 1969 production, directed by Keve Hjelm. Photo: courtesy Sveriges Television.

13 Miss Y (Ulla Sjöblom) and Mrs X (Gunnel Broström) in Strindberg's *The Stronger*. From the Swedish 1960 production, directed by Hans Dahlin. Photo: courtesy Sveriges Television.

14 The Officer (Uno Henning) and Indra's Daughter (Ingrid Thulin) in Strindberg's *A Dream Play*. From the Swedish 1963 production, directed by Ingmar Bergman. Photo: courtesy Sveriges Television.

15 Ingmar Bergman rehearsing Act II of Strindberg's *Thunder in the Air* for his Swedish 1960 production. From left to right: The Brother (Ingvar Kjellson), The Gentleman (Uno Henning), Bergman, The Confectioner (John Elfström), Louise (Mona Malm). Photo: courtesy Sveriges Television.

16 The Brother (Per Oscarsson) and The Gentleman (Ernst-Hugo Järegård) in Strindberg's *Thunder in the Air*. From the Swedish 1988 production, directed by Göran Graffman. Photo: Björn Edergren.

17 The Old man (Allan Edwall) and The Student (Stefan Ekman) in Strindberg's *The Ghost Sonata*. From the Swedish 1972 production, directed by Johan Bergenstråhle. Photo: courtesy Sveriges Television.

18 The Mother (Irma Christenson) and The Daughter (Gunilla Olsson) in
Strindberg's *The Pelican*. From the Swedish 1982 production, directed by Vilgot
Sjöman. Photo: Magnus Hartman.

Notes

Notes to Prologue: 2 Page, Stage and Screen

1   Cf. Elam's (p. 3) distinction between dramatic text ("that composed *for* the theatre") and performance text ("that produced *in* the theatre"), and Fischer-Lichte's (pp. 173-82) between literary text and theatrical text. In addition to these, we may distinguish between the performance text (the species) and the individual, factual performance.

2   Strindberg (1967), p. 37.

3   Cf. Hogendoorn, *passim*.

4   The shot, defined as "one uninterrupted image from a single static or mobile framing" (Bordwell & Thompson, p. 388), is the basic unit for all screen productions.

5   Although Bordwell's discussion of "The Viewer's Activity" (pp. 29-47) concerns film, it is highly applicable to the reception of television drama. Chatman (p. 125) gives the gist of Bordwell's in his eyes somewhat exaggerated standpoint when writing: "From the various cues streaming off the screen and loudspeaker, the audience 'constructs' the narrative through intricate hypothesizing, entailing the entire range of mental activity from perception to cognition."

6   Kowzan, p. 73.

7   Fischer-Lichte, p. 15.

8   Esslin (1987), pp. 103-5.

9   See, for example, Pavis (1997) who, polemising against a logocentric approach, argues so strongly for a "stage-centred" one that he even denies the value of "comparing a *mise en scène* with the text which seems to be its source" (p. 63) – the subject of this book. However, by taking this extreme position, Pavis places himself in opposition not only to the "philologists" but also to most stage-oriented researchers.

10 Elsaesser, pp. 137-8.

11 Fischer-Lichte, pp. 193-5.

12 Elam (p. 99) says it succinctly: "It should not be thought that a reader of dramatic texts constructs the dramatic world in the same way as a spectator: not only does the latter have to deal with more varied and specific kinds of information (through the stage vehicles), but the perceptual and temporal conditions in which he operates are quite different." – For a general discussion of the relationship between drama text and performance text, see Ubersfeld (pp. 13-23), and Pfister (pp. 13-39).

13 Bazin, p. 105.

14 Bazin (p. 92) defends the fixed camera in film, usually considered an undesirable 'theatrical' device, holding that it "springs from a reluctance to fragment things arbitrarily and a desire instead to show an image that is uniformly understandable and that compels the spectator to make his own choice."

15 Brandt, p. 27.

16 As a result, it is more difficult to disguise discrepancies on TV between the age of a character and the actor or actress incarnating him/her. Cf. Ollén (1971), p. 24, and Jensen, p. 48.

17 Gombrich (p. 5) points out that when looking at ourselves in the bathroom mirror, we have the illusion of watching our real head, although it will only be about half its real size. It is a fascinating idea that the size of television's talking heads will, in other words, often correspond to our own mirrored self.

18 "Five people on the set for any length of time is a producer's headache, meaning constant regrouping and cutting from shot to shot in order to show what the characters look like in close-up." Bussell, p. 103.

19 Cf. Willems' remark (pp. 69-70) that when televising Shakespeare "one should not underestimate [...] the specific problems attached to producing a Shakespeare play [...] for the benefit of a public whose expectations and rapport with the play are so different from those of its original audience." This is, *mutatis mutandis*, true also of Ibsen and Strindberg on the small screen.

20 Zitner, p. 37.

21 For an early statement on the discrepancies between stage-intended text versions and TV versions, see Chap. 3, "Die Veränderungen vom Schauspiel zum Fernsehspiel," in Elghazali.

22 TV *series* have recurrent characters but self-contained episodes. In TV *serials* the action is continuous from one episode to another. Cf. Brandt, p. 18.

23 McLuhan, pp. 22-32. While McLuhan regards both theatre and television as cool media and film as a hot medium, Hilton (p. 136) considers television, like film, a hot medium. The controversy illustrates television's in-between position.

24 Schwitzke, p. 124.

25 Ellis, p. 131.

26 Ellis, p. 24.

27 Eaton, p. 138.

28 Ivarsson, pp. 63-72.

29 Brandt, p. 8.

30 Ellis, p. 116.

31 Esslin (1980), p. 198.

32 Brandt, p. 22.

33 Brandt, p. 20.

34 W. & A. Waldmann (p. 110) distinguish four different types of TV drama presentation: (1) a pure documentation of a stage performance, (2) a pseudo-cinematic adaptation of a play recorded in an electronic studio, (3) a cinematic adaptation with interior and exterior scenes, and (4) a purely non-realistic electronic production.

35 The exception to the rule is Michael Darlow's production of *Little Eyolf,* included here to indicate the difference between those performances that have been made more or less directly for television and those based on a stage production.

36 Pavis (1992), p. 136.

37 Pavis (1992), p. 146.

38 Hanes Harvey (1998b), p. 28.

39 Pavis (1992), p. 140.

40 Ibsen (1983), p. 320.

41 Characteristically, Meyer's play translations are preceded by information about stage and screen productions first utilising them.

42 Strindberg (1997), pp. 8-9. – This attitude agrees with John Barton's (p. 218): "I always get a standard translation and then either a literal version or an advisor; and then I reword it as I want to or rewrite it myself." Barton has directed three Ibsen plays. – See also Ewbank (1998).

43 Esslin (1987), p. 9. – This neglect applies also to the reviewing of teleplays. "TV reviewers," Brandt (p. 6) points out, "are given grossly insufficient column space. By the time the review appears the broadcast has already receded into history. Since the review cannot serve as a shopping guide in the way theatre criticism does for the wavering playgoer, one may wonder what purpose the television critic serves." Valmin (p. 47) and Jensen (p. 5) make statements to the same effect. In the same way, television drama is still neglected in most theatre histories. Thus the final chapter in Marker (1996), despite its title – "The plurality of postmodern theatre" – pays no attention to it.

44 Pavis (1982), p. 111.

45 Unfortunately, the material is not easily accessible. Unlike cinema films, teleplays are seldom commercially available on videotape.

46 Esslin (1987), p. 7.

47 This applies especially to Strindberg who, often writing in a smaller format than Ibsen, has been hailed as "the world's greatest TV dramatist" – Anton Rønneberg in *Aftenposten*, quoted from Ollén (1971), p. 87.

Notes to: 3 *A Doll's House*

1 For an extensive discussion of this play and how it has been presented in different media, see Törnqvist (1995b). For an analysis of Palle Kjærulff-Schmidt's Danish TV production of *A Doll's House*, see Brøndsted.

2 Longum, p. 126.

3 This is reprinted in Ibsen (1961), pp. 287-8.

4 Sprinchorn (1980), p. 121.

5 For a floor plan based on the stage directions, see Törnqvist (1995b), p. 18.

6 Reynolds view (pp. 99-100) that the room expresses the taste and mentality of both Helmer and Nora is acceptable only if we realise that Nora has adjusted completely to her husband's desires.

7 Quigley, p. 93.

8 Hornby, pp. 114-15.

9 Hallingberg (pp. 170-76) compares the opening of Åke Falck's Swedish TV production, from 1958, with that of Sjöstrand. Borup Jensen (pp. 49-50) compares Ibsen's
   opening to Leif Panduro's 1973 TV version.

10 Styan's claim (pp. 93-94) that "performance makes the point" is slightly exaggerated.
   In a stage performance – Styan's concern – Nora's tipping, occurring far upstage, will
   barely be visible to the spectators, especially since she would most naturally turn her
   back to the audience at the time. A screen version can, through close-ups, reveal more
   of what moves Nora to her generosity but even there it will remain enigmatic, at least
   to the first-time recipients.

11 Bentley, p. 350.

12 Northam (1953), p. 19.

13 Johnston (1989), p. 145.

14 Quigley, pp. 99-100.

15 Sjöstrand actually consistently calls him by his first name, Torvald, a designation in
   line with his inclination to update the relation between husband and wife and to see
   the husband as an individual rather than as a pillar of male society.

16 Steene (1981), p. 297.

17 The hybrid nature of the production is indicated by the fact that whereas the
   pre-credits advertise it as a play by Henrik Ibsen, the post-credits call it a film by
   Werner Rainer Fassbinder.

18 Hayman, p. 144.

19 Quigley, p. 107.

20 Quigley, p. 91.

21 Quigley, p. 100.

22 Durbach, p. 44.

23 A tiny but telling example of how the director has not freed himself enough from the
   drama text to adjust properly to the TV medium.

24 Unlike Braad Thomsen (p. 82), I cannot see that Nora "turns" in the doorway.

25 Cf. Brunner (p. 176): "Noras Aufbruch [endet] mit ihrem Verharren im Dunkeln und
   dem Abwarten auf etwas: Diese Utopie wird im toten Bild des Stehens in der Tür
   gestaltet."

Notes to: 4 *Ghosts*

1 In Norwegian: "*Et Familjedrama i tre Akter*." Meyer (Ibsen, 1983) omits the subtitle.

2 Northam (1953), p. 60.

3 Aarseth (1977), p. 46.

4 Ibsen (1932), p. 139.

5 As the late Captain Alving's illegitimate daughter, Ibsen's Regine occupies a special
   place in Mrs Alving's house. This is indicated in the enigmatic description: "*i huset hos
   fru Alving*" (in the house of Mrs Alving).The enigmatic phrasing is hardly retained in

McFarlane's (Ibsen, 1961), Watts' (Ibsen, 1964) and Fjelde's (Ibsen, 1970) *"in service with Mrs. Alving,"* and lost in Meyer's *"Mrs Alving's maid."*

6   Downer, p. 163.

7   Meyer (Ibsen, 1983) similarly translates: *"she begins to water the flowers."*

8   Aarseth (1977), p. 49.

9   For practical reasons, notably to facilitate comparisons with the text, I have disregarded in my transcriptions the discrepancy between reader and spectator as to when a character is identified with a name. Obviously, Regine and Engstrand are, in the opening, simply 'A Young Woman' and 'An Old Man' to the first-time viewer.

10 Actually the intimate 'du' was not, in Ibsen's time, the pronoun a daughter would normally use when addressing her father. We here deal with a temporal signifier whose disrespectful flavour is lost to a modern audience.

11 The English form of the name is retained whenever I refer to the British translation used by Moshinsky.

12 Cf. Edvard Munch's purplish blue *Self-portrait with cigar* (1895), which may well have served as an inspiration. Moshinsky is often inspired by pictorial art in his TV productions. Vermeer, de la Tour and Watteau have all influenced his Shakespeare performances. Cf. Willis, pp. 141, 146, 160-61.

13 For an extensive discussion of Ibsen's ending, see Törnqvist (1979), pp. 50-61.

14 Hemmer, p. 37.

15 Ibsen himself gave the only correct answer to this question when he said: "That I don't know." Ibsen (1961), p. 475.

16 White sheets covering the windows of a house used to be a sign in Scandinavia that someone had just died there.

17 Cf. Ferguson (1973), p. 152.

Notes to: 5 *The Wild Duck*

1   Letter to Frederik Hegel on 2 September, 1884. Quoted from Meyer (1992), p. 553.

2   Cf. Chatman's observation (p. 51), with regard to film, that "the pressure to begin the action as early as possible has made it fashionable to start story time behind the titles, or even before they appear. Contemporary audiences expect the plot to start with the very first frame."

3   For the difference between a series and a serial, see p. 194, note 22, and Fiske, p. 150.

4   Cf. Widerberg's view that on the stage it is "the damned theatre dialect that destroys everything." Jensen, p. 70.

5   Quoted from Meyer (1992), p. 560.

6   Cf. Ibsen's observation that "Hjalmar must not be acted with any trace of parody. [...] His sentimentality is honest, his melancholy, in its way, attractive; no hint of affectation." Quoted from Meyer (1992), p. 559.

7   By contrast, Rudolf Noelte's stage-based West German TV version, from 1979, clearly favours Gregers at the expense of Hjalmar and Relling.

8   This is Meyer's rendering in Ibsen (1983).

9   This is McFarlane's rendering in Ibsen (1960).

10   When Meyer, in Ibsen (1983), has Gina refer to Gregers as "that repulsive little man," it may seem to be another implicit reference that Gregers is short in stature. But the translator's "little" has no counterpart in the source text.

11   Northam (1953), p. 89.

12   There is another one, as we shall see, in Strindberg's *The Father*.

13   Madsen, p. 257.

14   In Ibsen (1967) and Ibsen (1965) respectively.

15   For the significance of the opening speeches, in source and target texts, see Törnqvist (1978).

16   An exception to the rule was Ingmar Bergman's 1972 stage version at the Royal Dramatic Theatre in Stockholm, where the loft was placed at the front of the stage. Consequently, the audience could see how Hedvig, overhearing Hjalmar's conversation with Gregers, shot herself. Whereas Ibsen settles for identification between the male characters and the recipient, Bergman had the audience identify itself with Hedvig and function as *Besserwisser* vis-à-vis the men.

17   Brinchmann later took a risk when he showed the dead Hedvig in close-up. Although Relling assures Hjalmar that she is dead, the viewer can see her eyelids move slightly.

18   Letter 22 November 1884, quoted from Ibsen (1960), p. 439.

19   Høst (1967), p. 200.

20   Watts, p. 139.

21   This in contrast to Bergman, who in his 1972 stage production strongly suggested that Gregers intended to take his life when he had him leave the Ekdal home with the revolver in his hand that Hedvig had used on herself. Cf. Marker (1989), p. 154.

Notes to: 6 *Hedda Gabler*

1   Ibsen (1967).

2   Ibsen (1985).

3   This in contrast to, for example, Peter Zadek's stage-based TV version, produced in the late 1970s, where the play seems to be set in the 1950s. Old Miss Tesman wears pants and calypso music is being played on the record-player in the drawing room.

4   Høst (1958), pp. 147-8.

5   In this omission, as in many other ways, Garpe may have been inspired by Ingmar Bergman's famous 1964 stage production of the play.

6   Northam (1953), p. 155.

7   Nietzsche was introduced to Scandinavia through Georg Brandes' lectures in 1888.

8   Lyons, p. 53.

9   The resemblance to Hussein's opening is, in fact, so striking that it is hard to believe that Brinchmann has not been inspired by it. Both directors have probably been influenced by Ingmar Bergman's way of presenting Hedda alone in the preamble to his 1964 stage performance.

10 Cf. Bergman's abortive pantomime opening his 1964 stage version, where Hedda, in Markers' (1989) words, "pressed her hands to her abdomen, pounding it several times with the full force of her clenched fists" (p. 182).

11 Ibsen's Miss Tesman says "Dejlig, – dejlig, – dejlig er Hedda," which echoes the Norwegian Benediction's "Helig, helig, helig er Herren Sebaot" (Jes. 6.3).

12 In Ibsen (1960).

13 Retained by Fjelde in Ibsen (1965b).

14 Suzman, p. 103.

15 Ingmar Bergman approached a screen version by having Hedda face the prompter's box, representing the fireplace, in his 1964 stage production, so that the audience could see the expression on her face at this point.

16 Meyer in Ibsen (1985), p. 335.

17 Nelson, p. 205.

18 Suzman, p. 104.

Notes to: *7 The Master Builder*

1   The firmly established English title indicates an artistic supremacy on Solness' part lacking in the original's *Bygmester Solness*, literally "Building Contractor Solness," stressing the fact that Solness is not, like architect Brovik, someone who is professionally educated. He is a self-made man.

2   Northam (1953), p. 174.

3   Northam (1953), p. 175.

4   The frequent use of mirrors is characteristic of Ingmar Bergman's films. See Koskinen, pp. 61-153.

5   This sequence calls to mind the dreamlike Asylum scene in Strindberg's *To Damascus I*.

6   For a comparison between Solness and Knut Brovik, see Törnqvist (1972).

7   Hilde's line, which clearly refers to the Bible's *consummatum est* is here rendered as in the Authorized Version (John 19.30). The biblical reference is obscured in the translations. Ellis-Fermor (Ibsen, 1971), renders it as "For now, now it's done!," McFarlane (Ibsen, 1966) as "Now, now he's done it!," Meyer (Ibsen, 1983) as "He's done it at last, he's done it!," and Fjelde (Ibsen, 1965b) as "now, now it's fulfilled."

8   As Røed remarks (1977, p. 167), Ibsen had Herdal carry the shawl, since "it would have struck us as inappropriate if she [Hilde] had taken it from its owner."

9   Northam (1953), p. 183.

10 Cf. the double significance of Rebekka's shawl at the end of *Rosmersholm*.

11 See Törnqvist (1977).

Notes to: 8 *Little Eyolf*

1 Ferguson (1996), p. 407.

2 This is the tenor of the article by Davis & Thomas, pp. 54-7.

3 Ibsen's word is *"kratbevokset."* Ellis-Fermor (Ibsen, 1964) renders this as *"overgrown with copsewood,"* Meyer (Ibsen, 1988) as *"shrub-covered."*

4 Ibsen's word is *"lysthus,"* literally "house of pleasure." Its vine, we recall from *Hedda Gabler*, is a Dionysian symbol of joy in life.

5 Røed (1974), p. 73.

6 Cf. Jacobs (1984), pp. 608-9: "Alfred's unconvincing shame at not having a brother may mask a genuine need to subvert Asta's growing power to attract him sexually; but [...] the likelier explanation for this charade is that it appealed to him primarily as a narcissistic recreation of himself as a young boy, a boy as yet free from sexual desires and innocent of the world of adult responsibility. For Asta, one suspects that transvestism was not so much a means of changing sex as a way of getting closer to her beloved Alfred."

7 Cf. Ibsen's remark to his French translator, Moritz Prozor: "Little Eyolf, in whom the infatuation and the feebleness of his father are reproduced, but concentrated, exaggerated." Quoted from Northam (1953), p. 189, note.

8 Meyer, in Ibsen (1988, p. 222), claims that it is "the shock of Eyolf's fall" that "has rendered Allmers sexually impotent" – a somewhat misleading interpretation.

9 Valency, p. 215.

10 Cf. Northam (1973), p. 219: "Alfred is no hero, but he is not far short of one, and his deficiency must [...] be assessed in the context of his impossible predicament."

11 Weigand, whose analysis focuses on Allmers, provides what is hitherto the most devastating portrait of him: "a sorry wretch, part crank and part fraud" (p. 349).

12 This interpretation differs from Røed's (1974), p. 71: "It is Rita who is blond and Asta who is dark; and as the play progresses we realize that it is in Rita that the core is innocence, whereas there are dangerous undercurrents of passion in Asta."

13 Northam (1953), p. 188.

14 Valency, p. 216.

15 Jacobs (1984), p. 605.

16 Ibsen's word is *"saloppe,"* which was a morning garment for women in the eighteenth century.

17 Jacobs (1985, p. 607) observes that "so many stage directions specify eye movements [...] that the text often seems more like a twentieth-century film script than a late nineteenth-century play."

18 Valency, p. 217.

19 "Do you believe," Ibsen once asked Caroline Sontum, "that Rita will take on the rough children? Don't you think it's just a holiday mood?" Ibsen (1935), p. 184.

20 Ewbank (1994), p. 146.

21 Meyer (Ibsen, 1988), p. 220.

22 One of the Norwegian TV critics, Anton Rønneberg (p. 37), condoned this change partly because it was a way of getting rid of "the all-too-explicit symbol of the flag being hoisted."

23 In Britten's opera, as in Ibsen's play, a child falls to his death into the sea.

24 Cf. Ingmar Bergman's way, at the end of The Seventh Seal, of keeping Death invisible and showing only the reactions of the six characters he has come to fetch.

25 Meyer (Ibsen, 1988), translates this passage freely and omits several acting directions, among others Allmers' "*clenching his fists*" against Rita. Although this acting direction may seem both melodramatic and limiting, it is certainly the director's, not the translator's, task to ignore it.

Notes to: 9 *The Father*

1 Strindberg's word is "sorgespel," corresponding to German "Trauerspiel," that is, a drama in contemporary (bourgeois) environment with a tragic ending. Cf. Brandell, p. 164.

2 See Ollén (1982), p. 116.

3 On this issue, see Jacobs (1969).

4 Szondi, p. 23.

5 Ignoring these connotations Meyer (Strindberg, 1976), calls it just "*a room.*"

6 Brandell, p. 166. – The windows, we must assume, are in the 'missing' fourth wall.

7 Both Carlson (Strindberg, 1981), and Sprinchorn (Strindberg, 1986), assume that there are weapons of *different* kinds on the walls. But the most natural way of reading Strindberg's sentence is to see the guns (Sw. "gevär") as merely a specification of the more general term weapons (Sw. "vapen").

8 Cf. the diagonal arrangement of the guns in the 1908 production of the play at Strindberg's own Intimate Theatre. See Falck, p. 215.

9 Wirmark, p. 34.

10 After 1960, when women clergymen were permitted to the Swedish State Church, this does not necessarily apply to the Pastor.

11 Cf. *Miss Julie*, where Jean's brushing of the Count's pair of "*riding-boots with spurs*" takes place shortly after he has attempted to kiss Julie and some time before he has intercourse with her.

12 *The Father* was at one stage meant to be the first part of a trilogy, the second part of which, *Marauders*, had in fact been written already in 1886.

13 Wirmark, p. 34.

14 Cf. the description of the Captain, Edgar, in *The Dance of Death I*: "*He is dressed in a worn undress uniform with riding-boots and spurs.*" More obviously than in *The Father* this domestic dress contrasts with the uniform Edgar shows to the world: "*dress uniform, helmet, cape, white gloves.*"

15 For an extensive discussion of this part, as text and as presented in five different TV versions, see Törnqvist (1993).

16 After 1933 the Captain's Christian name has, of course, received very special, undesirable connotations.

17 To prove fatherhood you need, of course, to have access to the true father.

18 Breitholtz, pp. 181-90.

19 Trying to retain the meaning of the Swedish name, Sprinchorn (Strindberg, 1986)
translates 'Nöjd' with "Happy." But Happy, as Jacobs (1986, 116) points out, "sounds
like an affectionate nickname" rather than an ordinary surname. With regard to
charactonyms like Nöjd and Svärd a translator can choose either to keep the names of
the source text, in which case he sacrifices the thematic significance of these names.
Or else he can choose to find equivalents in the target language which, as the present
example demonstrates, is exceedingly difficult. In his French translation of the play,
Père, Strindberg changed the Swedish surname Nöjd into a French Christian name
(Pierre) – rather than into a nickname. Meaning 'stone,' 'Pierre' retains at least something of the original's charactonym.

20 Cf. Lamm, pp. 282, 295, 298.

21 In his combined film and TV version of the play (1971), Alf Sjöberg used the modern
form *Fadern* as title for his production.

22 In 1893 Strindberg, showing her his hand, told his second wife, Frida Uhl, about "an
innocent eczema" he had had since childhood. "When anything happens to me the
wound opens and bleeds." Two years earlier he stated in a letter that he had "suffered
for three years" from a "skin eruption" on his hands. Meyer (1987), pp. 313-14.

23 Lamm, p. 293.

24 Celebrating the birth of Jesus, the Christmas star reminds us of Joseph's dubious fatherhood.

Notes to: 10 *Miss Julie*

1 Martinus (pp. 111-12) considers this title a mistranslation and prefers the title *Lady
Julie*, used by Johnson in Strindberg (1970). But finding a functional English equivalent for the Swedish title is not easy and there is much to be said for retaining the traditional 'Miss.' Cf. Robinson in Strindberg (1998), pp. 293-4, note 69.

2 Cf. Karnick, p. 121: "Die Einheit des Orts wird zum Gefängnis, das nur noch einen
einzigen Ausgang hat."

3 Hjelm, *Svenska Dagbladet*, 2 July 1969.

4 This constellation had been used in an American segregational stage production
from 1950, set in a New Orleans plantation. See Ollén (1982), p. 146. Heany's production has, of course, quite the opposite aim.

5 Bengt Jahnsson, *Dagens Nyheter*, 27 December 1969.

6 The inclusion of the royal portrait was presumably inspired by little Jean's admira-
tion of the pictures of royalty in the Turkish pavilion.

7 Ollén (1972), p. 202.

8 See Törnqvist & Jacobs, pp. 96-97.

9 Sprinchorn (1966), p. 26.

10 As the term indicates, internal focalisation means that the experience is limited to one character. The range stretches from simple POV shots to shots indicating drunkenness, hallucination, etc. Cf. Branigan, p. 103.

11 Letter to the author 22 September 1888, in Strindberg (1961), 126, note 5.

12 Alf Sjöberg's famous 1949 stage version of *Miss Julie* at the Royal Dramatic Theatre in Stockholm was based very much on an allegorical reading of the play. See Sjöberg, pp. 115-32.

13 Carl Johan Elmquist in *Politiken*, 27 December 1969.

Notes to: 11 *The Stronger*

1 For a comprehensive analysis of the drama text, see Törnqvist (1970), pp. 297-308.

2 In the source text, the unmarried lady is called "Mlle Y." The title 'Mlle' was frequently used by Swedish actresses until the 1870s, when it was replaced by the corresponding but higher-ranking Swedish title 'Fröken.' Presumably the titular difference in the play is meant to indicate a certain class difference within the theatre between the two ladies. At the first performance of *The Stronger* – on 9 March, 1889 in Copenhagen – the two characters were listed as "Frk. [Miss] Amalie" and "Fru [Mrs] Helga". Janni, pp. 120-21.

3 Strindberg (1984a), p. 58.

4 Ollén (1982), p. 171.

5 Strindberg (1961), p. 263.

6 Ollén (1982), p. 170.

7 Strindberg is notoriously incomplete, careless, generous – choose your preference – in his stage directions.

8 Ollén (1982), p. 171.

9 Gavel Adams, p. 180.

10 Cf. Ollén's remark (1982, p. 173) on the 1960 TV production: "Since you rarely saw both of them at the same time, the silence of one of them never seemed unnatural."

11 Cf. the identical appearance of the brothers in Bergman's production of *Thunder in the Air*. See p. 149.

12 Bergman's film PERSONA (1966), which has a great affinity with *The Stronger*, has presumably been an important intertext.

Notes to: 12 *A Dream Play*

1 Pfister, p. 45.

2 Strindberg (1977), p. 152.

3 For an extensive discussion, see Lunin, pp. 182-8.

4 Törnqvist (1988), pp. 256-90.

5 In a letter to Gustaf af Geijerstam, 17 March, 1898. See Strindberg (1992), p. 624.

6 Prospero's words in *The Tempest* are quoted by Strindberg in the part of the "Explanatory Note" first published by Müssener, p. 26.

7   The name, of Greek origin, means 'chaste.' It became known through a saint who died as a martyr and who is usually depicted with a lamb (Latin *agnus*) at her side.

8   Chatman, p. 160.

9   Szondi, p. 29.

10 Insensitive to the significance of the key phrase, Paulson in Strindberg (1972, p. 340) remarks: "The phrase 'Mankind is to be pitied' can [...] easily become laughable [...] because of its frequent repetition in the play. For that reason I have thought it important to vary it somewhat [...]."

11 *Röster i Radio*, No. 17, 1963. – It is likely that the TV version helped Bergman to choose a chamber play format for his next, 1970 stage production of the drama.

12 Dyfverman & Löfgren, p. 143.

13 *Röster i Radio*, No. 17, 1963.

14 Törnqvist (1988), pp. 257-8.

15 It is significant that it was around this time that Bergman converted to "a world totally without god," his own characterisation of his film THE SILENCE (1963), shot just before he directed his TV version of *A Dream Play* and at an early stage called "The Dream." See Sjöman, pp. 191, 220.

16 His term of measure, ell, is characteristically obsolete – and fairytalish. In England 45 inches equal one ell.

17 Cf. Hamlet who, in Strindberg's view (1967, p. 102), "wants to know what one is not permitted to know; and because of arrogantly wanting to know God's secrets which have a right to remain secrets, Hamlet is punished by the kind of madness called skepticism, which leads to absolute uncertainty [...]."

18 For a penetrating discussion of the visual attributes in the play, see Bennich-Björkman, pp. 56-74.

19 Molander had used the same music in his stage productions.

20 Bergman's stylised, nightmarish recreation of the commencement ceremony here may be compared to the realistic version of it, set in the cathedral of Lund, presented in his film WILD STRAWBERRIES (1957).

21 Bergman, p. 33.

22 Bergman makes effective use of this device already in THE SEVENTH SEAL (1957), when he has Skat die with a mute scream. Törnqvist (1995a), p. 104.

23 Ollén (1971), p. 34.

Notes to: 13 *Thunder in the Air*

1   Anglo-American translators have suggested no fewer than four other English titles for Strindberg's first chamber play: *The Storm*, *The Thunderstorm*, *Storm* and *Stormy Weather*.

2   Carl Johan Elmquist in *Politiken*. Quoted from Ollén (1971), p. 20.

3 Jacobs (1988), who has noted the Gentleman's inconsistent reporting about the past, argues that "each version seems to bring him closer to the truth" (p. 26). Actually, the progression offered in the play is somewhat more meandering than this suggests.

4 The stage directions in the play are closely examined in Hanes Harvey (1984, pp. 185-245) in relation to the 1907 situation in the part of Stockholm, Östermalm, that Strindberg had in mind.

5 When writing the play, Strindberg was himself living in Östermalm.

6 Cf. Åke Perlström's remark in *Göteborgs-Posten* (23 January, 1960): "the austerely closed nature of Birgitta Morales' scenery interestingly reflected Strindberg's [suggestion of] constraint and cramped space around the characters of the play." It is, however, Bergman rather than Strindberg who suggests these things.

7 Ewbank (Strindberg, 1997, p. 17), assuming carelessness on Strindberg's part, amends this speech by giving the concluding question to the Brother.

8 This interpretation seems more likely and more meaningful than the other possibilities suggested by Ewbank in Strindberg (1997), p. 55, note 15.

9 Kvam, p. 53.

10 Cf. *A Dream Play*, where the Mother, who is soon to die, keeps trimming the burning candle in front of her, and where quickly alternating light (day) and darkness (night) represent the passing of time.

11 This was actually the original title of the play.

Notes to: 14 *The Ghost Sonata*

1 Strindberg (1967), p. 19. Actually, "subject matter" would be a better term than "motif."

2 For an extensive examination of the text as well as various translation problems related to it, see Törnqvist (1982), pp. 181-206, 220-41.

3 Strindberg had used it in an earlier play, *Crimes and Crimes*, to indicate the pangs of conscience afflicting the protagonist.

4 Strindberg (1967), p. 19.

5 At Strindberg's request copies of these had been placed at either side of the stage in the Intimate Theatre. See Falck, p. 53.

6 Bryant-Bertail, p. 307.

7 Rokem, pp. 66-68.

8 This is a mirror, found outside, not "inside," (Strindberg, 1955), old Swedish houses, enabling people indoors to see what is happening in the street without being seen themselves.

9 Cf. Delblanc, pp. 93-112.

10 Northam (1966), p. 41.

11 Strindberg (1918a), p. 1036.

12 Northam (1966), pp. 41, 48.

13 Ekman, concerned with how the five senses are related to the play, argues (p. 164) that Act I is mainly visual, Act II mainly aural, and Act III mainly gustatory and olfactory. This schematic sensual pattern seems contradicted when it is said (p. 199) that at the end "speech has been replaced by music." As we have seen, the play actually begins and ends with music, an aural framing that is highly meaningful.

14 He was to produce *A Dream Play*, very freely, for Swedish TV in 1980.

15 The actor who had played the part of the Old Man in the 1962 radio version did the same part in Bergenstråhle's TV version in a more Mephistophelian manner.

16 In *A Dream Play* – I quote from Walter Johnson's translation (Strindberg, 1973) – "the newborn whimper [Sw. kvida] / wailing, screaming / over the pain of existence."

Notes to: 15 *The Pelican*

1 Ollén (1961), p. 525.

2 *Röster i Radio/TV*, No. 10, 1982, p. 4.

3 In a recent English stage version, the two plays have been combined in such a way that *Toten-Insel* is used as a frame for *The Pelican*. See Strindberg (1994).

4 *Röster i Radio/TV*, No. 10, 1982, p. 4.

5 Cf. Maria, thumb in mouth, next to her doll's house in Ingmar Bergman's CRIES AND WHISPERS (1973).

6 Steene (1989), p. 66.

7 Strindberg (1991).

8 Steene (1989), pp. 63-5.

9 Cf. the explanation in Strindberg (1991), p. 460: "*carbolic acid* was injected into the blood vessels of a deceased person to prevent all too fast putrefaction."

10 Leifer, pp. 176-77.

11 This observation is Margareta Sjögren's in her review of the performance in *Svenska Dagbladet* 18 December 1973.

12 Cf. the symbolic life-saver at the end of WILD STRAWBERRIES .

13 *Röster i Radio/TV*, No. 10, 1982, p. 4.

14 The idea was never realised but the quotation appears at the beginning of *Toten-Insel* – see Strindberg, 1 (1918), p. 296 – intended to be a continuation of *The Ghost Sonata*. *Toten-Insel* was planned as a piece about the post-existence of the dead husband / father. This explains why Sjöman chose to reproduce the biblical quotation with Strindberg's old spelling.

15 Maria Bergom-Larsson in *Dagens Nyheter*, 29 October 1972.

16 More than three years earlier Nordwall's countryman Hans Dahlin had successfully directed an abstract, visionary TV version of the play in Norway, transmitted on 13 January 1970. Ollén (1982), p. 558.

17 Sjöman is responsible for some of the best interviews with Bergman. He has also, as earlier noted, published a very penetrating "diary" about the making of Bergman's film WINTER LIGHT (1963). See Sjöman.

18 Törnqvist (1995b), p. 161.

Notes to: 16 *Epilogue: Ibsen, Strindberg and the Small Screen*

1   Re Ibsen, see Törnqvist (1997b). – For Tennant (p. 62) the fact that Ibsen set his stage from the recipient's optical point of view – as did Strindberg – is a sign that he wrote his plays for the reader rather than the spectator. This is hardly convincing since the reader's and the spectator's – as well as the director's – optical point of view would coincide.

2   For dates of composition and English translations of Strindberg's plays, see Törnqvist (1982), pp. 250-54.

3   Bennett (p. 24) rightly remarks that "the acting style of naturalist theatre excludes audience intervention" but too easily accepts Brecht's view that the characters in these plays do not interact with the audience.

4   Williams (1990), p. 56.

5   Williams (1977) quoted from Fiske, p. 22.

6   Cf. Elghazali's remark (p. 39) that one-acters and chamber plays are regarded as "die wirkungsvollste Form für das Fernsehspiel."

7   Cf. the impressive number of Strindberg plays produced by Swedish television 1951-96 listed in Steene & de Nona, pp. 167-75.

8   Borup Jensen (1975) demonstrates (pp. 250-61) how the ideas expressed in the preface to *Miss Julie* and the "Explanatory Note" for *A Dream Play* fit the film medium.

9   For the problems related to the translation of Strindbergian imagery, see Törnqvist (1998), pp. 7-23.

10 See Johnston (1975), *passim*.

Productions

Unless otherwise indicated, all productions are in colour.

Abbreviations

Trans. = Translator
Adapt. = Adaptor
Dir.   = Director
Sc.   = Scenographer
Mus.   = Music

IBSEN

A Doll's House

1970   27 Dec. *Ett dockhem*. Sweden. SVT. Adapt. and dir. Per Sjöstrand. Sc. Bibi Lindström. *Torvald* Olof Bergström, *Nora* Solveig Ternström, *Kristine* Mona Andersson, *Rank* Olof Thunberg, *Krogstad* Sven Lindberg, *Nurse* Ann-Mari Adamsson. 1:48.

1973   23 Oct. *Et dukkehjem*. Norway/Sweden. NRK/SR. Dir. Arild Brinchmann. Sc. Christian Egemar. *Helmer* Knut Risan, *Nora* Lise Fjeldstad, *Rank* Per Theodor Haugen, *Mrs Linde* Bente Børsum, *Krogstad* Ole Jørgen Nilsen, *Anne Marie* Ingrid Øvre Wiik, *Helene* Unn Vibeke Hol. 2:26.

1974   3 March. *Nora Helmer*. West Germany. Saarländischer Rundfunk. Trans. Bernhard Schulze. Adapt. and dir. Rainer Werner Fassbinder. Sc. Friedhelm Boehm. *Helmer* Joachim Hansen, *Nora* Margit Carstensen, *Mrs Linde* Barbara Valentin, *Krogstad* Ulli Lommel, *Rank* Klaus Löwitsch, *Marie* Lilo Pempeit, *Helene* Irm Hermann. 1:40.

1992   21 Nov. *A Doll's House*. UK. BBC 2. Trans. Joan Tindale. Dir. David Thacker. Sc. Marjorie Pratt. Mus. Guy Woolfenden. *Helmer* Trevor Eve, *Nora* Juliet Stevenson, *Mrs Linde* Geraldine James, *Rank*, Patrick Malahide, *Krogstad* David Calder, *Helene* Sonja Ritter, *Anne-Marie* Helen Blatch. 2:16.

Ghosts

1978   29 Aug. *Gengangere*. Norway. NRK. Dir. Magne Bleness. Sc. Christian Egemar. *Helene Alving* Henny Moan, *Osvald* Bentein Baardson, *Manders* Finn Kvalem, *Engstrand* Rolf Søder, *Regine* Jannik Bonnevie. 2:07.

1987   14 June. *Ghosts*. UK. BBC 2. Trans. Michael Meyer. Dir. Elijah Moshinsky. Sc. Gerry Scott. *Mrs Alving* Judi Dench, *Manders* Michael Gambon, *Oswald* Kenneth Branagh, *Engstrand* Freddie Jones, *Regina* Natasha Richardson. 1:42.

1989   5 Feb. *Gengångare*. Sweden. SVT. Trans. Gurli Linder. Adapt. Margareta Garpe and Gunilla Jensen. Dir. Margareta Garpe. Sc. Bo Lindgren. *Helene Alving* Agneta Ekmanner, *Manders* Sten Ljunggren, *Osvald* Gerhard Hoberstrofer, *Engstrand* Gustav Kling, *Regine* Gunilla Röör. 1:40.

The Wild Duck

1973   20 Feb. *Vildanden*. Norway. NRK. Black-and-white. Dir. Arild Brinchmann. Sc. Per Schwab. *Werle* Georg Løkkeberg, *Gregers* Espen Skjønberg, *Ekdal* Ingolf Rogde, *Hjalmar* Tor Stokke, *Gina* Mona Hofland, *Hedvig* Anne Marit Jacobsen, *Mrs Sørby* Bab Christensen, *Relling* Joachim Calmeyer. 2:31.

1983   *The Wild Duck*. Australia. Adapt. Tutte Lemkow, Dido Merwin, Henri Safran. Additional material Peter Smalley. Dir. Henri Safran. Mus. Simon Walker. *Wardle* Michael Pate, *Gregory* Arthur Dignam, *Ackland* John Meillon, *Harold* Jeremy Irons, *Gina* Liv Ullmann, *Henrietta* Lucinda Jones, *Mrs Summers* Marion Edward, *Mr Roland* Rhys McConnochie, *Mollison* Colin Croft. 1:30.

1989   3-5 Sept. *Vildanden* (in three parts). Sweden. SVT 1. Dir. Bo Widerberg. Sc. Pelle Johansson. *Werle* Percy Brandt, *Gregers* Stellan Skarsgård, *Ekdal* Sten-Åke Cederhök, *Hjalmar* Tomas von Brömssen, *Gina* Pernilla Östergren, *Hedvig* Melinda Kinnaman, *Mrs Sørby* Mona Seilitz, *Relling* Mats Bergman, *Molvik* Claes Månson. 0:44, 1:12, 0:44 = 2:40.

Hedda Gabler

1972   20 Oct. *Hedda Gabler*. UK. BBC 1. Trans. Michael Meyer. Dir. Waris
        Hussein. Sc. Natasha Kroll. *Hedda* Janet Suzman, *Tesman* Ian
        McKellen, *Løvborg* Tom Bell, *Mrs Elvsted* Jane Asher, *Brack* Brendan
        Barry, *Aunt Juliana* Dorothy Reynolds, *Berthe* Rachel Thomas. 1:48.

1975   7 Jan. *Hedda Gabler*. Norway. NRK. Dir. Arild Brinchmann. Sc.
        Lubos Hruza. *Hedda* Monna Tandberg, *Tesman* Tor Stokke, *Mrs
        Elvsted* Henny Moan, *Brack* Knut Wigert, *Løvborg* Per Sunderland,
        Aunt Julle Ada Kramm. 2:04.

1993   27 Nov. *Hedda Gabler*. UK. BBC 2. Trans. Una Ellis-Fermor. Dir.
        Deborah Warner. Sc. Hildegard Bechtler. Mus. Per Nørgård. *Hedda*
        Fiona Shaw, *Miss Tesman* Pat Leavy, *Berte* Susan Colverd, *Tesman*
        Nicholas Woodeson, *Mrs Elvsted* Bríd Brennan, *Brack* Donal
        McCann, *Løvborg* Stephen Rea. 2:08.

1993   26 Dec. *Hedda Gabler*. Sweden. SVT. Trans. Klas Östergren. Dir.
        Margareta Garpe. Sc. Bo-Ruben Hedwall. *Hedda* Lena Endre,
        Tesman Göran Ragnerstam, *Mrs Elvsted* Gunilla Röör, *Brack*
        Lars-Erik Berenett, *Løvborg* Stefan Sauk, *Aunt Julle* Gunnel
        Lindblom, *Berte* Margreth Weivers. 1:40.

The Master Builder

1981   29 Dec. *Byggmester Solness*. Norway. NRK. Dir. Terje Mærli. Sc.
        Grethe Hejer. Mus. Kåre Kolberg. *Solness* Kjell Stormoen, *Mrs
        Solness* Rut Tellefsen, *Herdal* Joachim Calmeyer, *Knut Brovik* Bjarne
        Andersen, *Ragnar Brovik* Bjørn Skagestad, *Kaja Fosli* Tone
        Danielsen, *Hilde Wangel* Minken Fosheim. 1:52.

1988   15 May. *The Master Builder*. UK. BBC 2. Trans. Michael Meyer. Dir.
        Michael Darlow. Sc. David Meyerscough-Jones. Mus. Francis
        Shaw. *Knut Brovik* Sebastian Shaw, *Ragnar Brovik* Simon Rouse,
        Kaja Fosli Natalie Ogle, *Solness* Leo McKern, *Mrs Solness* Jane
        Lapotaire, *Herdal* Donald Churchill, *Hilde Wangel* Miranda Rich-
        ardson. 2:15.

Little Eyolf

1968   3 Sept. *Lille Eyolf*. Norway. NRK. Black-and-white. Dir. Magne
        Bleness. Sc. Olav Ile. *Alfred Allmers* Joachim Calmeyer, *Rita Allmers*
        Rut Tellefsen, *Eyolf* Hans Petter Knagenhjelm, *Asta Allmers* Lise

Fjeldstad, *Engineer Borgheim* Arne Aas, *The Rat Wife* Ragnhild Michelsen. 1:44.

1982   19 July. *Little Eyolf*. UK. BBC 2. Trans. Michael Meyer. Dir. Michael Darlow. Sc. Tony Abbott. *Rita* Diana Rigg, *Alfred* Anthony Hopkins, *The Rat Wife* Peggy Ashcroft, *Asta* Emma Piper, *Borghejm* Charles Dance, *Eyolf* Timothy Stark. 1:25.

1983   12 April. *Lille Eyolf*. Norway. NRK. Dir. Eli Ryg. Sc. John Kristian Alsaker. *Rita Allmers* Anne Marie Ottersen, *Asta Allmers* Tone Danielsen, *Alfred Allmers* Bjørn Skagestad, *Borgheim* Per Frisch, *The Rat Wife* Kirsten Hofseth, *Little Eyolf* Marcus Strand Kiønig. 1:37.

STRINDBERG

The Father

1985   22 Sept. *The Father*. UK. BBC 2. Trans. Michael Meyer. Dir. Kenneth Ives. Sc. Tim Harvey. Mus. Derek Bourgeois. Cost. Juanita Waterson. *Captain* Colin Blakely, *Laura* Dorothy Tutin, *Doctor* Edward Fox, *Pastor* Robert Lang, *Nurse* Irene Handl, *Bertha* Amanda Waring, *Nöjd* John Cording, *Batman* John Grantham. 2:00.

1988   2 Oct. *En far*. Sweden. SVT 1. Adapt. and dir. Bo Widerberg. Sc. Pelle Johansson. Cost. Gunnel Nilsson. *Captain* Thommy Berggren, *Laura* Gunnel Lindblom, *Bertha* Melinda Kinnaman, *Nurse* Majlis Granlund, *Pastor* Börje Ahlstedt, *Doctor* Ernst Günther, *Nöjd* Claes Månson, *Orderly* Michael Kallaanvaara. 1:57.

Miss Julie

1969   25 Dec. *Fröken Julie*. Sweden. SVT 2. Dir. Keve Hjelm. Sc. Kåge Andersson. Music Ture Rangström. *Miss Julie* Bibi Andersson, *Jean* Thommy Berggren, *Kristin* Kerstin Tidelius. 1:59.

1986   11 June. *Miss Julie*. South Africa/Sweden. Oy Yleisradio AB, TV 1/SVT 2/Epidem. Adapt. of stage version: Baxter Theatre, University of Cape Town. Prod. Mavis Lilenstein. Dir. Bobby Heaney. TV dir. Mikael Wahlforss. Mus. Joe Davidow. *Miss Julie* Sandra Prinsloo, *John* John Kani, *Christine* Natie Rula. 1:00

The Stronger

1960   3 June. *Den starkare*. Sweden. SR. Black-and-white. Dir. Hans
        Dahlin. Sc. Lennart Olofsson. *Mrs X* Gunnel Broström, *Miss Y* Ulla
        Sjöblom. 0:19.

1978   11 Sept. *Den starkare*. Sweden. SR 1. Dir. Gunnel Broström. Sc.
        Bo-Ruben Hedwall. *Mrs X* Margareta Byström, *Miss Y* Monica
        Nordquist. 0:20.

1991   25 Dec. *Silniejsza*. Poland. Ch.1. Trans. Zygmunt Łanowski. Adapt.
        and dir. Andrzej Wajda. *Wystapity* (Mrs X) Krystyna Janda, *Teresa*
        (Miss Y) Teresa Budzisz-Krzyzanowska. 0:27.

A Dream Play

1963   2 May. *Ett drömspel*. Sweden. SR (Nordvision). Black-and-white.
        Dir. Ingmar Bergman. Sc. Cloffe. Mus. Sven-Erik Bäck. *Indra's
        Daughter* Ingrid Thulin, *Officer* Uno Henning, *Lawyer* Allan Edwall,
        Poet Olof Widgren. Et al. 1:55.

Thunder in the Air

1960   22 Jan. *Oväder*. Sweden. SR. Black-and-white. Dir. Ingmar Berg-
        man. Sc. Birgitta Morales. *Gentleman* Uno Henning, *Brother* Ingvar
        Kjellson, *Confectioner Starck* John Elfström, *Louise* Mona Malm,
        Gerda Gunnel Broström. 1:25.

1988   9 Oct. *Oväder*. Sweden. SVT. Dir. Göran Graffman. Sc. Bo-Ruben
        Hedwall. *Gentleman* Ernst-Hugo Järegård, *Brother* Per Oscarsson,
        Confectioner Starck Björn Gustafsson, *Louise* Lena T. Hansson, *Gerda*
        Monica Nordquist. 1:30.

The Ghost Sonata

1972   30 Oct. *Spöksonaten*. Sweden. SVT 2. Dir. Johan Bergenstråhle. Sc.
        Bo Lindgren. Mus. Kåre Kollberg. *Old Man* Allan Edwall, *Student*
        Stefan Ekman, *Milkmaid* Lilian Johansson, *Colonel* Gunnar
        Björnstrand, *Mummy* Ulla Sjöblom, *Young Lady* Marie Göranzon,
        Johansson Per Myrberg, *Bengtsson* Sture Ericson, *Cook* Chris
        Wahlström. 1:31.

1980   23 Mar. *The Ghost Sonata*. UK. BBC 1. Trans. Michael Meyer. Dir.
        Philip Saville. Sc. Barrie Dobbins. Mus. Peter Howell. *Hummel* Don-
        ald Pleasance, *Mummy* Lily Kedrova, *Student* Clive Arrindell,

Daughter Nina Zuckerman, *Colonel* Ferdy Mayne, *Bengtsson* Vladek Sheybal, *Johansson* Oscar Quitak, *Fiancée* Sylvia Coleridge, *Dark Lady* Madlena Nedeva, *Nobleman* Orla Pedersen, *Cook* Bridgid Mackay, *Milkmaid* Debbie Linden. 1:35.

The Pelican

1973   17 Sept. *Pelikanen*. Sweden. SVT 1. Adapt. and dir. Yngve Nordwall. *Mother* Birgitta Valberg, *Son* Olof Willgren, *Daughter* Lilian Johansson, *Son-in-law* Hans Ernback, *Margret* Bellan Roos. 1:20.

1982   17 Mar. *Pelikanen*. Sweden. SVT 2. Adapt. and dir. Vilgot Sjöman. Sc. Birgitta Brensén. *Mother* Irma Christenson, *Son* Lars Green, *Daughter* Gunilla Olsson, *Son-in-law* Ingvar Hirdwall, *Father* Ernst Günther, *Margret* Margret Weivers-Nordström. 1:26.

Selected Bibliography

Articles and reviews in daily and weekly papers are listed only in the notes.

Aarseth, Asbjørn, "Scenisk rom og dramatisk erkjennelse i Ibsens *Gengangere*," in Leif Longum (ed.), *Dramaanalyser fra Holberg til Hoem*, Bergen-Oslo-Tromsø: Universitetsforlaget, 1977.
  "Peer Gynt" and "Ghosts": Text and Performance, London: Macmillan, 1989.
Barton, John, "On Staging Ibsen," in James McFarlane (ed.), *The Cambridge Companion to Ibsen*, Cambridge: Cambridge University Press, 1994.
Bazin, André, *What Is Cinema?*, Vol. 1, trans. Hugh Gray, Berkeley: University of California Press, 1967.
Bennett, Susan, *Theatre Audiences: A Theory of Production and Reception*, London & New York: Routledge, 1990.
Bennich-Björkman, Bo, "Fyrväpplingen och korset: Om symbolmeningen i Strindbergs *Ett drömspel*," in Gunilla & Staffan Bergsten (eds.), *Lyrik i tid och otid: Lyrikanalytiska studier tillägnade Gunnar Tideström*, Lund: Gleerups, 1971.
Bentley, Eric, *The Life of the Drama*, London: Methuen, 1965.
Bergman, Ingmar, *The Magic Lantern: An Autobiography*, trans. Joan Tate, Harmondsworth: Penguin, 1989.
Bordwell, David, *Narration in the Fiction Film*, London: Routledge, 1988.
Bordwell, David & Kristin Thompson, *Film Art: An Introduction*, 4th rev. ed., New York: McGraw-Hill, 1993.
Borup Jensen, Th., *Roman og drama bli'r til film*, København: Gyldendal, 1975.
  Indføring i dramalæsning, TV-spil, hørespil, København: Gyldendal, 1982.
Braad Thomsen, Christian, "R.W. Fassbinder: *Nora Helmer*," in Ulla Strømberg & Jytte Wiingaard (eds.), *Den levende Ibsen: Analyser af udvalgte Ibsen-forestillinger 1973-78*, København: Borgen, 1978.
Brandell, Gunnar, *Drama i tre avsnitt*, Stockholm: Wahlström & Widstrand, 1971.
Brandt, George W. (ed.), *British Television Drama*, Cambridge: Cambridge University Press, 1981.
Branigan, Edward, *Narrative Comprehension and Film*, London-New York: Routledge, 1992.
Breitholtz, Lennart, "Strindbergs Fadren och den sjuka viljan," in his *Monsieur Bovary och andra essayer*, Stockholm: Gebers, 1969.

Brøndsted, Henrik, "*Et Dukkehjem* – Tv-teatret 1974," in Ulla Strømberg & Jytte Wiingaard (eds.), *Den levende Ibsen: Analyser af udvalgte Ibsen-forestillinger 1973-78*, København: Borgen, 1978.

Brunner, Maria, "Fassbinder's Welttheater in *Nora Helmer* (1973) als Zeit-Bild," in Maria Deppermann et al. (eds.), *Ibsen im europäischen Spannungsfeld zwischen Naturalismus und Symbolismus*, Frankfurt am Main: Peter Lang, 1998.

Bryant-Bertail, Sarah, "The Tower of Babel: Space and Movement in *The Ghost Sonata*," in Göran Stockenström (ed.), *Strindberg's Dramaturgy*, Minneapolis: University of Minnesota Press, 1988.

Bussel, Jan, *The Art of Television*, London: Faber, 1952.

Chatman, Seymour, *Coming to Terms: The Rhetoric of Narrative in Fiction and Film*, Ithaca-London: Cornell University Press, 1990.

Davis, David Russel & David Thomas, "Liberation and Entrapment in *Little Eyolf*," *Contemporary Approaches to Ibsen*, Vol. 5, Oslo: Universitetsforlaget, 1985.

Delblanc, Sven, "Kärlekens föda: Ett motiv i Strindbergs kammarspel – bakgrund och innebörd," in Egil Törnqvist (ed.), *Drama och teater*, Stockholm: Almqvist & Wiksell, 1968.

Downer, Alan, *The Art of Play*, New York: Henry Holt, 1995.

Durbach, Errol, *A Doll's House: Ibsen's Myth of Transformation*, Boston: Twayne, 1991.

Dyfverman, Henrik & Lars Löfgren, *TV-teatern tio år: En krönika i ord och bild*, Stockholm: Sveriges Radio, 1964.

Eaton, Michael, "Cinema and Television: From Eden to the Land of Nod?", in Thomas Elsaesser & Kay Hoffmann (eds.), *Cinema Futures: Cain, Abel or Cable?: The Screen Arts in the Digital Age*, Amsterdam: Amsterdam University Press, 1998.

Ekman, Hans-Göran, *Villornas värld: Studier i Strindbergs kammarspel*, Stockholm: Gidlunds, 1997.

Elam, Keir, *The Semiotics of Theatre and Drama*, London-New York: Methuen, 1980.

Elghazali, Saad, *Literatur als Fernsehspiel: Veränderungen literarischer Stoffe im Fernsehen*, Hamburg: Bredow Institut, 1966.

Ellis, John, *Visible Fictions: Cinema, Television, Video*, London-New York: Routledge, 1992.

Elsaesser, Thomas, "Literature after Television: Author, Authority, Authenticity," in Jan Simons & Lucette Bronk (eds.), *Writing for the Medium: Television in Transition*, Amsterdam: Amsterdam University Press, 1994.

Esslin, Martin, *Mediations: Essays on Brecht, Beckett, and the Media*, London: Methuen, 1980.

The Field of Drama: How the Signs of Drama Create Meaning on Stage and Screen, London: Methuen, 1987.

Ewbank, Inga-Stina, "The Last Plays," in James McFarlane (ed.), *The Cambridge Companion to Ibsen*, Cambridge: Cambridge University Press, 1994. "Translating Ibsen for the English Stage," *Tijdschrift voor Skandinavistiek*, Vol. 19, No. 1, 1998.

Falck, August, *Fem år med Strindberg*, Stockholm: Wahlström & Widstrand, 1935.

Ferguson, George, *Signs & Symbols in Christian Art*, London: Oxford University Press, 1973.

Ferguson, Robert, *Henrik Ibsen: A New Biography*, London: Richard Cohen Books, 1996.

Fischer-Lichte, Erika, *The Semiotics of Theater*, trans. J. Gaines & D.L. Jones, Bloomington: Indiana University Press, 1992.

Fiske, John, *Television Culture*, London-New York: Routledge, 1987.

Gavel Adams, Lotta, "Maktkamp och kvinnokamp: August Strindbergs *Den starkare* och Dorrit Willumsens *Den stærkeste II*. En dialog över nio decennier," in Boel Westin (ed.), *Strindbergiana*, Vol. 10, Stockholm: Atlantis, 1985.

Gombrich, E.H., *Art and Illusion: A Study in the Psychology of Pictorial Representation*, Oxford: Phaidon Press, 1980.

Hallingberg, Gunnar, *Radio & TV-dramatik*, Lund: Gleerups, 1973.

Hanes Harvey, Anne-Charlotte, "Strindberg's Symbolic Room: Commanding Form for Set Design in Selected Strindberg Scripts, 1887-1907," diss., University of Minnesota, 1984.
"Strindberg and Scenography," in Harry Perridon (ed.), *Strindberg, Ibsen & Bergman: Essays on Scandinavian Film and Drama: Essays Offered to Egil Törnqvist*, Maastricht: Shaker, 1998a.
"Translating Scandinavian Drama – for Whom," *Tijdschrift voor Skandinavistiek*, Vol. 19, No. 1, 1998b.

Hayman, Ronald, *Fassbinder: Film Maker*, New York: Weidenfeld & Nicolson, 1984.

Hemmer, Bjørn, "Kaptejn Alvings Minde," *Edda*, No. 1, 1972.

Hilton, Julian, *Performance*, London: Macmillan, 1987.

Hjelm, Keve, "Hur spela Strindberg rätt?," in Ulla-Britta Lagerroth & Göran Lindström (eds.), *Perspektiv på Fröken Julie*, Stockholm: Rabén & Sjögren, 1972.

Hogendoorn, Wiebe, *Lezen en zien spelen: Een studie over simultaneïteit in het drama*, Leiden: Karstens, 1976.

Hornby, Richard, *Script into Performance: A Structuralist View of Play Production*, Austin & London: University of Texas Press, 1977.

Høst, Else, *Hedda Gabler: En monografi*, Oslo: Aschehoug, 1958.

Vildanden av Henrik Ibsen, Oslo: Aschehoug, 1967.

Ibsen, Henrik, *Samlede Verker* (Hundreårsutgave), Vol. 12, ed. Francis Bull, Halvdan Koht & Didrik Arup Seip, Oslo: Gyldendal, 1935.

The Wild Duck, trans. James Walter McFarlane, in James Walter McFarlane (ed.), *The Oxford Ibsen*, Vol. 6, London: Oxford University Press, 1960.

A Doll's House and *Ghosts*, trans. James Walter McFarlane, in James Walter McFarlane (ed.) *The Oxford Ibsen*, Vol. 5, London: Oxford University Press, 1961.

Ghosts and Other Plays, trans. Peter Watts, Harmondsworth: Penguin, 1964.

A Doll's House and Other Plays, trans. Peter Watts, Harmondsworth: Penguin, 1965a.

Four Major Plays, Vol. 1, trans. Rolf Fjelde, [includes *A Doll House*, *The Wild Duck*, *Hedda Gabler* and *The Master Builder*] New York: Signet Classic, 1965b.

Hedda Gabler (trans. Jens Arup) and *The Master Builder* (trans. James Walter McFarlane), in James Walter McFarlane (ed.), *The Oxford Ibsen*, Vol. 8, London: Oxford University Press, 1966.

Hedda Gabler and Other Plays, trans. Una Ellis-Fermor, Harmondsworth: Penguin, 1967 [orig. publ. 1950; includes *The Wild Duck*].

Four Major Plays, Vol. 2, trans. Rolf Fjelde, New York: Signet Classic, 1970 [includes *Ghosts*].

The Master Builder and Other Plays, trans. Una Ellis-Fermor, Harmondsworth: Penguin, 1971 [orig. publ. 1958].

Little Eyolf, trans. James Walter McFarlane, in James Walter McFarlane (ed.), *The Oxford Ibsen*, Vol. 9, London: Oxford University Press, 1977.

Plays: One, trans. Michael Meyer, London: Methuen, 1983 [orig. publ. 1961-62; includes *Ghosts*, *The Wild Duck* and *The Master Builder*].

Plays: Two, trans. Michael Meyer, London: Methuen, 1985 [orig. publ. 1962-65; includes *A Doll's House* and *Hedda Gabler*].

Plays: Three, trans. Michael Meyer, London: Methuen, 1988 [orig. publ. 1960-66; includes *Little Eyolf*].

Ivarsson, Jan, *Subtitling for the Media: A Handbook of an Art*, trans. Robert F. Crofts, Stockholm: Transedit, 1992.

Jacobs, Barry, "Psychic Murder and Characterization in Strindberg's *The Father*," *Scandinavica*, No. 1, 1969.

"Ibsen's *Little Eyolf*: Family Tragedy and Human Responsibility," *Modern Drama*, Vol. 27, No. 4, 1984.

"Strindbergs *Fadren* ("The Father") in English Translation," *Yearbook of*

Comparative and General Literature, Vol. 35, 1986.

"On Translating Strindberg's *Oväder*," *Scandinavica*, Vol. 27, No. 1, 1988.

Janni, Th. D., *August Strindberg: En biografi i text och bild*, Stockholm: Bonniers, 1973.

Jensen, Gunilla, *TV-regi Bo Widerberg: En TV-föreställning blir till*, Stockholm: Sveriges Radio, 1979.

Johnston, Brian, *The Ibsen Cycle*, Boston: Twayne, 1975.

Text and Supertext in Ibsen's Drama, University Park & London: Pennsylvania State University Press, 1989.

Karnick, Manfred, *Rollenspiel und Welttheater: Untersuchungen an Dramen Calderóns, Schillers, Strindbergs, Becketts und Brechts*, München: Wilhelm Fink, 1980.

Koskinen, Maaret, *Spel och speglingar: En studie i Ingmar Bergmans filmiska estetik*, Stockholm: Department of Theatre and Cinema Arts, 1995.

Kowzan, Tadeusz, "The Sign in the Theater: An Introduction to the Art of the Spectacle," trans. Simon Pleasance, *Diogenes*, No. 61, 1968.

Kvam, Kela, *Max Reinhardt og Strindbergs visionære dramatik*, København: Akademisk forlag, 1974.

Lamm, Martin, *Strindbergs dramer*, Vol. 1, Stockholm: Bonniers, 1924.

Leifer, Leif, "Den lutrende ild: En studie i symbolikken i Strindbergs kammerspil," *Samlaren*, Vol. 81, Uppsala, 1960.

Longum, Leif, "Ibsen på TV-skjermen – en ny Ibsen?", in Harald Noreng (ed.), *En ny Ibsen?: Ni Ibsen-artikler*, Oslo: Gyldendal, 1979.

Lunin, Hanno, *Strindbergs Dramen*, Emsdetten: Lechte, 1962.

Lyons, Charles R., *Hedda Gabler: Gender, Role, and World*, Boston: Twayne, 1991.

Madsen, Peter, "Den intrikate fordring – om Ibsens Vildanden," in Bertil Nolin & Peter Forsgren (eds.), *The Modern Breakthrough in Scandinavian Literature 1870-1905*, Skrifter utgivna av Litteraturvetenskapliga institutionen vid Göteborgs universitet, Vol. 17, 1988.

Marker, Frederick J. & Lise-Lone, *Ibsen's Lively Art: A Performance Study of the Major Plays*, Cambridge: Cambridge University Press, 1989.

A History of the Scandinavian Theatre, Cambridge: Cambridge University Press, 1996.

Martinus, Eivor, "Translating Scandinavian Drama," in David Johnston (ed.), *Stages of Translation*, Bath: Absolute Press, 1996.

McLuhan, Marshall, *Understanding Media*, London: Routledge, 1994.

Meyer, Michael, *Henrik Ibsen*, London: Cardinal, 1992.

Strindberg: A Biography, Oxford & New York: Oxford University Press, 1987.

Müssener, Helmut, *August Strindberg, Ein Traumspiel*: *Struktur- und Stilstudien*, Meisenheim am Glan: Hain, 1965.

Nelson, F.G., Review of Michael Meyer's translation of *Hedda Gabler and Three Other Plays*, *Scandinavian Studies*, Vol. 34, 1962.

Northam, John, *Ibsen's Dramatic Method*, London: Cambridge University Press, 1953.

Strindberg's *Spook Sonata*, in Carl Reinhold Smedmark (ed.), *Essays on Strindberg*, Stockholm: Strindberg Society, 1966.

Ibsen: A Critical Study, Cambridge: Cambridge University Press, 1973.

Ollén, Gunnar, *Strindbergs dramatik*, Stockholm: Sveriges Radio, 1961.

Strindberg i TV, Stockholm: Sveriges Radio, 1971.

"*Fröken Julie* i TV," in Ulla-Britta Lagerroth & Göran Lindström (eds.), *Perspektiv på Fröken Julie*, Stockholm: Rabén & Sjögren, 1972.

Strindbergs dramatik, Stockholm: Sveriges Radio, 1982.

Pavis, Patrice, *Languages of the Stage: Essays in the Semiology of the Theatre*, trans. Susan Melrose et al., New York: Performing Arts Journal Publications, 1982.

Theatre at the Crossroads of Culture, trans. Loren Kruger, London & New York: Routledge, 1992.

"Staging the Text," *Assaph: Studies in the Theatre*, No. 13, 1997.

Pfister, Manfred, *The Theory and Analysis of Drama*, trans. John Halliday, Cambridge: Cambridge University Press, 1988.

Quigley, Austin E., *The Modern Stage and Other Worlds*, New York-London: Methuen, 1985.

Reynolds, Peter, *Drama: Text into Performance*, Harmondsworth: Penguin, 1986.

Rokem, Freddie, *Theatrical Space in Ibsen, Chekhov and Strindberg: Public Forms of Privacy*, Ann Arbor: Umi Research Press, 1986.

Røed, Arne, "The Crutch is Floating," *Ibsen-Årbok*, Oslo: Universitetsforlaget, 1974.

"Right to the top – ?," *Ibsen-Årbok*, Oslo: Universitetsforlaget, 1977.

Rønneberg, Anton, *Ti års fjernsynsteater*, Oslo: Aschehoug, 1971.

Schwitzke, Heinz, "Das Wort und die Bilder," in Irmela Schneider (ed.), *Dramaturgie des Fernsehspiels*, München: Wilhelm Fink, 1980.

Sjöberg, Alf, "Existentialism och rollbyte i *Fröken Julie*," in Ulla-Britta Lagerroth & Göran Lindström (eds.), *Perspektiv på Fröken Julie*, Stockholm: Rabén & Sjögren, 1972.

Sjöman, Vilgot, *L136: Dagbok med Ingmar Bergman*, Stockholm: Norstedts, 1963.

Sprinchorn, Evert, "Julie's End," in Carl Reinhold Smedmark (ed.), *Essays on Strindberg*, Stockholm: Strindberg Society, 1966.

"Ibsen and the Actors," in Errol Durbach (ed.), *Ibsen and the Theatre: The Dramatist in Production*, London: Macmillan, 1980.

Steene, Birgitta, "Film as Theater: Geissendörfer's *The Wild Duck*," in Andrew S. Horton & Joan Magretta (eds.), *Modern European Filmmakers and the Art of Adaptation*, New York: Frederick Ungar, 1981.

"Sommarlovets hägring är inte nödvändigtvis översättarens vision. Om *Pelikanen*, Kulturspråk och Författarspråk," *Strindbergiana*, Vol. 4, Stockholm: Atlantis, 1989.

Steene, Birgitta & Elizabeth de Nona, "Filmatiseringar och TV-produktioner av August Strindbergs verk; En Strindbergsfilmografi," *Strindbergiana*, Vol. 12, Stockholm: Atlantis, 1997.

Strindberg, August, *Naturalistiska sorgespel*, in *Samlade skrifter*, Vol. 23, ed. John Landquist, Stockholm: Bonniers, 1914. [Includes *Fadren* and *Fröken Julie*.]

Komedier och enaktare, in *Samlade skrifter*, Vol. 25, ed. John Landquist, Stockholm: Bonniers, 1914. [Includes *Den starkare*.]

Kronbruden, Svanevit, Ett drömspel, in *Samlade skrifter*, Vol. 36, ed. John Landquist, Stockholm: Bonniers, 1916.

Kammarspel, in *Samlade skrifter*, Vol. 45, ed. John Landquist, Stockholm: Bonniers, 1917. [Includes *Oväder, Spöksonaten* and *Pelikanen*.]

En blå bok, 3, in *Samlade skrifter*, Vol. 50, ed. John Landquist, Stockholm: Bonniers, 1918a.

Samlade otryckta skrifter, Vol. 1, Stockholm: Bonniers, 1918b.

Six Plays of Strindberg, trans. Elizabeth Sprigge, New York: Doubleday Anchor, 1955. [Includes *The Father, Miss Julie, The Stronger, A Dream Play, The Ghost Sonata*.]

Three Plays, trans. Peter Watts, Harmondsworth: Penguin, 1958. [Includes *The Father* and *Miss Julie*.]

August Strindbergs brev, Vol. 7, ed. Torsten Eklund, Stockholm: Bonniers, 1961.

Open Letters to the Intimate Theatre, trans. and introd. Walter Johnson, Seattle & London: University of Washington Press, 1967.

Pre-Inferno Plays, trans. Walter Johnson, Seattle: University of Washington Press, 1970. [Includes *The Father, Lady Julie* and *The Stronger*.]

Eight Expressionist Plays, trans. Arvid Paulson, New York: New York University Press, 1972. [Includes *A Dream Play* and *The Ghost Sonata*.]

A Dream Play and Four Chamber Plays, trans. Walter Johnson, Seattle: University of Washington Press, 1973. [Includes *Stormy Weather, The Ghost Sonata* and *The Pelican*]

Plays: One, trans. Michael Meyer, London: Methuen, 1976. [Includes *The Father, Miss Julie, The Ghost Sonata*.]

Ockulta Dagboken: 1896-1908, Stockholm: Gidlunds, 1977.

Five Plays, trans. Harry Carlson, Berkeley: University of California Press, 1981. [Includes *The Father, Miss Julie, A Dream Play* and *The Ghost Sonata*.]

Fadren and *Fröken Julie*, in *August Strindbergs Samlade Verk*, Vol. 27, ed. Gunnar Ollén, Stockholm: Almqvist & Wiksell, 1984a.

Den starkare, in *Nio enaktare*, in *August Strindbergs Samlade Verk*, Vol. 33, ed. Gunnar Ollén, Stockholm: Almqvist & Wiksell, 1984b.

Selected Plays, Vols. 1-2, trans. Evert Sprinchorn, Minneapolis: University of Minnesota Press, 1986. [Vol. 1 includes *The Father, Miss Julie, The Stronger*, Vol. 2 includes *A Dream Play, The Ghost Sonata, The Pelican*.]

Ett drömspel, in *August Strindbergs Samlade Verk*, Vol. 46, ed. Gunnar Ollén, Stockholm: Norstedts, 1988.

Thunder in the Air, trans. Eivor Martinus, Bath: Absolute Press, 1989.

Kammarspel, in *August Strindbergs Samlade Verk*, Vol. 58, ed. Gunnar Ollén, Stockholm: Norstedts, 1991. [Includes *Oväder, Spöksonaten* and *Pelikanen*.]

Strindberg's Letters, Vol. 1, ed. Michael Robinson, Chicago & London: University of Chicago Press, 1992.

The Pelican & The Isle of the Dead, ed. and trans. Michael Robinson, Birmingham: University of Birmingham, 1994.

Three Chamber Plays, trans. Inga-Stina Ewbank, Leeds: Alumnus, 1997. [Includes *Storm* and *The Ghost Sonata*.]

Miss Julie and Other Plays, trans. Michael Robinson, Oxford-New York: Oxford University Press. [Includes *The Father, A Dream Play, The Ghost Sonata*.]

Styan, J.L., "The Opening Moments of *A Doll's House*: For Performance and Analysis in Class," in Yvonne Shafer (ed.), *Approaches to Teaching Ibsen's A Doll House*, New York: The Modern Language Association of America, 1985.

Szondi, Peter, *Theory of the Modern Drama*, ed. and trans. Michael Hays, Cambridge: Cambridge University Press, 1987.

Suzman, Janet, "*Hedda Gabler*: The Play in Performance," in Errol Durbach (ed.), *Ibsen and the Theatre: The Dramatist in Production*, London: Macmillan, 1980.

Tennant, P.F.D., *Ibsen's Dramatic Technique*, New York: Humanities Press, 1965.

Thomsen, C. Braad, "*Et dukkehjem*. R.W. Fassbinder: *Nora Helmer*," in Ulla Strömberg & Jytte Wiingaard (eds.), *Den levende Ibsen: Analyser af udvalgte Ibsen-forestillinger 1973-78*, København: Borgen, 1978.

Törnqvist, Egil, "Strindberg's *The Stronger*," *Scandinavian Studies*, Vol. 42, No. 3, 1970.

"The Illness Pattern in *The Master Builder*," *Scandinavica*, Vol. 11, No. 1, 1972.

"Ingmar Bergman Directs Strindberg's *Ghost Sonata*," *Theatre Quarterly*, Vol. 3, No. 2, 1973a.

Bergman och Strindberg: Spöksonaten – drama och iscensättning. Dramaten 1973, Stockholm: Prisma, 1973b.

"Individualism in *The Master Builder*," in *Contemporary Approaches to Ibsen*, Oslo: Universitetsforlaget, 1977.

"Ett dramatiskt dilemma," *Svensk Litteraturtidskrift*, No. 2, 1978.

"The End of *Ghosts*," in *Contemporary Approaches to Ibsen*, Oslo: Universitetsforlaget, 1979.

Strindbergian Drama: Themes and Structure, Stockholm: Almqvist & Wiksell International & Atlantic Highlands, N.J.: Humanities Press, 1982.

"Staging *A Dream Play*," in Göran Stockenström (ed.), *Strindberg's Dramaturgy*, Minneapolis: University of Minnesota Press, 1988.

Transposing Drama: Studies in Representation, London: Macmillan, 1991.

"A 'Play'-within-the-Play: The Opening of Strindberg's *The Father*," *Theatre Research International*, Supplementary Issue: Strindberg in Performance, eds. Willmar Sauter & Jacqueline Martin, Vol. 18, 1993.

"Ibsen on Film and Television," in James McFarlane (ed.), *The Cambridge Companion to Ibsen*, Cambridge: Cambridge University Press, 1994.

Between Stage and Screen: Ingmar Bergman Directs, Amsterdam: Amsterdam University Press, 1995a.

Ibsen: A Doll's House, Cambridge: Cambridge University Press, 1995b.

"Page, Stage and Screen: The Opening of Ibsen's *Gengangere* (*Ghosts*)," *Tijdschrift voor Skandinavistiek*, Vol. 17, No. 1, 1996.

"Strindberg och den intima teatern: *Pelikanen* som TV-drama," *Strindbergiana*, Vol. 12, Stockholm: Atlantis, 1997a.

"Ibsen's Double Audience," *Nordic Theatre Studies*, Vol. 10, 1997b.

"Translating Strindbergian Imagery for the Stage," *Tijdschrift voor Skandinavistiek*, Vol. 19, No. 1, 1998a.

"Screening *Hedda Gabler*," in Maria Deppermann et al. (eds.), *Ibsen im europäischen Spannungsfeld zwischen Naturalismus und Symbolismus*, Frankfurt am Main: Peter Lang, 1998b.

Törnqvist, Egil & Barry Jacobs, *Strindberg's Miss Julie: A Play and Its Transpositions*, Norwich: Norvik Press, 1988.

Ubersfeld, Anne, *Lire le Théâtre*, Paris: Messidor, 1982.

Valency, Maurice, *The Flower and the Castle: An Introduction to Modern Drama*, New York: Grosset & Dunlap, 1966.

Valmin, Stefan, *TV-teater*, Stockholm: Sveriges Radio, 1972.

Waldmann, Werner & Rose, *Einführung in die Analyse von Fernsehspielen*, Tübingen: Gunter Narr, 1980.

Watts, C.T., "The Unseen Catastrophe in Ibsen's 'Vildanden'," *Scandinavica*, Vol. 12, No. 2, 1973.

Willems, Michèle, "Verbal-Visual, Verbal-Pictorial or Textual-Televisual? Reflections on the BBC Shakespeare Series," in Anthony Davies & Stanley Wells (eds.), *Shakespeare and the Moving Image: The Plays on Film and Television*, Cambridge: Cambridge University Press, 1994.

Weigand, Hermann J., *The Modern Ibsen: A Reconsideration*, New York: Dutton, (1925) 1960.

Williams, Raymond, "A Lecture on Realism," *Screen*, Vol. 18, No. 1, 1977. *Television: Technology and Cultural Form*, ed. Ederyn Williams, London: Routledge, (1975) 1990.

Willis, Susan, *The BBC Shakespeare Plays: Making the Televised Canon*, Chapel Hill-London: University of North Carolina Press, 1991.

Wirmark, Margareta, *Den kluvna scenen: Kvinnor i Strindbergs dramatik*, Stockholm: Gidlunds, 1988.

Zitner, Sheldon P., "Wooden O's in Plastic Boxes," in J.C. Bulman & R.H. Coursen (eds.), *Shakespeare on Television: An Anthology of Essays and Reviews*, Hanover, N.H.: University Press of New England, 1988.

List of illustrations

15 Ingmar Bergman rehearsing Act II of Strindberg's *Thunder in the Air* for his Swedish 1960 production. From left to right: The Brother (Ingvar Kjellson), The Gentleman (Uno Henning), Bergman, The Confectioner (John Elfström), Louise (Mona Malm). Photo: courtesy Sveriges Television.

16 The Brother (Per Oscarsson) and The Gentleman (Ernst-Hugo Järegård) in Strindberg's *Thunder in the Air*. From the Swedish 1988 production, directed by Göran Graffman. Photo: Björn Edergren.

17 The Old man (Allan Edwall) and The Student (Stefan Ekman) in Strindberg's *The Ghost Sonata*. From the Swedish 1972 production, directed by Johan Bergenstråhle. Photo: courtesy Sveriges Television.

18 The Mother (Irma Christenson) and The Daughter (Gunilla Olsson) in Strindberg's *The Pelican*. From the Swedish 1982 production, directed by Vilgot Sjöman. Photo: Magnus Hartman.

Index